THANK YOU, LORD

GARY ATKINS

Thank You, Lord

Copyright © 2022 by Gary Atkins.

Paperback ISBN: 978-1-63812-272-2
Ebook ISBN: 978-1-63812-273-9

All rights reserved. No part in this book may be produced and transmitted in any form or by any means, electronic, or mechanical, including photocopying, recording, or by any information storage and retrieval system, without permission in writing from the copyright owner.

The views expressed in this work are solely those of the author and do not necessarily reflect the views of the publisher. The publisher hereby disclaims any responsibility for them.

Published by Pen Culture Solutions 05/23/2022

Pen Culture Solutions
1-888-727-7204 (USA)
1-800-950-458 (Australia)
support@penculturesolutions.com

PREFACE

The Author

Born in Melbourne, Victoria, Australia, in 1945, I was brought up in a Methodist family. I completed high school, trained to be a teacher on a scholarship, and then served the South Australian Education Department for four years as a teacher. I resigned, went back to university as a private student for one year, and then travelled to South East Asia at the time of the Vietnam War. On returning to Australia, I began a myriad of occupations. I married in 1971 and became a father of three sons. Following the birth of our first son, my wife was diagnosed as a paranoid schizophrenic. At that time, I began earning a living as a professional folksinger, songwriter, and publisher, and after seven successful years, we were able to make a deposit on a sixty-acre block of land in rural area near Adelaide, the capital of South Australia, and I began building a house there.

In trying to cope as a father with three sons and as a husband whose wife had a chronic mental sickness, I reached a point when I could no longer continue to earn a good living as a touring folksinger, and my successful business collapsed. Instead, I stayed at home most of the time and began casual work from home as a handyman. There was not enough money to keep up the mortgage payments.

I became a born-again Christian in 1980.

In 1981, my wife obtained custody of our sons and moved out, to live with her parents. In the same year, because I was unable to serve the mortgage on our land, the land was sold, and I became homeless, and destitute. A church family took me in. After a while, I began legal action to get the right to see my sons.

In 1982 my wife divorced me.

After many difficult years, I was successful in getting the legal right to see my sons, during which time I bought a block of land in a South Australian Outback town and built an underground house there, and I became an opal miner and the editor/publisher of the town's newspaper.

After ten years, I became reunited with my sons, and at peace with my former wife.

I remarried in 2012.

How the book was written

In 1995, an old friend whom I had not seen for about twenty years visited me. He told me that he had difficulty in understanding how I had become such a different person from when he saw me last. He suggested I ought to write a book to explain how such a change had come about. I was surprised to hear that I had changed so much and decided to follow his suggestion. And so, I began a task which was to span more than twenty years part-time, while earning a living. The task was made easier because I could refer to many legal documents that I had kept over the years, relating to my dealings with the Family Court of Australia in matters concerning access to, and custody of my three sons from my first marriage.

I began writing this book with pencil on paper. Then I met a man who told me he was already a published author. He told me that publishers only want to look at digital manuscripts. I enrolled in a word processing course, which introduced me to the digital world on a personal computer and subsequently the internet. Following that, I bought a PC and began making my digital manuscript.

I had difficulty in deciding at what point of time in my life the manuscript would begin. Most narratives I have read, began at a point in time, and progressed in time from that point. The one single event in my life that I thought would have triggered the beginning of the change in my life, which made my old friend have difficulty in understanding me in

1995, occurred in 1981. So, I began the manuscript with a description of that event. Then I realised that without a narration of my life story prior to that time, there would not be any comprehension by readers of the significance of that event in 1981. But to begin the story with an event which occurred in 1981, and then jump back to my childhood, and then go forward in time, up to the 1981 experience, and beyond, would defy convention. And so, after much thought, I decided that the description of that event of 1981 could still take first place in the book, but in a prologue, preceding Chapter One.

Book's goals

I came to adulthood at a time when the attitude of Australians was that everything was OK, and there was no need to worry about anything, just go to work, earn money, spend it, enjoy life, and leave everything to the government to handle. It was summed up as, "She'll be right, mate. No problems."

But in 1981, I found out that the Australian government had, six years previously, passed a law which: made adultery acceptable and adulterers unaccountable; threw out the principle that one is innocent until proven guilty, replacing it with exactly the opposite-that one is guilty until proven innocent; made it possible in a courtroom for a plaintiff to preclude a defendant from being present in the court when the court heard the case for the plaintiff.

That law has the name "Family Law Act, 1975."

No longer may informed Australians say, "She'll be right, mate, no problems."

I hope that this book will show Australians, and indeed, people in other Western nations (who have also passed a similar law) what devastating effect the Family Law Act has on everyday people.

I hope this book will give inspiration to others who are trying to deal with the cards of life that the Family Law Act has dealt them.

I hope that this book will encourage Christians.

I hope that this book will generate a desire in Australians to take an interest in politics and join me as I work towards the repeal of the Family Law Act.

I thank the Lord that I was able to survive the experience of being a defendant in the Family Court of Australia, and that I was able to fight back and clear my name, and that I was able to recover from financial collapse and subsequently write this book.

PROLOGUE

If someone were to ask you, when you were fifty years of age, what single day in all your life could you provide the most recollection of, you would probably wonder where to start.

But for me the answer is easy.

It is easy because I have in my possession documents and written references to one day in all my life when a personal crisis occurred-a traumatic event when, in a single split-second, I decided not to vent my anger on society for the wrong that it had done me that day.

I could not say off the top of my head the date of that day. The date is insignificant. It was about fifteen years ago. All I need to do to find the date is open my files under the heading of "Family Law Act–Private".

The evidence is all there: references and cross-references spanning over a period of ten years, starting with that one day.

Many personal experiences crowded my mind that day. My anger was immense. My mind raced to find a solution to the problem that was imposed on me.

The situation was resolved peacefully that day, but it could just as easily have resulted tragically with violence. I knew I had the capacity, under stress, to fight to the death, even though I was not in good health at the time. On that day, I was ready to fight literally or metaphorically, either way would have suited me. The choice was mine, the power was mine, and the determination to win was within me. Everything I had ever experienced up to then told me that I could not, *must not,* accept the personal injustice foisted on me.

It was on that day that I read, on the piece of paper that I held in my hands, a date which I was sure was the date of a day a couple of days previous.

I was not sure for two reasons-most times one is not sure of the date of the day, because for most people only one day is significant-their birthday. The other reason was that it seemed impossible to me that the legal document that I held in my hands would contain a mistaken date, being contained in a document that was dependent for its power on the dates being correct.

And if it was not a mistake then it was so unjust that it was unreal-a dream-such a thing could only happen in a work of fiction, or in a country overrun with tyrants and criminals.

To help eliminate the doubt as to whether the date on the document was mistaken, I decided to look at the wall calendar, and check the date of that day, which I was pretty sure was May 8. Even as my head turned in the direction of the calendar, I thought again that there must be a mistake, and so I had a doubt as to whether it was even worth looking at the calendar to check.

But that doubt was eliminated by me deciding to continue turning my head to the calendar. When I checked it, I found that my suspicions were correct-the date of that day was May 8, the date I originally thought it was.

Then I looked back to the document still in my hands to check if the date I had read two seconds previous was May 6. Yes, it was. The significance of that was, a court, (the Family Court of Australia) had informed me in the document, dated May 6, that was handed to me on May 8, that if I wanted to appeal against the judgement that the court had made on May 6, I would have to do it by 2.20 pm on May 6, two days previously!

I thought, either the date on the document was a mistake, or I had made a mistake when I had checked the day's date on the calendar. It was impossible to me that the date on the document was correct. That sort of situation would only occur in a comic, or in the weekly essay of a schoolboy with a vivid imagination but no maturity or sense of balance.

I have no clear recollection now of whether on that day about fifteen years ago, I looked again to check the calendar and then back at the document, but I suppose I must have done so. Maybe I did that several times before I finally concluded that my original conclusions were correct. On May 8, I was told that I could appeal against the May 6 court decision, if I did it by 2.20 pm on May 6, two days before they gave me the papers!

Much of the document was a copy of a statement-an affidavit-which was mostly about another person's opinion and assessment of me. I knew that many things in the document were mistakes, or rather, untrue, in the sense that, even though they were true, they were certainly not the whole truth, and most certainly not 'nothing but the truth'. It was therefore logical to assume that if most of the document contained mistakes, then the dates too were mistakes.

I guess I re-read and re-read the document, hoping that if the chronologically earlier dates were incorrect, then the last day mentioned was incorrect, therefore the whole document was a mistake and was not valid, and therefore such a great injustice had not really been dumped on me-I was imagining an injustice. This too was a logical possibility, because I was extremely depressed through experiences of previous weeks, and months, and years, and not well, and self-pitying, and alone.

But how could a government in a country like Australia do such a thing as I suspected had been done? Of course, it could not do such a thing. Australia is the land of my birth. Australia is the land where a person is innocent until proven guilty, rather than guilty until proven innocent. Australia is the land with a flag containing the representation of the emblems of Christian heroes; a tradition of good triumphing over evil; of truth always overcoming; of the underdog getting up and winning; of justice in the courts; a country to which migrants from the world's oppressive and tyrannical regimes flock, in the hope of a new and better life.

My father had always been a respected, small country town bank manager, my mother was a loyal, faithful wife, their parents were decent, law-abiding people. I was, to my knowledge, one of the most respected performers in the South Australian folk music scene. I had been a patrol leader in the boy scouts, a prefect at school, a group representative on a teachers college student representative council, then a teacher for four years before resigning to pursue different career paths.

The dates must have been wrong.

I would have checked them and read them in the awareness of the context of the affidavit, and my own knowledge of events leading up to the presentation of the affidavit, which obviously had been presented-courts had sat, judgments had been made, and actions had been authorised and then carried out by the relevant authorities as a result of the affidavit being accepted as being the truth, even though I had no knowledge that such things had taken place until I read the document, and not any knowledge that the events had been going to take place.

I would have looked again at the calendar, and then back at the document. Maybe an hour would have passed before I put the document down, out of my hands that had accepted it from the hands of the person who had served it on me. By then I would have realised that my suspicions were correct. Then I would have sat in the room, still alone, trying to recall the events of that day up to when I had accepted that document in my hands. I would have evaluated them in comparison with my situation a day ago.

The two days were radically different. On the one day, I was in control of my life, and responsible as a husband and as a father of three children, as a culmination of the previous nine years; the next day, the day on which my hands accepted a document from another person's hands, I had lost control of the power to make decisions concerning my wife and our three children.

My anger boiled up in me, and gave me a feeling of strength, but other than do something foolish, I could only remain seated until I calmed down.

Fifteen years later, as I write these words, they are blurring before my eyes with tears of gratitude to the Lord, who enabled me to make the choice to respond, rather than to react.

And right now, I am sobbing with joy.

Thank you, Lord.

1

The first friend that I can remember was a girl who, like me, lived in a main street house in the busy village of Berwick, twenty-five miles from Melbourne, Victoria, Australia, in the year 1950.

Then Mummy and Daddy and I moved to another house on the outskirts of the village, surrounded by lush green paddocks and many grazing dairy cows, and I did not see that friend again.

I got a baby sister, Jill.

Then we moved again, to the city, to a house by a railway line, in Blackburn, an outer suburb of Melbourne.

I got another baby sister, Patricia.

Blackburn Central School was about two miles away. My parents were happy to let me walk there by myself every day, but I had to memorise our home phone number and my Nana's, who lived in a nearby suburb. One day, walking to school, I somehow got to be thinking about what happens when life finishes, and I became very worried. Where did we go? All I could think of was a frightening, dark, deep quarry. I didn't want to die! When I got home, I told Mummy that I did not want to die. She said, "Don't worry-everyone has to die." She also said to me, "Books are your best friends." At school I was always the first to finish arithmetic, and always got a perfect score in a spelling test.

I made some new friends at school in my class, and some weekend friends from the house across the road. Blackburn in 1954 was surrounded by virgin bushland. On Saturdays, we could go and play there. I would take a big stick and go walking in the bush with my friends, trying to find snakes to kill. My friends thought I was very brave. I thought so too. One day, we decided to go snake hunting. On the way to the bush was a building where mentally sick people lived. One woman there had purple eyes, so we named her 'Old Purple Eyes'. Sometimes she was walking along the road when we were going to the bush. We used to tease her, calling out, "Hey, Old Purple Eyes!" One day we threw stones at her. She threw back accurately, two stones at once, one in each hand, so we didn't throw stones at her again. Little did I realise that many years later, mental sickness in the family would seriously impact my life.

My friends wanted me to take them snake hunting again on Sundays, but my parents wouldn't let me go out and play on Sundays-I was made to go to Sunday School instead. The grownups in charge of the Blackburn Methodist Sunday School read to us from books with lots of pictures, about a man called Jesus, who lived a long time ago, before electricity, in a far off, foreign country with no grass, and hardly any trees, and funny looking flat-roofed houses. Jesus always wore sandals, just like we did when we went to the beach for a holiday. When we came home from a holiday, we had to wear boots again, but Jesus only ever wore sandals. He always had something that looked like a bed sheet wrapped round him, and he had long hair and a long beard.

We also learnt from a book with very small printing and no pictures, called The Bible, about David, a small boy who defeated a giant, Goliath; and Lot, who chose the best land when offered a choice by his relative Abraham, but later lost the land, and had to be rescued by Abraham.

We learned to sing the songs *"Jesus Loves Me"*, *"The best book to read is the Bible"*, *"Jesus bids us shine with a pure, clear light"*, and *"Hear the pennies dropping"*. The teachers collected money from us while we sang the songs. I wondered where the money went. To me, Jesus wasn't real, just a man in a story in a book, just like Tarzan on the radio, or Superman in a comic. After all, what sort of a man would have such long hair and a long beard, and be dressed in a bed sheet, and wear sandals all the time? Sunday School for me was just a place where I had to go on Sundays, instead of going to school or hunting for snakes. Neither Jesus nor Tarzan nor Superman was ever talked about at home, and nobody ever read the bible, which had its place with many other books in the family bookcase. Every night before the meal we had to close our eyes and bow our head while we 'said grace'-"For what we are about to receive, may the Lord God make us truly thankful, for Christ's sake. Amen." Nothing could be eaten until grace was said. To me, we were talking to nobody, and we might as well have said any other words, before we could start eating.

Life at home was very secure-plenty food, three meals a day, clean clothes, nice house, peaceful, a mother and a father who provided everything. I was an avid reader. I was fascinated by the accounts in *The Swiss Family Robinson* and *Robinson Crusoe,* of how shipwreck survivors who made it to safety on a tropical island, managed to salvage a precious little thing like a knife blade from the wreckage that washed ashore, and use it to fashion a primitive shelter; and I enjoyed their daily struggle to make do with whatever came to hand, and eventually make a comfortable life using only what was provided by nature on the tropical island. I also had a King James Bible, given to me by the Sunday School, but it was difficult to read with all the old English words like *thee* and *thine*. Other children's classics in the family bookshelves were *The Testing of Jim McLean* and *Deerfoot in the Forest,* books given to Daddy when he was a boy. I was fascinated by the way Jim McLean survived alone, in a freezing cold, northern hemisphere winter in a remote rural area, by melting ice to drink and cooking the leather off his boots as his only available source of food. Many years later, I would be facing the same primitive circumstances, and I would have to find a way to survive.

After about two years at Blackburn, in the city, we moved what for us was a massive fifty miles to West Gippsland, to another house in the small country town of Bunyip. The friends I made at Blackburn, like the one from Berwick, disappeared from my life.

Daddy was the Manager of the Bunyip branch of the Commercial Bank of Australia. We lived in a nice house behind the bank chambers in the Bunyip main street. A woman came weekly to iron the clothes. Somewhere about this time in my life, Daddy impressed on me, "Don't trust anyone, not even your own father." At this point in my life, having lost every friend I ever had, to be told that, made me feel very lonely and isolated.

Mummy and Daddy continued to send us to Sunday School. At the Bunyip Presbyterian Sunday School, I became friends with one boy, who already had a very good friend, so I felt a bit left out when we were all together.

As a new boy at Bunyip State School, I had no friends. Most of the children had already been good friends for a few years, and it was an unhappy time for me trying to find a friend. Eventually I found one. He lived in a very small cottage that had no electricity, in a farming area on the Bunyip Swamp, right on the bank of the Bunyip River, with his mother and father and many brothers and sisters. At Bunyip State school, I had no problem in either getting the top mark, or near it, which made my parents very happy.

At the end of grade six, those who passed the exam went on to high school. For Bunyip kids, this meant travelling on a steam train to the town of Drouin, followed by a bus trip out to the new Drouin High School on the edge of the town.

My friend from the Bunyip Swamp did not continue to high school, and my Sunday School friend was only in grade five, so I started at Drouin High School with no friends.

Life was not happy for me at first, in my new school, with no friends. I was bullied a lot, being small. However, I eventually got a friend from Longwarry, the town on the railway line between Bunyip and Drouin. His older, married sister lived in Drouin. When the train got to Drouin in the morning, he and I would hide in the railway station toilets until the school bus left the station. Then we would come out from hiding, and go to his older, married sister's house in Drouin. He bought cigarettes and we smoked them at his sister's house. In the afternoon we walked to the railway station in time to catch the train home.

During the year, I always got very good marks in every subject, and many times I was in the top few students. But in Art I got a failure, because my friend from Longwarry and I were often wagging school on art lesson days. At the end of the first year at Drouin High, at the student presentation, each student who gained credit standard in any subject and who had not failed in any subject received an award. Several of the Bunyip kids got their award, but I was not able to receive any award for all my credits because I had failed in Art. It was a great disappointment for my parents. They expected much from me, because as a boy, Daddy was the Dux of the biggest high school in Melbourne, which meant that he gained the highest marks of all the students. He was also the winner of the Senior Athletics Cup.

One thing that I really enjoyed at Bunyip was going to the Boy Scouts, even though I had to start again with no friends. Our scoutmaster took us camping in his car. We would cook on an open fire and sleep in tents. We competed in inter-town troop competitions for boiling the billy, knot tying, tent pitching, and marching.

On one camping trip we were travelling in the scoutmaster's car through the mountain range near Bunyip. He saw a wombat ambling across the track ahead. Still driving, and holding the steering wheel in his left hand, he opened the door with his right hand and poked his rifle out the door window. He took a shot at the wombat, which dropped to the ground, dead.

He jumped out of the car. With his knife, he slit the wombat from the belly to the chest, ripping the animal open. The wombat's writhing, steaming, guts spilled out. The heart was still pumping, jumping off the ground.

On another camping trip, we went to Waratah Bay. The scoutmaster stopped his car on the side of a dirt road. We started at the roadside, with axes and machetes, and cut a path through the thick forest. Some way in from the road, we cut a clearing big enough to pitch our tent. We cut down small trees, and trimmed off the branches, and lashed them together with ropes, to make a frame to hang our tent on.

The evening meal was a mixture of tinned and fresh food, cooked in a billy on an open fire.

The next day we walked to the coast for fishing. For bait, we used the flesh from rock limpet shellfish that we prised from off the sea shore rocks. We caught fish, cooked them, and ate them. For that, we earned a scout 'proficiency' badge for fishing.

I earned another proficiency badge for collecting. My collection was matchbox labels. They were a black and white and red coloured series from the 1956 Melbourne Olympic Games.

Bunyip's annual rainfall was thirty-five inches, a lush, green land of dairy cows, crops of potatoes, peas, watermelons and corn, and orchards of apples and pears, a land of forests, swamps, rivers, and mountains, cloudy on most days.

On a rare, bright, sunny, late winter day in 1958, Mummy and Daddy, and my two sisters and the family dog left Bunyip in Daddy's Austin A50, and headed west. Daddy had been transferred interstate. We were going to Lameroo in South Australia, annual rainfall ten inches, bright and sunny most days, a wide, flat, dry, hot land of sheep and wheat and sand hills and stunted mallee scrub.

Once again, my friends were left far behind.

After two days driving from Bunyip, we arrived at Lameroo. It was pouring rain. Daddy's Austin A50 slipped sideways in the muddy main street. By late afternoon, we got settled in our new house, which was attached to the rear of the main street chambers of the Lameroo branch of the Commercial Bank of Australia. Next door, a party was going on. A girl climbed on the fence to get a look at the kids of the new bank manager. We got talking. I learned that as a Victorian, I had different words and pronunciation. My *'spiggies'* were South Australian *'spoggies'*; my *'cantaloupe'* was now a *'rockmelon'*; in *'castle'* and *'dance'*, the *'a'* was pronounced the same as *'ar'* as in *'car'*, instead of *'a'* as in *'cat'*.

The most distinguishing pronunciation difference was in the word *'school'*. It took me months of concentrated effort to alter my Victorian pronunciation of *'skuwel'* to the rounded South Australian *'school'*, so as not to be looked on as a stranger from Victoria.

Mummy impressed on me that in Lameroo, I was not just an ordinary child-I was the bank manager's son. "Come straight home from *skuwel*," she said. "Remember where you come from-you are the bank manager's son."

I was forbidden to make friends with children of the railway workers or any labouring 'class' family. Instead, I had to make friends with children of wealthy farming families. It became a dilemma for me, because I learnt in the Boy Scouts that, "A Scout is a friend to all, and a brother to every other Scout, no matter country, class or creed he may belong." Compounding the dilemma was the situation in which, as a child, I was regarded as 'seen and not heard', and I saw virtually no opportunity for discussion, because as a child, my duty was to obey my parents because they were always right, and I was only a child.

Lameroo Area School catered for boys and girls from grade one to 'Intermediate'–third year-at high school. My transition in mid-term, from a Second-Year high school class in Victoria to a First-Year South Australia Area school class was a hurdle, but I jumped it. The other students were familiar with 'theorems' after doing them for two thirds of the year, but for me it was a totally new world.

With unhappy memories of being bullied and teased at Drouin, I determined that it was not going to happen again in my new school. One day a tall, tough looking boy approached me. Straight away I looked him fair in the eye and said as tough as I could, "Scram, jam, or I'll spread ya!"

It worked! From then on, I was never picked on or teased or bullied. Quite the opposite, I became the boy whom the other boys came to for help when they were bullied.

Mummy and Daddy attended the Lameroo Methodist Church. I and my two sisters went to the Sunday School and the Band of Hope, with its games, and raspberry cordial, and recited promise to abstain from drinking alcohol until the age of twenty-one.

At home, we continued to 'say grace' before meals. But nobody ever prayed or read the bible, which appeared once again in its usual place in the bookshelves in the new house. The one and only reference ever made to the bible at home happened one day when Daddy said we were having "Hebrews 13:8" for tea. Daddy explained that Hebrews 13:8 was, "the same yesterday, today and forever", a cryptic reference to when we ate leftovers from the previous day. I asked Daddy what the Bible was, and he told me that it was a book of Jewish history.

In Lameroo, Methodists occupied all positions of social standing except the managers of the Community Hotel and the Post Office, who were Catholics.

In Lameroo, boys and girls paired off at a young age. Someone was always 'going steady' with someone, or 'breaking up' with someone.

I got to like the daughter of the Catholic hotel manager, but Mummy made it very clear to me that I was not allowed to have a Catholic girlfriend, and I could never marry a Catholic girl. And although there were no

Aborigines in Lameroo or nearby towns, it was also made clear to me that I was never to marry a 'black girl'.

There was no Boy Scouts in Lameroo. Mummy and Daddy said if I wanted to continue with the Boy Scouts, I would have to go to Pinnaroo, twenty-five miles away. When I said yes to that, they took it in turns each Friday night to drive me there. They waited in the car until it was time to drive back home.

In the Pinnaroo scout troop, I had to start off again as a new boy in a new town. I liked scouts with the badges and patrols groups and Red-Rover-All-Over games. I was made a patrol leader. The three patrol leaders took it in turn to pray at the start of each meeting. We prayed to 'God'. I didn't know what this God was, but it was easy enough to do when you were told how to do it, just like the saying of 'grace' before meals at night.

I befriended two boys from the Lameroo Methodist Sunday School. They had been friends for all their lives already, so I was an outsider. Quite often on Sunday after church I went with them to their family farms. I came back home with them when they went back to town for the night church service.

On the farms, both the boys drove tractors, trucks, and cars at the age of only thirteen. All I could do was sit in Daddy's lap and steer the car on the Friday night trip to Pinnaroo.

Sometimes my new friends came to my house after church. Mummy and Daddy had bought a tape recorder and microphone. We had it turned on while we were playing a card game.

One of the boys was looking at the turning spools. The first inch or so of the tape, where it was attached to the centre of the driving spool, was red. Someone said some 'rude' words. My friend jokingly said, "Ooh, look at the tape, it's turning red!"

The three of us liked singing. We recorded some songs, and I played them back and we had a good laugh. The three of us smoked cigarettes. At school, we would smoke in the toilet, between lessons.

In a science lesson while using the Bunsen burner, we would squat behind the workbench and 'light up'. Another friend was puffing away, down behind the work bench, and when the teacher saw the smoke drifting upwards from behind the workbench, he said, "Boy, are you smoking!"

Taken by surprise, he stood up and said, "No, sir." But as he spoke, the cigarette smoke belched out of his mouth.

At the end of Second Year, each student had to choose, for their Third Year, between the 'Area' course, and the 'PEB'-Public Examination Board- course. The Area course included Metalwork. It was designed for students leaving school at the end of Third Year to work on the family farm. The local teachers set the examination papers, and marked them, and told the students their results. The PEB course, however, was designed for academic students who would continue to university after Fourth and Fifth year. The examination papers were set in the capital city for all South Australian PEB students and marked in the city, and results were published in the *Adelaide Advertiser*, the one and only South Australian daily morning newspaper.

I liked Metalwork. I liked the idea of leaving school at the end of Third Year and working on a farm, but my hay fever was too severe for me to consider that occupation. I also wanted to work in the garage in the Chrysler motor dealership next door to the bank, but Mummy and Daddy said that was not an option for me. Another possibility was a career in the bank, like Daddy, but from what I saw of what Daddy did each day, that was not for me. In Lameroo the only other work options were the grocery shop, post office, police, minister, baker, railways, or teacher.

I liked my teacher and his sense of humour. On that basis, teaching became my choice of career, a last resort choice, so I went into the PEB course, and applied for a 'teaching scholarship', which would pay a small allowance for two more years at high school, followed by entrance to teachers' college, all dependent on satisfactory examination marks.

I wanted to continue with Metalwork, so I did it at night school, as well as extra Woodwork. One night during a break in classes, we decided to push the teacher's car around the corner of the building, so he would think it was stolen. It fell to me to be behind the steering wheel while the other students pushed. I went too close to a concrete tank stand and there was a sickening scraping sound. We disappeared quickly into the darkness on hearing the scraping sound, and while waiting to see what would happen, we tried to think what to say to the teacher. Nobody came out to see what the scraping noise was. We went to the car and found a scrape mark on a door handle. We didn't tell the teacher. Nothing ever happened about that.

Despite getting high marks for my subjects in Third Year, I never got top marks, which was once again a disappointment for Mummy and Daddy. Somehow Mummy had found out my results from an IQ test for PEB students, and she told me, "You are more intelligent than any of the other Lameroo students. Why don't you get the top marks in your studies?"

I had no answer for her. Boy Scouts was more interesting than school work, but I didn't say so.

I noticed that Mummy and Daddy had a predictable response when I disappointed them-Mummy would say, "Oh, my God," and Daddy would say, "You *fuwell* of a kid."

I continued to smoke cigarettes and disobey what I had been told about choosing my friends. Although I had some friends from farms, I befriended two other boys from the town who were sneaking out from their homes at night to break into shops and steal. Sometimes they sold the goods and gave money to someone older, to buy beer for themselves. I joined in with their breaking and entering and stealing purely for the excitement. We were never caught.

One day, at school, someone dared me to come to school drunk. I took the dare. Mummy and Daddy kept alcohol at home for their pre-ball parties. I got hold of a bottle of wine early one morning. I managed to swallow about two inches of it before going to school. I felt dizzy, and my eyes wouldn't focus properly. At morning recess, the kids got me to try walking a straight line in the playground. I could do it, but slowly. They all knew I was 'under the weather'. Somehow the teachers were not aware, nor were my parents.

I became a school prefect, and vice-captain of the school football team, and many times I was chosen best player. But I did not gain selection in the team to represent Lameroo in State Schoolboy football. There seemed to me to be no hope of ever being able to equal my father's schoolboy scholastic and sporting achievements. Only in the Boy Scouts did I feel that I achieved success.

With my mother's strong encouragement, at fourteen years of age in 1960, I achieved First Class and six proficiency badges. This was awarded with a Scout Cord, which I proudly wore on Friday nights. It was the first time in twenty-five years that a boy had done this in Pinnaroo. For the camping proficiency badge, I had to undertake a two-day hike with another boy, in open country, carrying our food and water, camping overnight, cooking at night on an open fire, and only using live coals from the previous night to start the morning breakfast fire. We kept a journal of the hike, including a list of what we carried, and a map of our walking path (with compass bearings and distances), and our menus.

I was chosen to be the Patrol Leader of a group of Pinnaroo scouts who attended an international Jamboree in Sydney. Later in the year I took part in the South Australian Boy Scouts participation of the celebrations of the Centenary of the Northern Territory. Again, I was chosen to be a Patrol Leader of a group of six boys, whom I had never met before, from various regions of South Australia, including Adelaide. About one hundred boys took part in the event, to travel by bus, nearly 2000 miles from Adelaide to Alice Springs and Ayers Rock and return, nearly all dirt road, camping on the roadside. Each night we erected latrines of logs and hessian. We cooked on open fires.

North of Pt Augusta, the main highway was dirt. The country was flat except for wide, flat-top hills known as tent hills. Heavy rain fell. Time and again we had to get out of the bogged buses and push them through the sticky red mud. The spinning wheels slid sideways, flinging cold, wet, sticky mud onto our uniforms.

After about two days, we arrived at a settlement named Coober Pedy, halfway between Adelaide and Alice Springs, consisting of a petrol station and a store and an opal shop. The main highway went between the petrol station and the store. I found a piece of opal on the road. I kept it in a tobacco tin. It was milky with flashes of green and red, about the size of a shilling.

In Alice Springs, we camped on an oval.

At Ayers Rock, we ran all the way up the Kangaroo Tail to the summit. From there, to look out over the vast Northern Territory virgin plains as far as the Olgas was unforgettable. On the summit of Ayers Rock, wedged in a small cairn of rocks, was a timber post that had four arms, each about four feet square. Nailed on each arm was a piece of tin, painted black, on which you scratched your name.

After returning to Lameroo, I wrote a story of my journey. The teacher published it in the LASRAG, a school newsletter. He gave it the title 'Willy's Walkabout'.

Another memorable journey was with the Pinnaroo scouts. We went on an historic camping adventure, a five-day walk across fallow farmland, and through mallee scrub, from Pinnaroo, eighty miles directly south to Bordertown. The feat had been attempted many years ago by the Pinnaroo scout troop, but after about one day the effort was abandoned, and the group had to return to Pinnaroo.

For our walk, a spotter light aircraft was hired to fly over late each afternoon and check the progress and safety of the walk. We had to carry enough water for five days, the time estimated to complete the eighty-mile walk. There were eight boys. Two boys at a time took turns to carry the water in containers suspended on a log supported on their shoulders.

A few miles from Pinnaroo, the leader realised we were all carrying too much weight. All the mothers had made sure we had plenty clothes and other things we might need. We shed much of it and buried it under a pile of rocks, to be picked up after the journey was over.

We used a local map which showed farmland property borders, approximate distances, and prominent landmarks. In open country with no marked roads, we used a prismatic compass.

On the fourth night, we were very low on water. We reckoned we were at a soak, as shown on the map. We dug in the sandy soil in the soak for a couple of feet, looking for water but there was none. That night, for a cup of tea, we used the water we had boiled eggs in.

On the fifth day, when we walked into the town of Bordertown, we were met by a reporter from an Adelaide newspaper. He took photos and interviewed us. The story appeared in the *Adelaide Advertiser*.

After attending the Lameroo Methodist church and Sunday School for over two years, I was asked if I would like to become a member of the church. There didn't seem to me to be any point in it. We had been taught something of the Ten Commandments, and I knew that some of the church members worked on a Sunday, and that didn't seem right. I said I did not want to become a member.

Over the Christmas school holidays, I worked in the railway yards branding and sampling wheat bags. In January, the results of the PEB examinations were published in *The Advertiser*. I read that I had passed everything, with some credits. Soon after, I received notification by mail from the South Australian Education Department, that my application, made more than a year previous, for the Leaving (fourth year high school) Teaching Scholarship at a high school in Adelaide, was successful. I was to attend Unley High School, the biggest high school in South Australia. My simple, country life was coming to an end, and it frightened me.

My parents arranged for me to board in Adelaide with a Methodist family. I was to go to a capital city where I did not have a single relative. Not only was I once again going to leave my friends behind, this time I was also leaving my family behind. It was the biggest challenge of my life thus far. The only consolation was that I had already spent most of my life leaving friends behind, so I was getting used to it.

2

Mum and Dad drove me to Adelaide in early February 1961. After about eight hours travelling at first through flat countryside and then through the rural Adelaide Hills with its thick forests of gum trees, I saw the great plains of the Adelaide suburbs stretched out in front of me, right down to the sea. I felt as if I was on a train, heading for a destination not of my own choosing. I wanted to get off the train but I did not know how.

Soon we were at the house where I was to be boarding, a house in a row of similar houses. Across the street was another row of houses, in a suburb of houses, surrounded by many other suburbs of houses. To me, it was endless and monotonous.

A very excited and confident, youngest of three brothers answered the door and welcomed us. But I did not feel welcome. I felt very small. He took me to my bedroom. I put my things down and sat on the bed, wondering how I was ever going to survive.

The family gave me directions to get to Unley High School. They told me about Cross Road, which I thought meant a crossroad. To me there were hundreds of crossroads, but later I found out that 'Cross' was the name of the road.

I had to ride my pushbike four miles to school along the bitumen roads, between endless rows of houses. A sign saying 'Hail Bus Here' puzzled me—was that where you caught a bus if the weather was too bad to walk in the hail?

On my first day, I stood in the school yard and stared at the masses of students. Somehow, I found myself in class 4D with about 30 other students. At Unley High School in 1961 there were about 2000 students. After a few weeks, I discovered two that I had met previously, one boy from the Pinnaroo Scouts, who stayed with his relatives in Adelaide, the other, also from the Scouts, who was in my patrol on the Alice Springs trip. He lived at home in Adelaide with his parents.

We had to order our books and stationery. I had never heard of things like Manila folders and Spring-back folders. I had never heard of Physics and Chemistry-General Science was the only one I knew. Maths I and II were familiar subjects, as was English. Why I had to take English Economic History was another mystery.

At the end of my first day at my new school, I found my way back 'home'. Two men from the Sturt Football Club, a team in the biggest football league in South Australia, were waiting for me and got me to sign up to play for the club.

On Sundays I went to church with my host family, at a Methodist church, because that was what my parents said I had to do. The people were friendly. Everyone had known each other for years. I felt insignificant. I went to the Unley scout meeting on a Friday night. Some boys from Unley High School were there.

Each night after school, there was plenty homework to be done. I did it in my room at a little desk, while I smoked 'roll-your-owns'. At age fifteen, I was an addicted smoker.

Slowly and steadily, I got used to the city life. Football was the highlight of my week. I trained twice a week on Unley Oval with the Sturt Junior Colts. I got selected a few games after the season started. It was very exciting to be in the team. Then I was dropped for a few weeks. I lost interest. The team selectors promised me a game. The next Saturday, I was first reserve, ready to go on the field to play. Some Unley High School A-graders turned up at the last minute after a forfeited game. I was dropped. That was it for me. I left and joined a club in the Amateur League, in a parklands club of Sturt 'leftovers', and got a game every week.

One of the players was a boy who also attended the same Methodist church as me. After playing football one day, we were walking home together, on the footpath alongside the main road which led to Lameroo.

Ahead on the footpath, I could see a matchbox. I kept my eyes on it, intending to pick it up, hoping it would be one from a new series that I had started collecting in Lameroo.

As my companion and I came closer to the matchbox, I noticed that our paths were converging, and then I saw that he also seemed to be looking ahead at the matchbox. When we both bent over to pick it up, I said, "Do you collect matchbox labels?"

"Yes," he answered. "I have a few thousand from all over the world. I'm a member of an Australian club of matchbox label collectors." I found it hard to believe him. My father collected stamps, as did his father before him, but I wanted to be different and collect matchbox labels instead. I had never heard of anyone besides me who did it. He asked me if I would like to see his collection, and we went straight to his home and he showed me. I was amazed that there were serious collectors all over Australia, and from all around the world. My education in 'Philumeny' began that day, and our friendship began

My friend's mother smoked cigarettes; his father smoked a pipe. My friend and I smoked too, in the family lounge room while watching TV. From that weekend on, I spent nearly every weekend with the family. I made friends with another student, who was also from the country.

At end of term I got a lift back to Lameroo in a car driven by a university student whose parents lived at Lameroo. As we reached the outskirts of the suburbs, I felt greatly relieved, no more confronted by all the houses and streets. But two weeks later, as we again came out of the rural hills and descended once again into the suburbs, I felt sad and lonely. Plenty homework and football matches helped pass the time.

I turned sixteen at the end of my first year at high school in Adelaide, and over the holidays in Lameroo, I passed my driver's licence.

One day I was driving my father's car in the town. My father and my mother were in the car. I went faster than the speed limit because it was a clear road with few houses.

"Slow down," they said.

"Why? There's nothing around here," I answered.

"Never mind, it's the Law!" they said, annoyed, with voices raised.

I slowed down to the speed limit. I really wanted to ask, "What is the Law?" but I knew it was no use to try because they were annoyed, and I thought they might tell me to stop driving and let them take over.

The Leaving exam results came out in *The Advertiser* newspaper: I read that I had passed all subjects except Mathematics.

The following year, I passed Leaving Honours English and Chemistry and a repeated Leaving Maths I and II. This gave me enough subjects for university enrolment and to continue to receive an allowance while studying at a teacher's college. I chose Wattle Park Teachers College for my teacher training. It was well-known that this tertiary college, the college of preparation for infant and primary school teachers, had a ratio of three girls to one boy, which was for me an exciting prospect.

My parents bought me a new leather satchel with my initials stamped on. No doubt they were pleased that their son was heading into a steady, safe career as a teacher, studying his books while on the train from the Adelaide Hills to Adelaide, and then on the bus from Adelaide to Wattle Park each day. But I had other ideas, and finally they agreed to let me buy a motorbike for my commuting. My parents found another Methodist family to board me in the Adelaide Hills.

One of my two Unley High friends enrolled at a different college for training as an art teacher. The other one went back to the family farm.

I was to start 1963 at Wattle Park Teachers College without knowing any other student.

3

On Sunday, the family I was boarding with went to the local Methodist church. At age seventeen, I was not interested. I had a credit in high school chemistry. 'God', to me, could not be proved, or analysed in a test tube.

It was exciting driving my motorbike every day up and down the winding, hilly road to the teachers' college and to Adelaide University in February 1963. But when I could not start the motorbike one day, I was helpless, with no tools and no mechanical experience. Somebody helped me get it started. I decided that I would have to follow in my father's footsteps-he had no mechanical experience either-and joined the Royal Automobile Association so I could get emergency roadside assistance. I bought an Adelaide street directory and marked on it every public phone box location on my daily route.

Not long after I started at WPTC, I began going steady with another student. She and my motorbike took over my life. I asked my girlfriend's father if he believed in God, because even though I did not believe in God, I was still curious, having had a church upbringing. He said he didn't believe in God. His answer reinforced my atheism. Perhaps, if he told me he was a believer, I would have been influenced.

I entered fully into the social life on the campus-football for WPTC, Bushwalking Club outings, running a sweep on the South Australian Football League each week. My study time decreased proportionally.

In my first year at WPTC, my student group elected me as their student representative. Each month I attended the night meeting of the

Students Representative Council. But my meeting procedure knowledge was poor. I was very intimidated by the social and debating skills of other representatives, and I did not utter one single word in any meeting during the whole year.

At the end of the first year, I passed well in teachers' college subjects that I had a natural talent for, music, health, and physical education, none of which I spent any time studying for, but I failed my university subjects, Geography and History. I passed my professional teaching subjects 'Principles and Practices of Teaching', and Educational Psychology 1A, which was worth half a unit in a ten-unit Bachelor of Arts degree. I thought that if my parents transferred to Adelaide in the Commercial Bank of Australia, I would do better in life, staying at home instead of boarding. They had no say in where they were posted. All they could do was promise me they would retire in Adelaide.

But one night in my second year at WPTC, they phoned me to say they were being transferred back to Victoria, to a place called Warracknabeal. Mum said, "What will you do?"

At age 18, after being apart from my parents and sisters for three years, and well used to making quick decisions on my own without fear of failure, I said, "I'm staying here. All my friends are here, and I'm well into my teacher training." As soon as I said it, I knew I was heading further into isolation, but I had learnt to believe in myself, and once I said that, I knew I couldn't go back on my decision.

Riding my motorbike to college and university was fun, but I did have an accident that landed me in hospital for a few days. It didn't stop me though. Soon I was back on the motorbike to my lectures.

I broke off with my girlfriend. It was as if my accident and loss of memory of events of that evening, immediately prior to the accident, triggered a lack of feeling towards her. Apparently, I had taken her to a place where she wanted to visit, and dropped her off there, and driven off, and then I was run down from behind by a motor car.

On nearly every vacation, I went on a WPTC Bushwalking Club hike. Rarely did I go home to see my parents.

After two years at the college, I passed enough subjects to qualify as a teacher, Classification B. If I had passed every subject, I would have been able to do a third year of training and gained Classification A, which meant a higher salary and an increase in possibility for promotion.

My next step was to make written application for a teaching appointment, stating what age students I would like to teach (I was qualified for ages eight to twelve) and in which locality in South Australia, either in the suburbs or, if in the country, which region. I applied to teach children any age between eight and twelve in the Eyre Peninsula region, which was as far away from Victoria as I could go, an area which I had no knowledge of, where I knew nobody. After the academic year was finished, I packed up my belongings and rode my motorbike to Warracknabeal to stay in my parents' home and wait until I received my teaching appointment.

The Warracknabeal branch of the Commercial Bank of Australia was like the ones at Bunyip and Lameroo-in the main street, with the manager's house attached to the rear of the bank chambers. Once again I was the bank manager's son, once again in a new town, knowing nobody except my parents and sisters, who had been to the Warracknabeal school a year already and had made new friends, whom I had never known. My parents were still regularly attending the local Methodist church, but I did not join them.

In January 1965 I received notice from the South Australian Education Department of my appointment to an Eastern Eyre Peninsula Area School as a Junior Assistant on Loan, which meant that I was to teach secondary students, notwithstanding that I had been trained to teach primary students. I also received a letter from one of the town's football clubs congratulating me on my appointment, and welcoming me to the town, and expressing the hope that I would play football for the club. A country teacher was expected to play a major role in the social life of the town.

I borrowed some money from my father, and on his recommendation of the trustworthiness of a car dealer who was a bank customer of his, I bought a twenty-year-old, second hand, Austin A50 sedan. A few days later I drove away from Warracknabeal, alone in my Austin, to Adelaide, and up to Port Augusta with its familiar tent hills that I remembered from my boy scout trip to Alice Springs. Then I headed west to Eyre Peninsula, where the landscape was wide and flat mostly, and almost treeless, with dry, rocky, creek beds and saltbush plains, like the country to the north, on the way to Coober Pedy.

Everything was new. It was an adventure. I was healthy and strong, full of confidence, on a teacher's salary with superannuation. My job was secure and commanded respect. It mattered little to me that I would be working many hundreds of miles from any friends or family.

4

Late in March, as football training was starting for 1965, my male fellow teacher boarder and I decided to attend the training evening of both the town clubs, before deciding which team to play for. Both clubs were keen to get the new teachers. Sport was a major part of the life of a country town, and most teachers were good footballers and in demand. We went to a training session of one of the clubs on a Wednesday, intending to attend the other club on Thursday, but on Thursday morning our landlady told us that we could not board in her house any longer because we had been seen training with the club that she did not support. The football club that we had trained with arranged board for us three teachers at a supporter's house about half a mile from the school. We moved there in my Austin.

I was the class teacher for a class of five boys and twenty-five girls. The students had all been promoted to this class regardless of their scholastic scores, as was the practice in this small, remote, country town, to avoid any stigma of some children not being scholastically as bright as others. When I started to teach them English, I realised that many of them were at a standard of about grade four instead of grade eight. Algebra for some of them was incomprehensible. I tried very hard to bring the lowest students up to standard, but it was impossible, and I came to be regarded as a not very good teacher because of the failure rate of many of the students during the year.

No Science textbooks had arrived for 1965, because of late ordering in 1964. The headmaster said I should do without them and just teach from my knowledge of the curriculum. But there was no curriculum available, and I had no training for it, having done a course for primary students only. And that wasn't all I was asked to do. In this district, the teachers had to make a survey of the government property they were using-the number and size of windows in the classroom, the doors and the cupboards. And on top of that, each week the students brought pocket money, and the teachers acted as bank clerks for the State Bank and made entries into each student's State Bank passbook. Adding to that, with marking of essays, and lesson preparation at night, life became a battle to survive until the Wednesday afternoon of each week. By then I knew that the back of the week had been broken, and football and weekend beer drinking were getting closer and closer.

At the start of my second teaching year, I moved out to a farm to live rent free on the farm and drive a private contractor's school bus. During football season, I drove back in to the town for training and to coach the Colts. I picked up bread from a bakery for the farms along the bus route and got paid one cent per loaf in the new Decimal Currency, when Australia changed from pounds, shillings, and pence to dollars and cents. My living quarters on the farm was a brick building in the house yard. At shearing time, the shearers stayed with me.

Often on weekends, I helped on the farm. The farmer and I talked about the possibility of me leaving the Education Department and working on the farm. However, I was contracted as a teacher for three years, and if I left before that, I would have to pay back a proportion of my four years of student allowances. I had no money saved to be able to do that.

The woodwork teacher was always well dressed. He spoke nicely. He had a warm smile and shining eyes. He did not play sport in the town. He was a non-drinker, which would have made it impossible for him to be involved in local sport.

He said to me one day, "Gary, you ought to believe in Jesus."

I told him there was no proof Jesus rose from death. I told him that if a person prayed to God for something and was granted it, it could have been a coincidence, and if it wasn't granted then the person would say that it wasn't God's will to answer the prayer-to me, that meant of a lack of proof of God answering prayer. I had a bible in my growing collection of books, but whenever I started to read in Genesis that God created the world, I stopped reading, because how could anyone prove that God created anything? Were they there to see the creation? If so, who created them? Who created God, anyway? For me, Science and Evolution were the answers. The only thing they didn't provide an answer to was the question of life after death, but what did that matter-if you are dead, you are dead, and everybody must die, as I had been told by my mother. I decided that I was coping well enough with my life without any help from prayer, or from taking on a belief system that negated one's self reliance.

After two years, I got reasonable control over the extra workload of teaching secondary students rather than primary ones. Sporting life and drinking were good antidotes to difficulties in the job. Joining in with fishing on the weekends with football teammates, and many invitations to farms for meals, made my life full. My fellow teacher boarder and I went everywhere on weekends together, getting drunk. We went one evening to a local professional's house. He fed us more beer, and tinned frog legs.

For the Christmas holidays, I stayed at my parents' home interstate, occupying my time playing lawn tennis with a local professional, and examining his stamp collection, and looking forward to a third year as a teacher in the same South Australian town.

5

Late in January 1967, I received a telegram from the South Australian Education Department instructing me to go immediately to Adelaide and sit for an Education Department bus driving test, because I had been transferred to another town where they needed a driver for a government school bus. It seemed to me that the government regarded me more as a bus driver than as a teacher. I was very disappointed that I could not return for a third year at my first appointment town, not only because I had made friends there, but because a third year doing the same job that had taken me two years to get used to, would have made my life easier.

A few days later in Adelaide, I sat and passed the test, and then drove to the new town, on the East-West railway line across Australia, where I stayed on a farm about twenty kilometres out of town, where the government bus was based.

On my first day of duty, as we were walking across the school yard, the headmaster put his arm around my shoulder and told me he would be relying heavily on my support. He gave me the positions of school treasurer and sports master. Then he took me into the rundown science laboratory and told me he wanted me to upgrade it for the modern mini-chemistry course, and he told me to fit the laboratory out with Bunsen gas burners. I did not have any experience as a plumber or gasfitter, nor did the headmaster ask me about that, but I was expected to do the job. As far as my core job of teaching went, I was to be teaching many of the secondary subjects, quite often a mixture of first, second, and third year high school students, all in the one classroom, all at the same time, quite often with subject combinations of English, Geography and Science. As well as that, on occasions, I was to relieve the infant teacher if she was absent, and the art teacher, and if the headmaster had to go away to a conference, my position was to be the headmaster in his absence. With all these extra responsibilities, which I was willing to undertake, I expected an increase in pay. But there was no mention of that, nor did I have any experience in negotiating any increase in pay. I was starting to think I would be better off in a different job, but I still had another year of service to complete before I had fulfilled my three years teaching obligation. I had no choice but, as they say, to grit my teeth and bear it.

There were no Woodwork or Needlework teachers or facilities at the school, so the high school students had to be driven to a larger school in the next railway town, thirty kilometres away. That was my job also. It meant that in addition to my Monday to Friday sixty-five-kilometre daily bus run starting at the farm and going to the school and back, I also drove from the school to the next town and back on a Wednesday morning. I would leave the farm on Wednesday about 8 am, drive a bus to the school, get out of it, and get straight into a different bus, and head straight off to the next town in time for 9 am lessons. After about three hours in that school staff room doing lesson preparation, or marking essays, I would leave the town, after buying my lunch there, and take the students back to their school in my lunch break, eating on the way. On arrival, I would get out of the bus, and go straight into a classroom and start my afternoon teaching. When that was finished, I would get into my regular bus and drive out to the farm.

The most difficult lesson I had to teach was a combination of three third year PEB Geography students, plus sixteen second year students doing science experiments involving the use of Bunsen burners, plus twelve first year students writing an English essay. In one of these lessons, everything was going 'normally'. Suddenly a one-metre-high, blue gas flame erupted at one of the science desks. With a dull roar, it kept burning at a metre high. I sprinted across the classroom through the fear-paralysed students, and turned off the gas tap.

A few weeks into term one, the headmaster told me that there was a rationalization of the bus run because of a fall in student numbers. I had to take the bus and move to yet another farm, stay with the family, and design a new bus route. After about one week, I presented a new route and timetable for consideration, which was accepted.

The football season started again. The local team was the bottom team in the league, with a rundown clubroom and a tradition of heavy drinking. One Saturday it rained heavily for the whole of the first half of the football match. At the break, everyone was soaked and shivering. Someone brought out a couple of flagons of wine. Everyone drank eagerly, getting a nice, warm feeling. We continued drinking, getting warmer and warmer. Then the umpire started to encourage everyone to resume the match. Nobody listened. No matter how hard he tried to explain that it was necessary to complete the match, nobody could be bothered. He gave up, and play was abandoned.

One day in a match, I leapt high against other taller players attempting to mark the ball. We all fell to the ground, and my leg got squashed. It felt like I got a sprained ankle. I realized that my match was over. I limped to the boundary and sat alone. No trainer or first-aider came to me. That night, with my leg swollen near my ankle, I drove to a local dance and even had one dance, leaning on my partner's shoulder.

On Sunday morning I was in a lot of pain, with increased swelling near my ankle. The farmer drove me to a church founded Bush Nursing hospital, for an X-ray, which revealed I had a broken leg-a fractured tibia. The nurses splinted my leg after forcefully straightening it, and then packed it in ice. Later they plastered my leg from hip to ankle. At night time, a nurse came to my bedside with The Bible, ready to read to me, as was the practice in a Bush Nursing hospital. I told her, "Go away, I don't need that stuff." I knew I was tough enough without The Bible.

After discharge from the hospital, the farmer came and picked me up and took me to stay in a house in the town, and I walked to work each day. Somebody else drove the bus.

After six weeks, the plaster was taken off. The fracture had fully healed. I went back out to the farm and resumed the bus run. On weekends, I played golf until my leg was strong again, with most of my scores being on the 'nineteenth hole'. I played the last two football matches of the season.

The broken leg wasn't the only illness I had that year. I came down with many minor things that held me back. I felt really rundown. I applied for a transfer to a town close to north-western Victoria, near to where my parents lived. My request was accepted, and I transferred to another Area School, only about two hundred kilometres from where my parents lived. I boarded with a farming family, but I did not have to drive a school bus.

My new class was a grade three group of thirty students, average age of seven, nine years younger than my students in the previous town. Instead of teaching students how to prepare materials ready for doing a science experiment, and make observations and come to conclusions, I had to teach them how to write-how to hold a pencil! "Start on the line, go slowly up nearly to the next line, turn around, and come down again to the line," I would say to them while watching them, as I did it with chalk on a blackboard, showing them how to do a lower-case cursive 'l'. It was a test of my patience.

My playing football on Saturday, and Saturday night drinking, in the previous two towns, continued in this town. I found willing friends in two other teachers who were weekend drinkers. They were friends with another drinker, a farmer who lived with his wife on their family farm. One Saturday night after a few beers, my teacher friends invited me to go with them, out to their friend's farm for more beers. The farmer was a tall, strongly built man, used to hard farm work. After some beers, he decided that I needed to be 'initiated' into their drinking group. The three men tied my ankles together and hoisted me upside down and left me swinging from the rafters in an implement shed. Later in the evening, we were in a car, drinking. We started wrestling, in fun at first. But the farmer got me in a headlock, and it was very painful. I bit his wrist, and he let go.

Another Saturday night with my teacher friends, after a few beers, we went to another teacher's house and stole his school bus. We drove along a dirt road and came to a railway crossing. I thought it would be a challenge to drive the bus along the railway line. It was easy enough to get partway over the crossing and then make a right turn where the ground level was nearly up to the height of the railway line, and then go along the line. But when we tried to drive off the line, the wheels just span around, and we got nowhere-there was too much difference in height between the sleepers and the railway line, and between the ground and the sleepers. We were stuck! It was about 2 am on Sunday. There was very little chance that a train would be coming in the next few hours, maybe not even for half a day or so. But the bus had to be returned to the teacher's residence in time for the Monday morning school run. We decided that the only option was to go to our drinking farmer friend and convince him to bring his tractor and pull the bus off the railway track.

We walked back along the track to the car and then drove out to the farm. The farmer obligingly got out of bed and brought his tractor and pulled the bus off the railway line. Two hours later we were greatly relieved to park the bus outside the teacher's house. Nobody found out about the episode.

I went to a local hospital for an examination of an infection. The doctor said I would need an operation to remove the infected flesh, and a skin graft over the wound. He assured me that he could do the operation, but I declined his offer. I got sick leave, and went to Adelaide, and had the operation there. I was not able to be at work on the last day of the school year. I was told that it meant I could not receive any holiday pay. It was unbelievable that I should be penalized for that reason, considering all the unpaid work I had done in my time in the school in the previous town.

I went into the Education Department Head Office and asked to speak to someone about the situation. A youngish man behind a desk told me that it was correct that I was not eligible for any holiday pay. I asked him if I could see the specific regulation. He said it was not possible for him to show me. But I insisted, so he brought out a folder of government papers and pointed to a couple of clauses. I read them. There was absolutely nothing there about denial of holiday pay. In the end, he admitted that I was correct, and my holiday pay was reinstated.

During the Christmas vacation, I went with three teacher friends to the tropical area in the north of Australia for about six weeks. We stayed in youth hostels with many people our age. There I met a girl who was training to be an infant teacher. She was from Sydney, New South Wales. To me, she was very pretty, always happy and smiling, attractive, intelligent. We had a wonderful, stress-free few weeks together. I fell in love. We got engaged. I stayed with her at her parents' house for a week in late January 1968.

In February, back to work, I was allocated a combination grades four/five class. It was my fourth year of teaching. Not once in any one of those years did I have the luxury of teaching consecutively the same subjects to the same age range.

My beautiful fiancée rang me to break off our engagement. I was shocked. She didn't want to talk about it. I did not believe her when she said she didn't love me anymore. I thought her parents were influencing her. I thought if I went to her house in Sydney, I could sort things out. She posted back the engagement ring.

Without telling anyone what I was going to do, let alone discussing the situation with anyone, I decided to take a few days off, to drive to Adelaide, fly to Sydney, and hire a car and drive to her parents' home to find out why she had broken off our engagement. I made lesson preparations for a few days and left them, and a note of explanation at the school, to say that I was taking leave for 'personal reasons'.

But my effort was all to no avail. The family would not even let me in the house. In the meantime, my headmaster boss had contacted my father and told him about my disappearance, saying that he believed I had had a nervous breakdown. My father came to Sydney. We stayed in a hotel until he assured himself that the small-town rumours of my supposed nervous breakdown were unfounded. He told me that the headmaster had ordered me not to return to the school, but to report to the Education Department in Adelaide first, to senior staff, and explain my behaviour. He also said that, on no account, if I was offered my position back, was I to accept the offer.

Back in Adelaide with senior Education Department staff, I related my story. They offered me my position back. I thought that if I accepted the offer, even though I was told not to, it would give me a chance to go back to the little town and prove to everyone that I was quite OK, and that I had not had a nervous breakdown. Anyway, nobody had given me any reason why I should not resume my position. I got to thinking that if I never went back, then whatever anyone had said about me in my absence would never be challenged. Having spent most of my adult life making independent decisions for myself without input from others, I decided to disregard what I had been told to do, and I accepted the offer.

On returning to the school, I found that the headmaster had instructed his staff to have very limited contact with me. At staff meetings, I was not permitted to speak. I was not able to stay with the same family as a boarder.

The family of another farmer took me in as a boarder for the rest of the school year. The farmer said teachers were just glorified public servants, but he didn't mind having one in his house.

I was not in good physical health. I had inflamed eyes. A doctor diagnosed conjunctivitis, prescribing eye ointment. After several days, there was no improvement. I drove to Adelaide alone, with the bad eye covered, and went to an eye specialist, who said I had a dendritic ulcer on my cornea, and if it was not operated on quickly, I was in danger of losing my sight in that eye. The specialist scraped off the ulcer and I returned to work.

The headmaster called me into his office. He was very angry with me. He said that my actions had had the effect of threatening his opportunity for rapid promotion. He told me that he had been advised by his superiors that I was to be put "on probation". To me, that was saying that all the very hard work I had done as a teacher for four years, in three schools in remote situations, was not appreciated. To me, my boss had 'cooked it all up to save his own skin'. I knew from conversations I had with colleagues during vacations that my four years had been much harder than theirs, because they had done all their teaching in the city, most of them staying at home with their parents.

I had money saved. I had completed my service to pay back for my four years of paid training. I was single. I had learnt what life was like as a public servant. I did not want to continue in that life. Once again, without any consultation with anyone, I decided to resign my position as a teacher, and cash in my superannuation, and withdraw the money that I had saved in a teacher's savings fund.

In the last week of the teaching year, I sent my resignation to the Education Department on the appropriate form. It was accepted. My superannuation funds were returned to me, without interest.

In late December I drove away from the farm house, leaving behind my drinking friends and an aborted teaching career, and headed for my parents' home in Warracknabeal.

6

My parents saw that I was not in good health. They allowed me to stay with them for some weeks to recover. Then they said it was time for me to get up out of my 'pit' and start my life off again.

I got the idea that I wanted to be a writer. I had read a book about it. There was a suggestion that life as a taxi driver would be a good experience on which to draw from. I packed my possessions and headed off to Adelaide, to get hold of the information outlining the requirements for obtaining a taxi driving licence.

I rented a room in a boarding house. The house had a community kitchen. In the toilet were toilet rolls fixed to the back of the toilet door, each one with the owner's name. I found it depressing sharing a house with a lot of strangers.

I was studying a map of Adelaide in preparation for the taxi license one day, when I had a visit from a former teacher colleague, who had also resigned. He was preparing to attend Adelaide University as a private student, while staying at home with his parents. He said it would be alright with them if I came to stay too, and I could go to university and we could study together. Having spent all my life, from age four to twenty-three, in a school situation, I found it difficult to get out of it, and my resolve to be a taxi driver vanished. I left the boarding house and moved into his parents' home, just in time for the start of the scholastic year at Adelaide University, where I selected Geography I, Geology I, English I and Philosophy I, paying all my fees as a private student.

Public opposition to the Vietnam War was strong in Adelaide in 1969. Two former WPTC students who had done a tour of duty in Vietnam and had been discharged, had resumed their interrupted studies at Adelaide University. They were also former WPTC bushwalker friends. They had little to say about the anti-war demonstrations on campus. Every day, agitators harangued the lunchtime crowds. I listened. I watched. I saw that when it came to a street demonstration, the ones who spoke strongly on campus were never in the front lines of masses of demonstrators walking ten to fifteen wide along the main city streets. They always walked along the edge of the crowd, close to the shops, using loud hailers to urge the crowd forward. It was a distraction from my studies.

As the year progressed, I saw as a private student that the academic life I was embarking on was not what I wanted. I bought a discounted university student air fare to Indonesia, looking forward to the opportunity to leave Australia, where I felt there were no more challenges for me. I went to Melbourne for Bahasa Indonesia language orientation, and to arrange home stays in Djakarta. There I met a sophisticated Melbourne University law and politics student who had travelled to South East Asia a few times. He told me about a way to travel separately from the main group of students in Indonesia. He mentioned Thailand, Laos, Cambodia, and Vietnam. I thought that this would be my opportunity to visit those countries and find out for myself what was really going on there, instead of relying on information from campus spruikers.

Without waiting for my exam results, I left Australia, and on Christmas Day 1969, I arrived in steamy Djakarta, a city smelling of sewerage and musk.

The itinerary was for twelve weeks-ten weeks in Java and Bali, followed by two weeks in Singapore. We all went to Jogjakarta and bought saris and silverware. Then I left the main group. I travelled alone to the east end of Java by bertchak. In some places, I was the only white man. There was still some bad feeling towards the Dutch. When the locals found out that I was Australian and not Dutch, they were friendly. I learnt to sing, in Bahasa Indonesia, the song about how the Indonesian people took back the burning provincial city of Bandung from the Dutch in 1945. Singing this song helped me everywhere I went in Indonesia. It was the equivalent of an Indonesian passport. Dutch colonialism and Communist atrocities were still in recent memory of some Catholic nuns whom I met at a student hostel. They recalled hearing digging sounds in the night, which, as they found out later, were men digging graves for the important people of the town who were to be slaughtered the next day. I went from Java to Bali and back in a sail-driven dugout canoe, a djukung, and then I headed back across Java to Djakarta. From there I took my scheduled flight to Singapore, ten weeks early.

In about mid-January 1969, I walked across the bridge from Singapore to Malaya, and started walking northwards towards Thailand. There was a 10 pm curfew due to Communist insurgency in Malaya, but I got a lift on a timber truck right through to Bangkok, Thailand, travelling all night.

In Bangkok I got hold of a map of Thailand. I walked northwards out of Bangkok, towards Vientiane, capital of Laos. Several lifts in local vehicles got me there.

A stark Vientiane newspaper headline, *"Plain of Jars Falls"*, was a reminder that a war was going on in Laos. A strategic airfield was located on the Plain of Jars, near Vientiane, and it had been overrun by Communist forces. Scuttlebutt was that there were two half-brothers, Prince Souvanna Vong and Prince Souvanna Pouma, vying for control of Laos. Communists were helping one, Americans the other.

I hitch hiked south from Vientiane, back into the middle of Thailand, and then headed east, and crossed the Thailand/Laos border and reached the town of Pakse, where I slept the night in a Laotian army barracks.

The next night, I lay awake in the barracks bed. Someone was snoring. A lone mosquito buzzed. The air was still and humid. Then the peace was shattered by a high pitched, descending whistle followed by an ear shattering explosion. Everyone sprung bolt upright in bed. There was another screaming whistle and explosion. And another. And another.

The soldiers scrambled for their boots and rifles. I groped for my passport and wallet. I counted seven explosions. Then there was silence for several minutes. It seemed as if the attack was over.

We got out of the barracks. The soldiers assembled and lined up in the parade area. I stood there with them. The commanding officer explained that the Pathet Lao, the Communist rebels supporting Prince Souvanna

Pouma, had attacked a nearby airfield with mortar bombs. He said I should leave the area. He would provide a jeep. I said I did not want to go overland by jeep through the jungle, because I had heard that, only a day or so ago, some nurses were evacuated by jeep from a conflict area, and they were ambushed and killed. The commanding officer agreed. I was crammed in with the parcels in a single seater light aircraft on a 'milk run' to the Thomas Dooley Foundation Hospital, further down the Mekong River, near the Cambodian border.

Arriving at the hospital, I was shown to a rest room. The words of the song, "*Hang down your head, Tom Dooley*" went over and over in my mind. Little did I know that the hospital was founded by a Christian missionary doctor, Thomas Dooley, nothing to do with the song.

I went to the bathroom. Each of the nurses had a towel rack with her name by it. There was one rack ironically labeled, "Pathet Lao."

Next day I decided to leave the hospital and head for Phnom Penh, capital of Cambodia, and from there take a flight to Saigon, and another to Singapore. My twelve weeks South East Asia trip was nearly over.

There was no transport available from the Thomas Dooley Foundation Hospital. There was only one way out-a walk along the road through the jungle, over the border into Cambodia.

As I walked alone, along the road through the jungle, I could hear spasmodic rifle fire, from all directions. My eyes narrowed. I saw every leaf in every tree. I was looking for the shine of sunlight on a steel rifle barrel. What I would have done if I saw it, I did not know, but I knew I had to at least be ready. I was frightened, but I just had to keep on walking. The narrow road was bitumen, with the jungle close to the edge. It was a hot day. The ground under the trees was dry and dusty, and I could smell it. I passed a few milestones. Soon I saw the border sign. I crossed the border. I was in Cambodia, and relative safety.

Some kilometres more walking took me into the town of Stung Treng. Many of the town buildings had rusty corrugated iron rooves, with quite a few sheets missing. The walls needed paint. There were holes in them. From there I bused to Phnom Penh and took a Cambodian Airline flight to Saigon, capital of South Vietnam.

For a place to stay at first, I went to a police barracks. Nobody could speak English. I used sign language. First I pointed to my chest. Then I put my palms together and inclined my head and rested it on my palms. Then I pointed to the ground in front of me. They understood that I wanted to sleep in the barracks. They said it was OK.

Next day I made my way to the 'Hotel Canberra', the Australian Army accommodation quarters in Saigon, which was fronted by rows of concrete-filled 44-gallon drums painted white, topped with barb wire, and manned with a machine gun sentry duty.

I was told to surrender my backpack while my identity was verified. After it was established that I was indeed a bona fide tourist, the officer in charge returned my backpack. He said I was free to do as I wished. He advised me to "keep your head down". Viet Cong in civilian clothes were known to strap plastic explosives onto bicycles; when the cyclist started pedaling, a deadly explosion went off.

Out in the streets of Saigon, I walked alone. Away from the 'Hotel Canberra' area, Saigon was like any other city in peacetime-pretty girls walking to work in the early morning, busy traffic of cycles, motorbikes and cars, footpaths crowded with pedestrians.

I made my way to the United States PX. Armed guards stood at the entrance. I did not know what to say, so I looked straight ahead and kept walking. I entered the PX unchallenged. What a delight it was to sit down to a delicious omelette and a milkshake, after weeks of boiled water and powdered milk coffee, and watermelon, as my daily food.

After three days of wandering around Saigon, I boarded a plane to Singapore, where I met up with the student group. I heard how they had all stayed in peaceful comfort in Java for two and a half months, sightseeing, and had then spent two weeks in a nice hotel in Singapore while getting fitted for a suit. They had experienced a wonderful, relaxing holiday, paying maximum dollars. Contrastingly, I had, at minimum expense, a far more diverse international experience, with great personal challenges of languages and cultures, going to places where few Australians had ever been or would ever be likely to go. I had exposed myself to great personal danger in a civil war in Laos, and Communist insurgency in Malaya, and been close to the Theatre of War of Vietnam. I learnt that life means little in a warzone, that there is little to be learnt in those zones other than to survive.

I had come through everything unharmed. My strength and my intelligence and my courage and my self-belief had brought me through far greater challenges than those that the other students had faced on their overseas trip.

7

On returning to Australia in March 1970, I went to Adelaide, and found a house to rent. I began a series of jobs as I tried to find a way to make a living. The jobs were all casual, unskilled and part-time, and each job never lasted more than a few weeks. They included builder's labourer, farmhand, salesman, labourer.

My first try as a builder's labourer was the shortest job I ever had. On a building site, the foreman, with a sideways glance and a nod of his head, said to me, "Shift that pallet there."

I looked where he was looking. There was no pallet in sight. I was wondering why an artist's palette would be in amongst all the rubble on a building site. I said, "What palette-I can't see any palette."

"That's it. You're fired!" he said.

As an ex-teacher, it was difficult for me to get a good job other than what I had trained for, and I found it difficult to relate to people who did not have the same training as I had. I visited another teacher with whom I was friends in our training years, when we were both members of the college bushwalking club. He also had taught for a few years and then resigned. He was living at home with his parents as a student, and he had stayed at home during his teaching years in an Adelaide school. He had started a bushwalking club for former students at WPTC.

I joined the club, and I went on several bushwalks and hikes, and a canoe trip partway down the Murray River, the biggest river in Australia. I went to some club social parties. Through these events, I got to know

Wendy Smith, a teacher living in Adelaide, whom I had a faint memory of from when we were students at WPTC. She was very pretty, with long, straight, dark hair, like my mother had.

She was a confident, happy woman, who had also travelled out of Australia. We started dating, going to dances, and the drive-in, and bushwalking club functions. After about four months, during which time I often had meals with her in her rented apartment, we agreed that it would be cheaper for us to share an apartment, rather than each of us paying rent in separate apartments. I moved out of my place, and we started living together in her rented flat.

A few months after that, she took me to meet her parents, who operated a dairy and an orchard in the rural hills just outside the Adelaide suburbs. I liked visiting them because it reminded me of my boyhood times when I visited my relatives on their orchard and dairy. Wendy had two brothers who were both taller than I. After a few visits, we went to her father, and I told him we wanted to get married. I did not think to ask any permission- Wendy and I were both independent thinking people who made our own decisions.

A church wedding was arranged, in the church building where Wendy had attended as a child, and where her mother still attended. Neither Wendy nor I had been in a church since childhood. The ceremony was held in May 1971. The minister gave us a bible after the ceremony.

After a brief honeymoon, we rented a cottage in the rural hills near the city. Wendy stopped her teaching job and stayed at home in the cottage while I earnt casual wages as a fruit picker.

There wasn't enough money coming in. Wendy got a job operating a loom in a knitting mill. On a day off from fruit picking, I went for an interview for a permanent job as a shop assistant for an educational bookseller, in the Adelaide CBD. The chief salesman asked me, "What do you do for a job right now?"

"I'm picking grapes," I answered.

"What makes you think you will be suitable as a shop assistant for an educational bookseller?" he asked, bemused.

"I was a teacher with the South Australian Education Department for four years," I said quietly but confidently.

"Right, you've got the job!" he said.

It was my first decent job opportunity in nearly three years.

I bought a motorbike and went down to the city each day to the shop assistant job. Through the job, I heard of a house for rent, that had a very large yard, in Oakbank, the home town of the annual South Australian horseracing and social event, the Great Eastern Steeplechase. We moved there.

I did well in the bookshop as a shop assistant. The owner of the business put me in charge of the bookshop on the first floor. He gave me a key to the leased, two-story building.

I got the idea that if I used Wendy's VW Beetle and my Hillman Imp as trade-ins, we could buy a new VW Transporter, and I could fit it out to live in, so we could stay in caravan parks and pay less rent, and then use the saved money towards buying our own home in the Adelaide Hills. Wendy agreed. I made a deal with a car dealer in an outer suburb named Paradise, and I came home one day with a new VW Transporter. We bought an Electrolux gas/electric fridge and a gas stove, and I fitted them.

I got promoted to Salesman with a company car. I worked under the supervision of an older salesman until I created my own sales schedule, and then I began calling on teachers in suburban and country high schools, showing them the latest educational publications from publishers in Australia, and USA, and English imports.

On country sales trips, the company let me use the car. They paid for my motel accommodation. I built up the business to such an extent that the manager did not require me to report first thing each morning. In my spare time, I grew gherkins on the quarter acre property of our rented house, on contract with a pickle company.

The bookselling company did some renovations in their leased building. They let me take home all the timber and masonite offcuts, and some carpeting. I got enough to complete fitting out the transporter.

A former teacher friend asked me to join him in rehearsing Australian folk songs, and we started Sunday night appearances in a coffee lounge. The coffee lounge was in a cellar. There was only one entrance and exit door, at the bottom of a steep, narrow stairway. Above the doorway was a sign: *Abandon hope, all ye that enter here.* Not having any personal expectation of hope for life after death, it was not a problem for me to enter.

My friend played banjo and I played guitar and we both sang. Gradually we built up a repertoire and a following and a small income. Then we got regular paid engagements with a folk club, as it moved from one hotel to another, under the auspices of the South Australian Folk Federation. Income from entertaining, and from gherkin sales topped up my salesman wages.

The interstate-based company that I worked for during the day did very well in South Australia with an innovative method of selling. Other Adelaide based educational book suppliers then refused to supply our bulk orders. My boss found a loophole in his lease agreement with the owners of the building. He put a sign up on the locked front door: *Closed for stocktaking*. Overnight, we loaded about 90% of the stock of books onto trucks. We sent them to the company's stores interstate. We took the rest of the books to a single room office on the second floor of a building in a nearby street. The company put off eleven staff–managers, clerical staff and store man. Only the older salesman and I and an office girl remained.

One morning some months later, I arrived at the office at my usual mid-morning time to be told by the older salesman that I had been sacked. He was furious with me, because through my sales efforts, he had a very free life as a senior salesman, calling on publishers. I was very disappointed when I found out that the reason they sacked me was apparently because the office girl had told a company executive, in an interstate phone call, the reason I was not at work at 9 am each morning was because I was growing vegetables in my spare time.

It was very disappointing to hear that I had lost the full-time job, after working for the company for nearly two years, but it was comforting to hear that the company would pay me three months wages in lieu. If I had known anything about unfair dismissal, or if the company's reason for sacking me was a valid one, or appealing my case, I might have gone to the bother of complaining and defending myself. But as it was, I was happy to walk out of the office with three months wages. I had no debts, and I owned a mobile home.

Wendy and I kept on renting, living off our savings. We had a small amount of income because Wendy got night-time work as a waitress. At Easter, we rented out the quarter-acre house yard to some campers who came to South Australia for the annual horseracing and social event of the

Great Eastern Steeplechase. I continued in paid entertaining on Friday nights with my friend, who had now become my business partner, in the folk clubs in Adelaide hotels and on Sunday nights in the coffee lounge, and we made a few paid television appearances.

Although we were not in financial difficulties, our long-term income prospects were not good. Nothing of any significance came up in a period of about two months after I got the sack. Then one day my business partner said that he thought we could make a good living as Australian folksingers performing in schools. He told me that he knew quite a few teachers who were interested in promoting Australian Studies in schools, but there was very little material in the curriculum. He asked me if I would be willing to help him put on a performance of Australian folk songs for review by a panel of teachers. Then, if we got a favourable review, he planned to submit the review for publication in the *South Australian Teacher's Journal*, following which we would mount a sales campaign to South Australian schools, selling our performance of Australian Folk Songs for an agreed student charge, offering a percentage of our takings to the schools.

I agreed to work with him and give it a try. His entire plan was successful, and early in 1973, we completed arranging our first tour. We were to put on our first show in a suburban Adelaide primary school in the morning, and then head north out of Adelaide on a two-week country tour starting that afternoon in Pt Pirie, followed by Pt Augusta, Leigh Creek, Marree, William Creek, Coober Pedy, and Woomera. Wendy and I would live in the Transporter. My partner would live in another van. We would camp on the roadsides.

8

Wendy became pregnant. She was in good health, and she said that the plans to be living in the Transporter, travelling, and camping on the roadsides, would not be a problem for her.

We stopped renting and started living in the Transporter. We drove down to the city to meet up with my business partner, and we put on our first school performance. It went well. We counted the money. With about 400 students at ten cents each, less 10 per cent for the school, we were left with $18 each. It was petrol money to start our first tour.

Most of our shows were in the daytime for school students. In Marree we also put on an evening show, for the Marree Camel Club.

The dirt road from William Creek to Coober Pedy became impassable because of rain. We had to camp and wait with other stranded travelers. After two days we set off again. The road turned into a series of detours around clay pans. We managed to get through to Coober Pedy, where we put on a show for the children in the school.

In the town, I met up with an opal miner with whom I had played football years ago, on Eyre Peninsula. He took us out to the Seventeen-Mile opal field claim where he was working with his wife and her brother. Underground, we watched as he drilled holes ready to set off explosives. Next day we went back down to the fresh working and found a seam of opal in the wall. It was a beautiful blue-green with plenty of flash, much better colour than the piece I picked up in the main street of Coober Pedy as a Boy Scout in 1960.

Back in the town there were people everywhere in the main street. A lot of opal was being found around Seventeen-Mile. Miners had plenty of cash, from selling their rough opal, and a local night club was full and rowdy. Remembering how I wrote a little story about my Boy Scouts trip which passed through Coober Pedy in 1960, the thought came to mind that I would like to stay in Coober Pedy and start up a local newspaper. But we had our tour bookings to complete, and we needed the money from them to survive.

My partner had a hand operated duplicator. He and I each wrote a song about Coober Pedy, and he ran off copies of the words, which we sold in the street as we walked along singing the songs and playing our guitar and banjo. That night we went to the crowded nightclub. The manager offered us all the beer and food we wanted, for us to put on a free show. We stayed there singing and playing for hours, willing troubadours looking for experience, getting more and more drunk, not receiving a single cent for our work.

Next day we left Coober Pedy and headed south, performing in schools all the way down. It was a very successful tour. After paying all the travelling expenses, we had enough money to last for a few months. Wendy and I stayed in a caravan park, which was to become our Adelaide base for more tours during the year. We bought a canvas annex to attach to the Transporter. It was good to be self-employed, and touring, and to be saving money towards our own home.

One afternoon Wendy started to get labour pains. On the way to the hospital her waters broke, but I got her safely there. She spent seven hours in labour. I stayed by her side for the whole time, and for the birth. She had a son. We named him Dary. It was Friday, the thirteenth of July 1973. After the birth, I left the hospital and went to my usual Friday night folk club hotel venue to do a paid performance. After the hotel closed, I went to a 'folkies' party in a house in the CBD for more beers and singing and guitar playing.

In a room at the front of the house I performed some of my original songs to a few people. Then, while I was telling them the stories of how I came to write my songs, loud shouting broke out in the house. Someone stormed out the front door, yelling, "You'll be sorry. We'll be back with our mates."

The owner of the house locked the front door and the party continued. Soon after, there was a loud splintering noise. It sounded like the front door had been smashed in. Then the door of the room I was in crashed inwards and whacked into the wall. A fierce, wild man stood in the doorway and scanned the people in the room. Looking at me, he said to other wild looking men behind him, "He's OK, leave him."

He left. A mob wielding lumps of wood surged past the doorway and towards the rear room of the house. Screaming broke out. Someone yelled, "Call the police!" I could hear furniture being smashed in the rear room, and terrified screams, and dull, whacking sounds. Carrying my guitar, I went down the corridor. My idea was to warn the mob that they'd better get out quick because someone had gone for the police. I reasoned that because one of the mob had earlier said I was "OK", the mob would listen to me, and take my advice, and get out before the police came. The house was only one street from the Police Headquarters.

As I walked into the kitchen to give my advice, someone behind me grabbed the guitar from my hand and pushed it into my back, forcing me into the middle of the room. I felt a powerful blow behind my right knee, and I sank to my knees on the floor. Another blow from a lump of wood crashed into my nose and knocked me sideways to the floor. The mob set in to kicking me in the head and stomach. I writhed on the floor, hunched up, trying to avoid the deadly boots. I managed to get to my feet. I stood facing a couple of crazy faced individuals who grabbed anything at hand-a large knife, a chopping board, a saucepan. They hurled them at me. I dodged. The things crashed against the wall behind me. I didn't have time to be scared-all I wanted to do was survive.

Then there was a sound of a bottle being smashed, and everything fell silent, and everyone was still. Across the room, I recognised a man well known in folk circles. He was barefooted as usual, wearing his customary loose, tattered clothing. He was clutching the jagged, broken neck of a beer bottle that he had just smashed on the kitchen table. He looked serious. Everyone knew he was about to inflict terrible wounds. In the brief lull, I dashed out of the kitchen into the garden at the rear of the house, and I squatted under a bush, gasping and in pain.

Several minutes later I felt a cold sensation around my backside. My fear had manifested itself in me passing my bowels. I stayed under the bush, resting. Police arrived, but the murderous gang had already left. I limped to the Transporter and drove to the caravan park. Sometime in the night I sat bolt upright in bed and spat out a huge mouthful of blood and mucous that had slid from my injured nose into my airway, nearly choking me.

Next day my face was swollen, and a black eye had started. I was limping. I went to the hospital to see Wendy and Dary.

A nurse came to me and said the doctor wanted to discuss something with me about my wife before I went in the room to see her. The doctor told me that Wendy had not slept well after the birth, and they had given her medication to help her sleep, and now she was suffering from post-natal depression.

"What's that?" I asked.

He said, "It's like, she might be breast feeding the baby and suddenly think the baby is a red back spider, and then fling it to the ground. She'll have to go to another hospital, and to have shock treatment."

I didn't know anything about shock treatment. It sounded terrible. I went to Wendy's room and sat down at her bedside. She glanced towards two nurses nearby in the ward. She said to me in a low, serious, confiding voice, "They're talking about me." She looked frightened. She kept staring at the nurses. She did not look at me. She looked as though she thought the nurses were about to approach her to do her harm. I looked at the nurses. I could see that they were talking to each other, occasionally looking around the ward. They looked to me like they were doing the kind of thing they did every day as a normal part of their job-discussing patients as if they were changing shifts and updating each other. They certainly were not focusing attention on Wendy, and did not make any movement in her direction, but she kept her eyes on them, and eventually they moved away and continued their rounds of the ward. Wendy said nothing. She just lay on the bed, her eyes moving around the ceiling. She seemed unable to do anything else but lie there. I knew absolutely nothing about depression other than what the doctor told me. I said to her, "Look, what makes you think the nurses were talking about you? How on earth can you tell that?"

"I know," she said, "because I could tell by the look on their faces."

I was baffled. I thought she was overtired and imagining things. I kept thinking about the doctor's red back spider explanation. Wendy stayed lying down, emotionless, staring at the ceiling. I sat there with her. She had nothing to say about the birth, or about the baby, or about any pain or discomfort or happiness, or anything. I didn't know what to say to her.

A nurse came and told me that Dary was being cared for while Wendy was under medication, and he would be brought to her for breastfeeding. The nurse said Wendy would be taken by ambulance the next morning to another hospital, where she would be given shock treatment. I was very confused. I had never experienced anything like this before.

The previous day, Wendy was what I might call a 'normal' person, having conversations, talking rationally about the things of everyday life- the weather, how she felt, how was I going, how the new baby was doing. But this day, she was talking about things that were apparent to her but not to anyone else; or else she lay quietly, like she was in a daze on the bed, with her eyes open.

It was all a mystery. One thing was plain to me, that this 'shock treatment' was a real cause for concern. I knew I had to stay with her when she went the next day for it, and make sure she was alright.

The next morning at the hospital, I got into the ambulance with her, and we went to another hospital. Sitting in the waiting room, Wendy was quiet, and sat still and said nothing, just staring blankly ahead. I noticed a couple of women dressed in hospital nightwear wandering slowly along the corridor. They looked dazed. I thought they must have been through the shock treatment. I did not like the idea of this happening to my wife.

A doctor approached with some papers to be filled in. Wendy was to sign to give permission for the hospital to give her the shock treatment. I asked her if she knew what it was all about, and she said that she didn't know. I said to the doctor, "You can't expect her to sign this. She doesn't know what it's for! She doesn't know what's going on!"

"Well, you sign it for her!" he said impatiently.

"No, I won't!" I said back to him.

"What!" he said angrily. "You know, I need this fixed straight away. I'm leaving today on a plane for Europe, to give an international talk on shock treatment. Now just sign the paper!"

"NO!" I said. "I refuse to sign this!"

"Alright," he said, his voice raised, "if that's the way you want to do this. But I warn you, if she doesn't have the treatment, she will be taken to a psychiatric hospital and be put on medication, and she may be there for weeks."

I knew I couldn't put up with being bullied by an impatient, loudmouth of doctor, into accepting some treatment for Wendy that I didn't understand, and didn't even understand why such treatment was necessary, so I got up and took Wendy by the hand and I walked her out of the hospital and we went back to the birthing hospital in the ambulance. From there, Wendy was taken, with Dary, to what I was told was a psychiatric hospital, by ambulance.

I went alone back to our mobile home in the caravan park, trying to get my head around the situation of my wife and our newborn baby being confined under a doctor's order, and hospitalised indefinitely. It was as if events were preordained that I would not be able to have any say about my wife. The only kind of explanation about the whole situation that had been given to me was the little story about the red back spider. Everybody involved apparently knew what had to happen in such a situation, but I knew nothing, and it made me feel helpless, and I did not have any idea what to do other than accept that the doctors and specialists knew what they had to do with Wendy. It certainly was apparent to me that she was not functioning as a person aware of her own condition. I could understand how Wendy, being on strong sedative medication, would appear to be dazed, but the business of her thinking that people were talking about her, and her being afraid that people were going to do her harm, when it was obvious to me that such a situation did not exist, I could not understand. All I could do was get on with my life, and to look after myself.

9

Wendy and Dary stayed in the psychiatric hospital for about two months. The doctors said she was a paranoid schizophrenic. They said there was no cure. They assured me that the medication she was on was not going to affect Dary through the breastfeeding.

For the first month when I visited, Wendy was drowsy and not interested to talk about anything, as though she didn't care. The nurses were bringing Dary to her for breastfeeding, and then they would take him away from her and care for him until the next breastfeed.

Gradually, day by day, I saw that she became more aware of her situation, that she was a mother with a new baby to look after. Then one day she said, "They're going to let me go home soon." What she said, and how she said it, made me think that she thought she was talking to a friend who was visiting her in hospital, rather than to her husband, and that the person she was talking to was not familiar with the whereabouts of the place she called 'home'.

While Wendy and Dary were in hospital, I did some shows in Adelaide schools with my folk singing partner, and we appeared regularly at a folk club.

The day finally came for my wife and new baby to come home. Wendy was a little bit slow in her movements, but she was alert and aware of everything. She was still on medication, which was to be continued indefinitely at gradually reduced amounts. She was to report back as an outpatient every few months, and pick up her pills, Imipramine and Tryptonol.

I took Wendy and Dary out of the hospital, and we settled in to the Transporter and annex in the caravan park. Dary slept in a bassinet over the two front seats. Wendy only ever moved slowly, but she coped.

We planned another two-week country tour. I thought Wendy was well enough to come with us.

The tour was successful and profitable. Teachers and students had asked us for recorded copies of the songs we had been singing. My mind flashed back to the fun my boyhood friends and I had when we recorded our singing on the tape recorder at home in Lameroo. I said to my partner that I would like us to make a recording of the songs that we were presenting, and to have it on sale at our concerts. He agreed, and we contracted with an Adelaide recording studio to hire their studio, and for their staff to record and mix our songs, and to produce 500 copies of a mixture of traditional Australian Folk Songs and our original songs, on a twelve-inch vinyl long playing (LP) recording. A friend took a photo of us for the sleeve of the LP, and my partner and I supplied the text.

Within a few weeks, we took delivery of 250 copies each. The LP was pressed locally, and the sleeve was printed locally. We had enough spare cash to pay in full, up front, for the production.

We did some more successful and profitable shows on country tours, and day trips for Adelaide schoolchildren audiences. The LP record sales were steady. Not having to pay rent while we were travelling, because we camped on the side roads, and minimum rent while in a caravan park, most of the takings from the concerts and record sales were savings. Wendy and I had a joint bank account, and the spare money went into it. We were saving towards getting the amount that was necessary for us to receive the government First Home Owners Grant. Wendy never got around to asking how much I earned, nor was she aware of how much we had in our joint bank account. It was enough for her to cope with just looking after herself in her life as a new mother, still on medication for paranoid schizophrenia, resting a lot of the time, recovering from the effects of the medications. My partner and I spent more time together practicing and working than Wendy and I did as husband and wife.

Most of the time in our concerts, my partner and I worked as a duo. Then one day he started doing a small section by himself, involving a home-made puppet snake, which invited interaction between itself and the audience. Through this theatrical device, he could promote some of his personal philosophies. I would go somewhere out of view while he and the snake held the audience spellbound. When he finished, he would signal me to return, and we would resume our duets.

One time in a show on a country tour, he and the snake were taking more than the usual time. I was thinking that it would be necessary for me to make a big impact on return, not only to be able to capture my 'share' of the audience's attention, but also my partner's.

I remembered a little old man from one of the country towns I lived in as a boy, who walked into the town occasionally and spoke in a very parochial way. He pronounced 'Adelaide' as 'Adelid', and 'Good day' as 'nay'. He had a nasal voice. He did not appear to have had any education other than at primary school. He did not seem to have traveled anywhere in his whole life other than the two kilometers from his hut on the edge of the town into the town itself. In the town, he used to be regarded by some as an iconic link to the past, and by others seen as a village idiot.

I had an old overcoat and a scruffy hat in the Transporter. I put these on and waited for my partner's signal to return to the stage.

He called to me. I shuffled onto the stage, hunchbacked, hat pulled down over my eyes. I said nasally, "Nay."

My partner knew it was me, but he played along with the deception, and said, "Who are you?"

"Perce," I said, "Rabbit Trapper Perce."

'Perce' stayed on for a few minutes and then went away to get 'me', and I returned, having disgarded the overcoat and hat.

Thus, the character of Rabbit Trapper Perce was born, and he became a fixed feature in our tightly run forty-minute show.

Towards the end of the year I said to my partner that, with a baby now, I needed to get more income. He said he was not interested in increasing the amount of work we were doing. We agreed that we would part ways. He told me I would have to increase my repertoire a lot, to be able to survive on my own. I took his comment seriously, and bought a banjo, a dulcimer, a concertina, a button accordion, some mouth organs, two microphones and stands, and an amplifier and public-address system. I made a T-chest base and a lagerphone. I spent weeks teaching myself to play the new instruments and learning many new songs.

I wrote a new, forty-minute concert of three parts: I would play each instrument and sing; Rabbit Trapper Perce would come on as raconteur and cook a 'johnnycake' on a small kerosene stove, using 'blowfly juice' for cooking oil, followed by a tasting of the cake; I would get children from the audience to accompany me in an impromptu Bush Band, with children playing the T-chest bass and the lagerphone and a cow bell and bones.

Just before the start of the new school year in 1974, I spent some cash on printing flyers and booking forms and reply-paid envelopes, and I did a mail out to hundreds of South Australian Infant, Primary, High, and Area Schools. In a few weeks, the engagements started coming in, and I could see that I would have enough work in the year ahead to be confident of success as a lone performer in my own right. I was looking at a very big increase in the number of country tours and city engagements.

Each time I had a run of heavy engagements in city schools, our family life was badly disrupted, because each time I went out to work, all the instruments and the amplifying system and speaker columns that were stored in the Transporter annex had to be packed up and put in the Transporter, and I would drive away leaving Wendy and Dary in the annex. That became unsuitable, so we changed plans and packed up the annex too and Wendy and Dary came with me and waited in the Transporter until I finished work. After the show, we went back to the caravan park and erected the annex and moved all the work gear into it.

Then I bought a half-ton box trailer and used that as a permanent storage area for the concert things, but we still had to pack up the annex for each engagement, and then erect it again after the show.

Then I bought a second-hand Morris Minivan. With all the concert things crammed into it, I would go to work in it, in the Adelaide suburbs, while Wendy and Dary stayed in the Transporter and annex. I also took the Minivan on country tours, while Wendy and Dary stayed in the caravan park. Each night while on tour, I would take out the concert things and put them outside the van, under cover, and I slept in the van, and I camped on roadsides instead of paying for accommodation. Many of the engagements were in tiny towns, all over South Australia. The individual concert takings at these small towns were small, but I was fully booked each time I went away, and the total weekly income was usually in the hundreds of dollars.

When the Minivan needed repairs, there was always plenty advice and help close at hand in the caravan park. I had to start buying tools and spare parts. There was too much to store in the trailer. I found a place to hide them under some bushes along the riverbank next to the caravan park. Eventually this lifestyle became too hard, so we rented a house. We saved less money, but we were more comfortable.

I alone had to promote my business, plan the itineraries, drive the vehicle to the venue, set up the concert, do the concert, pack everything up again, drive home, do the banking, and keep all the business records. I knew the regular expenses of the household, and so I knew when there was a few hundred dollars spare for a few weeks, or days, and I would put the spare cash into high interest building society accounts. CBS and REI were two that had offices in many suburbs, so it was no trouble to call into one or the other on my way home from a concert, and I deposited the cash. Wendy never asked what happened to the money-she didn't know that I was putting spare money into the building society accounts.

I bought some fowls, for eggs for eating in the home, and built a henhouse in the garden of our rented house, and grew some home vegetables, and got a contract with the pickle company again, for a patch of about 120 square metres.

Over a period of about eighteen months, Wendy kept up her prescribed medications, with several visits to the outpatient clinics. She was never able to live life in the same way as she did before her first onset of post-natal depression and committal to the psychiatric hospital. She was never the same happy, confident person that I remembered her being before the mental sickness came.

When a Friday the thirteenth arrived, it reminded Wendy of the day and date of the month when Dary was born, the day when her mental problems started, with the result that she could not get out of bed. Her voice was like a weak whine. She said, "I'm no good, I'm no good," and asked me to take her and Dary to her mother's place, where she could stay in bed while her mother looked after her and Dary. I agreed, because for me to look after our little son, and at the same time give my attention to Wendy as she lay in bed too depressed to get up, and do my concerts to earn a living, was an impossible task. I took her and Dary to her mother, and they stayed for about a week.

Several other times that year, she would ask me to take her and Dary to her mother to be looked after. I took them, and then came back home to live alone for a week or so each time, and to concentrate on my work. I was still occasionally able to sell copies of the LP that my partner and I had made the previous year, but with my heavily booked, one man show, there was a demand from the schools and teachers for recorded copies of my original songs. I had enough original songs to fill a new, forty-minute LP. I decided to do it. There was no discussion with Wendy about it. She was not an effective business partner, because her medications and side effects rendered her capable of nothing much more than looking after herself and our son, and even that was too much for her at times.

For the new LP, in order to save on studio rental and mixing costs, I bought two tape recorders, and recorded separate tracks of vocals and instrumentals, and mixed them in a room in the rented house. Once satisfied with the mix, I was ready to hire a studio and record single tracks and give instructions to the mixer as to how it should be arranged. Through the South Australian Folk Federation, I found a recording studio, run by an ex-Australian Broadcasting Corporation recording engineer, in his house. He quoted me a price for one thousand copies of an LP. It was a considerable proportion of the money that Wendy and I had saved for our own home, but it seemed to me to be an investment likely to give a good return in a reasonable time-the LP I did with my folk singing partner showed a profit after only a year.

Because of all the preparation I had done at home, it took only about two weeks in the hired studio to complete the final master tape and hand it over for the pressing. A few weeks later I took delivery of the one thousand LP's, and I started to sell them at concerts to individual customers, and to distribute them wholesale to city and suburban and country record shops, and city department stores.

Besides doing day concerts in schools, I had other performing jobs: on live and recorded television on every channel in Adelaide, and on radio, in an ABC orchestra, in festivals in Adelaide and Canberra, in night clubs and restaurants and art exhibitions, and in a pilot for a TV series. But the highlight of all of them for me was to be the lead singer and instrumentalist for two choirs, performing in the biggest auditorium in South Australia, the Concert Hall of the Adelaide Festival Centre, which seated two thousand people. The show consisted wholly of songs that I had composed.

At rehearsal in the empty Festival Theatre auditorium, I tested the microphone by making a small popping sound with my lips. The greatly amplified sound filled every corner of the auditorium. As the leading performer, I had my own change room. As time came closer for the first performance, an usher came to my room and told me, "Ten minutes Mr Atkins," then five minutes, two minutes, one minute. Then I walked along the corridor to the rear of the stage, then across the stage in front of the assembled choir, and sat at my seat at the front and centre of the stage, behind the curtain, and picked up my guitar and licked my lips, my heart pounding so loud I thought the microphone might pick up the sound.

The curtains rolled back. An introduction was given. Then there was absolute silence. I could see the two thousand faces in the low auditorium lighting, but I fixed my eyes on a position straight ahead and above the highest auditorium seats.

I started, picking out individual melody notes on the guitar, and then I did an accompanying whistle. Every note I picked was clear and clean, and the whistling was faultless. I sang the first verse, strumming a rhythm guitar accompaniment. The choir joined me to sing the chorus. After a couple of bars of my singing the second verse, one or two people in the audience started to clap with the rhythm of my guitar strumming. For an instant I wondered if the clapping was a sign of approval or of disapproval. Then others joined in, and within seconds, the whole auditorium clapped in unison with my strumming, and I knew straight away that the show was a success.

After the show, it was hard to adjust to the silence and being alone. I drove back home to Wendy and Dary. Wendy showed very little interest in hearing about the show. Her apparent apathy about life in general was very depressing for me, and even more depressing when it extended to her attitude to my success as an entertainer. I would so much have appreciated some encouragement, or congratulations, even some criticism, but Wendy was so involved in her own sickness that she was incapable of looking beyond it.

When Wendy became pregnant again, I contacted my high school friend, whom I heard had returned from studying art and exhibiting his paintings overseas, and I invited him home for a meal. He knew about Wendy's time in the psychiatric hospital after Dary was born. He said to her, "Now don't you go and do what you did before, when Dary was born."

Our second son Andrew was born. Soon after, Wendy was again admitted to a psychiatric hospital on a doctor's order.

10

Wendy came home again after about a month in the psychiatric hospital, once again on high doses of prescribed drugs. She was very drowsy for many weeks.

I often took her and the boys to her mother's house for a few days at a time, where she rested most of the time, while her mother looked after her and the two little boys, and I kept at my concerts and correspondence and bookkeeping. The business had got to a stage where I paid an accountant to do my tax.

The time came when we had saved enough to qualify for the First Home Owner's Grant. Wendy's parents added some money, and we got a bank loan to buy a one-hundred-year-old cottage on two and a quarter acres on the edge of a town in the rural hills near Adelaide.

The business continued steadily. The revenue for LP record sales far surpassed the original investment amount. Sometimes I collected amounts of hundreds of dollars from concerts with large audiences. If we didn't have any bills to pay and if the house loan wasn't due, I would keep on putting the spare cash into high interest building society accounts for a few weeks or even a few days. Wendy rarely knew the state of our finances, most times being barely capable of full time home duties. She stayed frequently at her mother's house. I had so much spare cash that I paid cash in full for a forestry covenant, which is usually purchased by installments over a few years.

I signed again with the pickle company. I contracted a local farmer to disc plough half the vacant land on our property. I bought a new, three-HP petrol tiller and worked the ground and planted three quarters of an acre of gherkins by hand. The narrow window of the gherkin growing season in the hills required that planting be done in the first fortnight of November- earlier than that, the risk of frost was high; later, the picking season was too short. With the onset of the summer vacation, my concerts in schools decreased, but it fitted in well with gherkin growing. Small cheques from the pickle company started coming in late January each year, and increased in value each week until early March, then decreased week by week until the end of the picking season, usually in the first or second week of April. By this time of year, I was doing regular concerts in the suburbs again, and doing country tours.

I was doing around 150 concerts a year, and I got confident enough to allocate a few minutes towards the end of a concert, when I knew that I had the audience on-side, to ask for requests. Most times I could accommodate the requests. One day I got asked to sing "Jesus Loves Me". The song from my childhood in Sunday School had faded from my spontaneous memory. I had to ask to be excused for that request. I felt a tinge of guilt that I had forgotten my upbringing.

With Wendy's mother as a backup to help look after our two little sons, I had a free hand at keeping my entertaining and publishing business going, while Wendy spent a lot of time at her mother's house. She was committed two more times to the psychiatric hospital in the two years following our second son's birth.

A pattern of behaviour emerged, leading up to her committals. Things would start off with a few consecutive nights of broken sleep, in which Wendy would get out of bed and go for a bath, or she would try doing some housework. It broke my sleep too. Then she would need to catch up sleep during the day. I was more interested in the business than doing housework and looking after two little boys. I used to help, but begrudgingly. My idea of a marriage was that the wife stayed at home looking after the children while the husband earned the money to provide for the family. Wendy was not capable of earning any sort of living, so whatever I earnt, that was our only source of income. I saw Wendy's prescribed drug taking as the cause of her not getting out of bed in the mornings to do housework. I reasoned that if the drugs were gradually decreased, then she would gradually be more and more capable of doing her housework, and in the end, do away with the drugs and have a healthy, active life again. After some sleepless nights and sleepy days, she would get to the point where she would be lying awake in the bed beside me when I woke in the morning, and she would say, "I'm no good. I'm no good. I can't do anything. I can't get up. You'll have to look after the children." Her voice would be a whine. Her look was one of hopelessness. She would not move out of bed. She would lie in bed, sometimes awake and staring, sometimes dropping off to sleep. If I did not have a concert, I would do some housework, but I did not have the time to take over the housework and keep on earning a living as well.

She would stay in the bed for days. She would talk about how terrible she was, how terrible her life was, how she was 'no good'. I usually finished up taking her to the local doctor, who would write an order for her committal to the psychiatric hospital. It usually took about two months to go from her initial sleeplessness to her being committed to the psychiatric hospital. Her stay there was usually for two months. After her hospital discharge, on high-dose medication, she took two or three months to get back to normal. Then, some months later, it would start all over again.

It was a matter of endurance for me to have a wife with such a chronic (long term) illness. She was never happy, never cheerful, never of a positive attitude. It was a paradox of a life for me-my regular job was to make people happy, but I could not achieve that in my own home, and if it wasn't for help from Wendy's mother in looking after the children, I would not have been able to continue to earn a living.

11

I joined the South Australian Folk Federation and was elected Honorary Treasurer. Our committee arranged the 1977 National Folk Festival, which was held in Adelaide. We hired the Adelaide Festival Theatre, and sections of the campus of the Adelaide University, and several smaller theatres in the city, as venues for the national and international performers that we engaged for the festival.

On the first night of sales of tickets, we collected thousands of dollars. Someone said that it would be good if we could use some of the cash to buy beer to sell at the performance venues, and then make extra money for the Federation. As treasurer, I said it would not be right, because it was not part of the constitution of the Federation to use its funds for that purpose. Others on the committee agreed. We talked around the subject, and it turned out that I was the only one who had enough spare private funds to risk on buying beer for resale at the venues. The committee agreed that I could supply the money. The beer was bought and resold, and I made a handsome profit.

During the festival, Wendy was at her mother's house with Dary and Andrew; I was alone in the house. The phone rang. The voice was clear. It was an uncle calling from England, where Mum and Dad had gone for a retirement holiday. He said, "Your mother has something to tell you."

I knew before she spoke that something had happened to Dad. Then Mum said, "Dad's had a heart attack. He died this afternoon. There's nothing you can do."

I stopped smoking that day, something I had tried to do unsuccessfully for years.

I rang my sister interstate. She rang my other sister, also interstate. Several days later, with money given to me by an aunty and uncle, I flew to England with my sisters and one of their husbands for a cremation service for Dad. We went to England and back in a fortnight.

We had been living in the house for a few years. The combined noises of a nearby railway level crossing signal, the long goods train engines, the nearby factory sirens, and tipper trucks constantly going past our property for a nearby freeway construction, became too much for me, and I decided that I wanted to sell and move somewhere that was quiet. A local grazier had subdivided his extensive grazing property a few kilometres away from our property, to raise money to buy a sheep station in Outback South Australia. He was offering private mortgagee finance. Wendy signed the contract with me to buy a 60-acre selection of the grazing property. We sold our property at a good profit, and we paid off the bank loan completely. We paid the grazier a $12,000 deposit and bought the selection with a private mortgage with the family who owned the grazing property.

The purchase happened at the end of a very rare three-year drought in the Adelaide Hills. A creek, which ran through the middle of the property, had stopped running. In the creek bed were a few shallow pools with tadpoles and a red-bellied snake at the side of a pool. Sheep had grazed every blade of grass, leaving the ground bare and brown.

I dismantled a shed from our property, and took the pieces to our new property, and erected it, over late summer and early autumn. We had no electricity or plumbed water at the selection. We used kerosene lamps for lighting, and a wood stove for cooking and heating water. We took drinking water to the block, and we used creek water for washing. There was plenty firewood on the ground, from dead branches, at the base of every one of the scores of huge, old gum trees on the property.

Not long after we moved there, the drought broke. Young gum trees sprouted everywhere, and the block took on a green tinge as the grasses grew. I rigged up a siphon from a spring for our drinking water.

I had the phone connected. I kept up the business promotion and the concerts. I signed again with the pickle company and put in a half acre of gherkins, irrigating it by pumping water from a permanent water hole in the creek.

Four years after our second son was born, Wendy became pregnant again. Our third son was born in the local hospital. Soon after, Wendy was committed to the psychiatric hospital again. She was released in a few weeks, again on high dose medication, again unable to do much in the home. Gradually, over a period of months, she got better.

We got to know a couple who lived on a nearby farm. They seemed, in contrast to Wendy and me, a very peaceful and happy couple. We accepted their invitation to visit their local Seventh Day Adventist Church. The visit was very pleasant, with lots of families enjoying a lentil-based lunch. They explained that they did not believe in eating meat. Although I liked the people and the good fun, I did not want to go again to the church meeting and not be able to eat meat at a community meal.

I was still doing concerts, despite having a policy of not leaving home unless I was guaranteed a minimum of $80. I was keeping up the payments on the private mortgage. But Wendy wanted a reliable car of her own, so she could be independent. We did not have enough spare cash to buy a reliable car. The only way we could do it would be to enter a hire purchase agreement with a car dealer. I knew that to do so might put us in financial difficulties if my concerts slackened off, which sometimes happened. Eventually, to keep the peace, against my better judgement, I gave in. We signed a hire purchase agreement and bought a new VW Golf sedan.

For a while, I was earning enough to service both the monthly mortgage and the fortnightly hire purchase repayments. Then we got to a time when the concerts were not so frequent. We did not have enough money for both payments, so I got a Bankcard loan, which carried us through another few months of mortgage and hire purchase repayments. We were booking up food in a local grocery store, and fuel at a garage. I was earning enough at the time to make the minimum monthly payments on the Bankcard loan, but not enough to pay any of the principle. Then we came to a time which I dreaded, and which I foresaw before I agreed to go into the hire purchase agreement, when the mortgage and hire purchase and Bankcard repayments all became due at the same time and I didn't have enough money.

The only way out was to take the new car back to the dealer and hand it back and cancel the agreement, and thus forfeit the payments we had already made. At least then we could continue to make the mortgage payments. But when I took the car back, the dealer explained that I would still be liable for the combined amount of the unpaid principle plus the interest for the full term of the four-year loan. They would have to sell the car at auction and subtract what they got for auctioning the car from what I owed, and bill me for the difference, and require me to make regular monthly payments until it was all paid off. I had no choice but to surrender the car. So, they auctioned it, and somebody bought it 'for a song', and I was left to make payments that were nearly as high as if I was still in possession of the car, but I no longer had the car.

Another month passed. Then the mortgage repayment became due, as well as the payments for the car that I did not have, as well as the Bankcard minimum monthly payment, but I did not have enough for all three. I contacted the grazier and said that I couldn't make the payment on time. They said to pay it when I could, and so we got some 'financial breathing space'.

I got Wendy to arrange for her mother to look after the three boys while we had some 'time out' together, and we stayed a couple of nights in a motel. In the motel room was a book titled, *"Your Bible and You"*. On the cover was a picture of a blissful family scene. The artist's perspective was from behind and to the side of a prettily dressed wife happily ironing clothes on an ironing board in her kitchen. Her neatly dressed husband could be seen through the curtained kitchen window, standing on a beautifully manicured lawn next to a tidy garden bed of colourful flowers. He was chatting with another man standing in the street outside the white picket fence. The husband in the garden and the wife in the kitchen both looked very happy. The picture represented exactly the kind of life I was searching for. However, it was the exact opposite of the kind of life I was living.

A notice in the book said it could be freely taken from the motel, if the guest contacted the publisher to say from which motel it had been taken so that the publisher could replace it. When we left the motel, I took the book and contacted the publisher. At home, when I got the chance, I read from the book. The style was contemporary. The content related to everyday situations of ordinary people who, when confronted with overwhelming problems, prayed to God, and received miraculous help-a passenger ship's captain trying to navigate in a thick fog without instruments; a farmer facing eviction in time of drought.

The book related how Mr Kellogg, of Kellogg's Corn Flakes, and Mr Wrigley, of Wrigley's Chewing Gum were both committed believers in Jesus Christ as the Son of God. Of course, I had never met either Mr Kellogg or Mr Wrigley, but at last I had finally found examples of people that I could relate to, who believed in God and in Jesus.

The book went on to ask the reader what he would decide at that instant, now that he had read about other people who had decided to believe in Jesus-would the reader believe or not?

I could not answer straight away.

I looked back on my life and couldn't understand how it had got to this: that at thirty-four I was having to pay for a car that I no longer owned; that my cumulative life's savngs had been paid out on a deposit on a block of land and a few loan repayments, and now there was not enough money to keep up the loan repayments; that I was living in a tin shed in a remote part of the Adelaide Hills, seven kilometers from a town, at the bottom of a steep 250 feet valley without a formed access road, without electricity, without a refrigerator, without flooring; that I had a wife who was so sick and in hospital so frequently that she was more like a fourth child to look after than a wife to help me.

To me, there was no hope for the future. There was no other avenue of financial assistance. There was nobody I could ask for help. My self-confidence, that I had relied on since I was a young boy, had disappeared, as had my strength, and my courage. I had no answers. My life was a failure.

In all my life, during my childhood years of church and Sunday school attendance, and in adult life in many discussions with others, there had never been one single instance of anyone directly asking me to believe in Jesus.

I said, "Yes."

12

Having decided to believe in Jesus, I thought the next logical thing to do would be to start going regularly to a church. I told Wendy that I wanted to do that. Her response was her usual-she wasn't fussed about it, wasn't interested. There seemed to be only two possibilities-my background was Methodist, Wendy's was Church of England. Neither of us were familiar with the Catholic church, and we had already tried the Seventh Day Adventist church. Hopefully, either a Methodist minister or a Church of England priest would be able to help us.

First up, I went to see a minister from a local Methodist church, and I told him that I had recently decided to believe in Jesus, and that I was looking for a church for me and my wife and children to attend. He then asked me about myself and my family, and my situation in life. I told him how I was in financial difficulty, and about my wife's mental sickness, which was threatening the stability of our marriage.

His response was in no way what I thought it ought to be. It took me completely by surprise. He said, "Look, we've got enough problems in our church already. We don't need any more, thanks." Well, what could I say to that? I said nothing. I just turned around in disgust and walked away.

Wendy and I tried another Methodist church, and then a Church of England. We could not agree on which one to go to, with the result that we went to neither.

One day I was talking to someone who told me that if I didn't take Wendy and the boys out of the shed and into a nice house in the town, she would leave me. I took their comment seriously. I found a nice rental cottage in the nearby town. It was like the one in the picture on the cover of the book that I took from the motel. We moved there. In the well-established garden was a big, old walnut tree. I used a long stick to knock the nuts off the tree, and I collected a wheat bag full, and kept them in the house.

Wendy said we needed marriage counseling. I told her I didn't believe in that sort of thing.

On another day, uninvited and unexpected by me, a social worker called at the cottage, and asked how we were coping. I told him I had enough money for living expenses, and I showed him the vegetables I was growing and the bag of walnuts. I said that my wife would not do what I said or what I asked. He said I should divorce her. I told him that I thought divorce was wrong, and I wouldn't do it. The social worker seemed satisfied and he went away.

The grazier phoned and said he wanted to help us. I assumed that he was going to offer a longer time to pay off the mortgage, so Wendy and I visited him. His solution to the problem of us falling behind in our mortgage payments was, however, not to offer extended time, but to tell us that we ought to sell the property and pay the whole of the mortgage off with the proceeds of the sale. I said that was unacceptable, and we went back home.

A few weeks later a man came to the cottage and said he knew we were in financial trouble, and he offered us cash for the block. His offer was less than our original mortgage price. I rejected it.

Wendy wanted me to stop touring and stay at home all the time to help in the house and with the boys, while she rested in bed. I had been touring for seven years, away from home for much of each of the years. Though the opportunity to continue earning a reasonable living was there, it was always based on 'you're only as good as your last show', which could be stressful at times, particularly if there was a lot of stress and sickness in the home. Perhaps it was time for a change. I agreed to stop touring. I stopped doing promotions for my concerts. The work stopped coming in.

I painted "Gary Atkins-Home Handyman", and my phone number, on the door of my HK Holden Ute that Wendy had paid for with money she received from selling her shares that her parents had bought for her. Work started coming in. A local land agent agreed for me to do all his maintenance and odd jobs on the rental properties he handled. He gave me permission to clean up scrap on a block of land with an abandoned house, in the next street. I took the scrap to our 60-acre property.

There was not enough regular money coming in from the odd jobs to keep up the mortgage payments, so I decided to rent a narrow-front shop in the main street of the town and start up a business as a music teacher and instrument retailer. A solicitor was using the shop on Saturdays. I offered to build a moveable partition that could be turned around 180 degrees. On one side would be my music things, on the other, a plain wall suitable as a rear wall for a small solicitor's office. The shop owner agreed, and I got a very cheap rental. I went to Adelaide to some music shops that I had dealt with over my seven years as a professional folksinger, and bought some mouth organs, guitar strings, guitar spare parts, and some music teaching books. Soon I had a few music students and was selling music things and doing guitar repairs, and we had enough money for rent and household expenses, but still not enough for the mortgage payments.

Then I got the idea of offering for sale, for $25 each, pre-paid copies of a limited edition, numbered, personally autographed LP recording of my own songs. I put in the shop window a notice advertising the deal, and a boxed chart with 2000 boxes, each one representing an LP record. Customers could choose their own numbered copy. If I sold only half the LP's, I would have enough to pay off the mortgage completely, ahead of time. Each time I received $25 dollars, I coloured in the box of the number that the customer had chosen. As the weeks passed in the shop, I made good progress on pre-paid LP sales, and more and more boxes got coloured in.

A Christian coffee lounge had started up in the town main street. Wendy and I had still not yet found a church to go to. I had recently begun regularly reading the bible which was given to us when we were married, which had not been opened for about eight years. One day I went in to the recently opened coffee lounge, and I found out that three couples from local churches had started it up. One of the husbands turned out to be a schoolboy acquaintance from my Lameroo days. We got talking. I told him about how my professional folk singing started off in a coffee lounge in Adelaide. Another husband asked me to bring my guitar along to the church he was attending. I did it, the next Sunday, and they got me to join in with the regular church musicians. All the songs we played accompaniment for were very short and simple. I knew all the musical chords and the rhythms. It was very, very easy for me.

The singing in the church was enthusiastic and uplifting for everyone. They clapped, they raised their hands. They enjoyed singing in church. It was spontaneous-sometimes a song would be sung a second or third time, sometimes the last one or two lines were repeated one or two times, all at the discretion of the song leader. The pastor asked me to come again the next Sunday. I did, and after that I was there playing my guitar, every Sunday. The meetings were held in a local hall, as an outreach of an Adelaide church which was part of a worldwide church called Assembly of God. Wendy and the boys never came to the meetings.

I was familiar with the pattern of behaviour which led up to Wendy being committed to Glenside: gradual daily increasing depression, followed by sleepless nights and listless days; taking of increased medication to try to help sleep; not being able to get out of bed for a whole day; saying 'I'm no good, I'm no good,' and wanting someone at her bedside to listen to her complaints and problems, which she elaborated on and wanted sympathy for; apathy about life; staying in bed for a couple of days. After about five or six of her committals to a psychiatric hospital, notwithstanding the months-long crippling effect they had on everyday life each time they happened, I developed a kind of acceptance to them. Each time it happened it was 'easier' to handle.

There had been none of that pattern of behavior in recent weeks. Instead, one day, while we were at her parents' house, Wendy started raising her voice in accusations against anyone and everyone. This tirade went on ceaselessly for about ten minutes. It became unbearable to listen to.

She raised her voice even more, and she started talking faster. Her very loud voice increased to a scream, and the words were coming out so fast it was hard to understand. I wasn't sure where our sons were, but they were not in sight. I couldn't take it anymore. I got out of the house and walked deliberately but aimlessly along the long street. I reached a glasshouse market garden area on the edge of the town. Wendy's screaming voice echoed in my ears the whole time. I came across some people working in the glasshouses. They were all Asian. I thought I was back in the middle of the civil war in Laos. I waited for the mortar bombs to come screaming down. None came.

I made my way back to the house. Two strange men were grappling with Wendy. She was fighting against them, still screaming. One of the men had a hypodermic needle. Eventually they held her still long enough to be able to make an injection.

Suddenly she stopped screaming and struggling. At least there was peace and quiet again, but this radically different kind of behavior, which I had never experienced, or even heard of before, caught me completely by surprise. I became very angry, realising that after all the years it had taken me to become accustomed to a pattern of behavior which my mentally sick wife exhibited, I was now going to be confronted with a totally new kind of behavior.

I walked out of the house again. I picked up a cricket bat lying on the lawn. I went to the house garden and smashed flower heads off with the bat, and I smashed the bat on the vegetables. Then I threw the bat down and went back into the house. Wendy was being helped into an ambulance. Someone said to me that I had better go in the ambulance too, so I did.

We went away from the Smith's house, past the outskirts of the town, and onto the freeway, and headed for Adelaide. Wendy was quiet and calm. I began to relax. It was good to be a passenger. It was good not to have to think about the cost of the trip or how to get to the destination. It was good to know I had nothing to do but sit in the ambulance and relax.

We went into the grounds of the psychiatric hospital. I recognised each building there, because I had visited Wendy in some of the buildings over the years when she had been admitted there.

Wendy was taken from the ambulance. We went further into the grounds. "Where are we going now?" I said.

"You'll see," was the terse reply.

Suddenly I realized that my pleasant, relaxing passenger ride to accompany my wife to a psychiatric hospital for yet another of her admissions, and then be driven back to her parents' home and our sons, was not so pleasant after all. It looked to me that I was also going to be detained, but I wasn't sure about that because nobody had said anything to me to indicate that.

I was ushered into a small room. A man sat down with me at a table. He put what looked like a hospital admission form on the table. There were several chairs in the room.

He asked me my name. I told him. He asked me my age. I told him. He asked me my address. I told him. He asked me my children's names and ages. I told him. He asked me my mother's maiden name. I said nothing.

He asked again. Again, I said nothing. I thought he would ask again, and I made up my mind I was not going to answer. I thought that he was compiling a list of all my relatives so that we would all be rounded up like what happened to Jews in times past, and be put to death.

Before he could ask again, I grabbed a chair by the back and lifted it up, ready to strike at anyone who got in my way. I was going to get out of the room and out of the hospital and go and warn my family of a coming persecution. Instantly the door burst open and several burly men rushed in, knocked me to the floor, held me down, and shoved a hypodermic needle into me. I felt my body slump, and I must have lost consciousness.

When I opened my eyes, I was lying on my back on a bed in another room. I could feel my blood pumping through my body, and my heartbeat was loud and strong. I thought that any minute the blood pressure would explode through a weak section of a wall of one of my blood vessels and spurt out all my blood, and my life would be over.

I closed my eyes and lay still so as not to put pressure on my blood vessels and I cried softly, repeatedly, "Oh, God, Oh God, Oh God ..."

Eventually my blood stopped pumping so strongly. The crisis had passed. I had not bled to death.

I was taken to another room and told to take off all my clothes. By that time, I realized that I was indeed detained in the psychiatric hospital, even though nobody had told me so. They took all my clothes away. They brought me hospital clothes and hospital toothbrush and toothpaste. They did not leave with me a single personal item. I felt that I was now the property of the hospital, devoid of my own identity. They brought me medication and watched me as I swallowed it. Later a bell sounded. It was time to go to the community mess and have a hot drink and biscuits. The bell sounded again later for an evening meal in the mess. Later, another bell-it was time for another supervised medication dosage.

I settled into life in the hospital. About a week later I felt comfortable enough to join in with conversations with other patients at meal times and in the patient recreation area. One day we had an outdoor barbecue. We could see across the hospital grounds, and beyond the low stone perimeter wall and into the street, where people walked along the footpath and cars were being driven along the road. The situation reminded me of a joke about a mental hospital patient who was allowed out of the hospital grounds for a short, unsupervised walk. The patient had walked past a house where a man was working in his garden, putting cakes of cow manure on and around his strawberry bushes. The patient asked the gardener, "What are you doing?"

"I'm putting cow manure on the strawberries," was the answer.

The patient said, "You ought to come and stay with us. We put cream on ours."

Each patient knew all about the other patients-the circumstances leading up to admission, how long the admission was for, how each felt about life in the hospital, whether they wanted to leave, what life after hospital would be like.

After about a fortnight in the hospital, a nurse told me that I did not have to take any more medication and I was free to go anytime I liked. I said I'd go that day. I got back my clothes and personal things. My discharge papers were signed. I left the hospital and went straight back to the rented cottage, where I stayed alone, the boys still with Wendy's mother, Wendy still in hospital.

13

The day after my discharge, I started again in the music business in the rented shop. I was earning enough to pay living expenses, but I realized that the possibility of paying off the mortgage from money collected by selling pre-paid LP recordings was diminished, seeing I had not been in the shop for more than two weeks, so I contacted a land agent and told him to put our property on the market, and I told the grazier what I had done.

Two weeks later, Wendy came home from hospital to the rented cottage. She asked me to take her to her mother's house. I took her. She said she needed to stay there for a while. I went back to the rented cottage and stayed there alone. After a few days, I went to see the boys. I found out that Wendy had been sending Dary and Andrew to the local school there. I said that was unnecessary, because I could look after them. I took them home. Wendy stayed on at her mother's. I took Dary and Andrew back to their original school, and I told the teachers that the boys would be staying there, even though they had been recently attending a different school.

One morning, I sent Dary and Andrew off to school and took Ben to the music shop as usual. Ben was two years old. I knew he had to be watched all the time, but for a moment I turned away from him in the tiny shop to attend to something.

Next minute when I turned around I did not see him in the shop. I thought he must have wandered out into the street. I went out of the shop and looked to the left. He was not there. There were only two shops to the corner, and I thought he wouldn't have had time to walk that far and around the corner, so he must have gone along the footpath to the right.

I looked to the right. I saw a few people walking along the footpath, but no little boys. There were many shops to the right, and the next street was about thirty meters away. I thought Ben must have gone to the left after all, and around the corner, so I turned around and started walking towards the corner.

Two men came around the corner and walked towards me. One was the social worker who had been to the cottage, asking how I was coping with finances. The other man was a stranger to me. As we came closer to each other, the two men looked as though they were going to speak to me. I wanted to walk past them and go around the corner to look for Ben, but the stranger spoke to me. He said, "Are you Gary David Atkins?"

I had no idea why he was asking me such a question in such a way, but I said, "Yes."

He said, "We've got Ben, and we've taken Dary and Andrew from school."

I stared at him. I felt paralyzed. He said, "I have some papers for you."

He stretched his arm towards me. In his hand were some papers. I took them out of his hand. The men turned around and walked back the way they came. I turned around and slowly walked back into the music shop and sat down, in a daze.

14

I sat down in the shop for about ten minutes, in shock. I wasn't sweating, or feeling cold and shivery, or feeling dizzy. I was simply unable to do anything except sit down and consider what had just happened-earlier on in the morning I was looking after my three sons because my wife was sick; I had sent the two oldest to school; I was minding the youngest, two years old, who was out of my direct sight for a matter of about two minutes only. Now, mid-morning, without any warning, without any reason to think that such a thing might possibly be going to happen, a stranger had walked up to me in the street and told me that he had taken my two year old son away from me, from virtually under my nose, and that he had gone to the school where I had sent my six year old and eight year old sons, and without my permission, had taken them from the school, without the teacher telling me that he had gone to the school, without the teacher telling me what he wanted to do, without the teacher telling me what he had done! Surely, this was not true. Surely this did not happen. But, yes, it was true, it had happened!

Now, why had it happened? How did a stranger have the power to do what he had done? How could I get answers to these things? Who could I ask?

I was still holding the papers from the stranger. Yes; therein should be the answers. On a first, quick look at them, I saw that there were three separate documents: each one had the words, "Family Law Act." One was titled "Affidavit", another, "Application for Custody," another, "Court Order."

The words, "Family Law Act", sounded to me like an official government title. So, all this that had just happened to me that morning, was something to do with the government, therefore it had authority. But how could a government have authority to step into the everyday life of my family and take away my children while I was looking after them because my wife was sick? What about my wife, the mother of my sons-what did she know about this? Perhaps she gave permission and forgot to tell me-maybe I would find something in the documents about that.

The paper titled 'Affidavit' was dated 4th May, which was four days previous, the present day being 8th May. The first sentence said the document contained some statements made by my wife, "presented to the Family Court, in support of her Application for Custody, which she requested to be heard ex parte as a matter of urgency." Well, I had never heard of such a thing as a 'Family Court', but nevertheless, it obviously did exist, because it was referred to in the government document. The next thing that confused me was the words, "Application for Custody." To me 'custody' meant being in prison. I couldn't understand why my wife would want to apply to be put in prison. Further confusion came with the words 'ex parte', which I had never heard of, which was, I thought, from the ancient Latin language, but which now had some legal meaning that I had no idea about.

All I could do was skip over that part of the document. Maybe I would understand it if I read a bit more, and then returned to that part.

Then there was a series of numbered statements attributed to my wife. In the first one, she mentioned the date of our marriage, and then said we 'separated' on 7th April. Well, that was news to me, whatever the meaning of separation was. It sounded like it was a legal term. It probably meant that we were apart from each other. If that was the case, then to put a date like 7th April as when we were apart, had little or no meaning to me, because there were probably fifty other times during the years of our marriage when we were 'separated'-the many times Wendy was in hospital, the many times she stayed resting at her mother's house while her mother looked after the children, the many times I went away from home on tour for sometimes up to a fortnight at a time. Her statement said that the 7th of April was the date when she "departed the matrimonial home." When I read that bit, I began to get an idea of what all this paperwork was about-if one 'departs' a matrimonial home, one is not going to hospital, or to one's mother's house-one is abandoning the marriage! The only problem with that was, it would only have been my wife and her solicitor and perhaps her parents who were aware that she was abandoning the marriage, on 7th April. I certainly was not told anything about such a thing prior to, or on, 7th April, or on any other day, for that matter.

Wendy's next statement annoyed me, because it simply was not true: "The said separation was the result of several years of deterioration of the marriage arising from quarrels over the shortage of money to provide basic essentials for the care of the children." Sure, we had trouble sometimes, making the mortgage payments on time, but I know there was always money for food and clothes and shelter. Anyway, most of the time Wendy was incapable of managing any kind of household budget, because she was in the psychiatric hospital around about once every year, and for much of the time when she was at home, she was under medication and sleeping a lot. I doubt if she ever consistently knew what the financial situation of the family was.

Her next statement annoyed me too. It did not represent the whole truth, only part of the truth, and as such, it conveyed the impression that she was a woman who was always at home working hard to care for the children, and that her husband did not contribute much to the family life, and that there was one time when she desperately sought the help of her parents: "we separated briefly in February 1981 when I left him and took the children to my parents' home for a few days to get over a particularly difficult period." But the whole truth was that her parents helped many, many times, by looking after the children, and looking after her too, in their home. She was often so depressed that she could not get out of bed; she was often committed to a psychiatric hospital; I often tried to help in the house while continuing to run my business and earn a living.

Wendy's next statement made me very angry. She stated that I had been unable to "retain a steady job or income". How could such a statement be reconciled with the fact that for the first two years of the marriage I worked for a company, with a fortnightly pay packet. Then for the next seven years, I worked for myself as a folksinger and publisher and for four of those years I also grew gherkins on contract with a pickle company. In my best year, I earned over $10,000.

I saw that the Affidavit so far, through both misinformation and plain untruths, was painting a very bad picture of me as a father, and one of her as a caring, worthwhile mother, but there was nothing in the Affidavit about her chronic psychological illness and committal to a psychiatric hospital seven times in nine years.

Wendy said that I was looking after our youngest son while teaching music three nights a week. This statement was simply untrue-I was not giving any music lessons at night at all-the lessons were all in the daytime.

Her next statement, "I believe the husband has been unable to pay rent", was very misleading, because I was regularly paying the rent.

Then for Wendy to state, "I intend that I and the children reside with my parents in their comfortable, well-appointed, four-bedroomed house at Frank Street Murray Bridge" was a continuation of the implications that I as husband and as a father was not looking after my family, and, as far as I could see, a deliberate omission of the fact that I was already paying rent for a comfortable, well-appointed, three-bedroom home in a well established residential area of a country town.

Wendy's final statement was to me the most misleading one: "I am able to devote all my time to their supervision as I do not work." The plain fact of the matter was that Wendy did not work, and did not need to work, for the last eight years of the marriage, the simple reason being that my income was sufficient to provide for the family. And for Wendy to use the words "all my time" was ridiculous to me, but of course if her solicitor had not been made aware of how much of Wendy's time was taken up with having many breakdowns, being hospitalised, recovering from high dose medications, then the words "all my time" had relevance. And if Wendy's solicitor was aware that she was a diagnosed paranoid schizophrenic, then he was deliberately implicit in compiling a deceitful series of statements.

Wendy's final statement, that "her mother was well, and able to assist her in the care of the children at such times as may be necessary," would more accurately be expressed as "whenever I have an acute attack of depression, which occurs quite often, resulting in me being detained in a psychiatric hospital for weeks at a time, and after discharge, being required to be on high dose medication for many weeks, I would have no fear for the well being of my children, because my mother is in very good health and able at any time to take over their care, for extended periods of time, as may be necessary."

After reading the whole of the document, although I did not yet understand the significance of the Latin expression "ex parte", right at the start of the document, the associated words "as a matter of urgency" conveyed to me that Wendy, working with her solicitor, urgently wanted the matter dealt with, before I had a chance to find out about what had been said about me and my role as a husband and father, and before anyone had any opportunity to take into consideration that Wendy was a mentally sick woman.

15

Nobody had come into the shop so far. I put down the first document and picked up the second, the "Application", dated 5th May, which was three days prior. It was an Application, made by Wendy, for several Orders to be made, by the Family Court, under the authority of the Family Law Act.

The first Order that Wendy applied for was that she be given sole custody, care, and control of our children. As soon as I read that, I realized that the word 'custody' had a different meaning from being in prison, as I had originally thought. I also then realized that the taking of the three boys from me that morning had been at the request of my wife. She had also requested that an Order be made for me to "return forthwith" the children to her custody. Those words implied to me that the stranger who gave me the papers ought to have come to me and told me that my wife had applied for an Order to be made, that I return the children to her. If that had happened, I would have been able to ask him when the Family Court was going to sit to hear Wendy's Application for the Order to be made, and I could have gone to the Family Court and objected to the Order being made, because my wife was a paranoid schizophrenic, and ought not to be given sole custody, care, and control of our children.

But the stranger did not give me any such opportunity. Instead, he had gone to the school where I had sent my two older sons that morning, and taken them from the school, presumably with the consent of the teachers, and without my consent, and somehow grabbed my two year old son without me seeing him do it.

I could not understand how all this could have been legal, because there was nothing in the Application to say that the Family Court had heard the application, let alone anything to say that the Family Court had agreed with Wendy's request, and had made the Orders. Maybe there was something in the third document that would explain everything.

I continued to read the second document. I could hardly believe what I read next: that Wendy had requested for an Order to be made by the Family Court that I be "Restrained", and that an Injunction be granted, restraining me from removing the children from Wendy's care and control, or removing them from the State of South Australia. She also requested that the Family Court make an Order that an Injunction also be granted which would restrain me from "in any was assaulting, molesting, harassing or interfering with the wife or the said children" or "Entering upon or remaining upon or in the vicinity of premises or place at which the Wife may reside from time to time." It was all just simply unbelievable-no matter what I might try to do, to object, to go and plead my case, to go anywhere near where Wendy and our children were staying, I would be breaking the law, and be liable to be arrested! I could do nothing except sit there in the shop and wonder what my life had turned into.

At this stage in my reading of the document, I had not yet read anything to say that the Family Court had made any Orders as requested by Wendy. I was still trying to get to an understanding of how the morning's events had been able to have had any chance of the possibility of being able to have taken place. Nothing I had read so far had explained that.

Then, I saw at the end of the document, a heading "TO THE HUSBAND." Aha! This was surely going to explain everything. Of course, it would have to be assumed that the husband, on or before the day when the document was written, would have seen the document, because it said that the Application, "has been set down for hearing by the Family Court ..." Now, here, I read the date of the day when the Application would be heard, and when I read that, my eyes nearly bulged out of their sockets, and I just stared in disbelief at what I read. It said that the Application has been set down for hearing on 6th May! How could that be? Today was the 8th of May! The Family Court, according to the paper I held, had already heard the Application!

Compounding this unbelievable situation, the next sentence said that, if I wanted to contest the Application, or seek some other Order, I may do so. What! How could I contest the Application two days after the Application had already been heard!

It was at that time that I thought there must have been something wrong with the document. As an ex-teacher I had noticed a few typing errors in the document. I thought that maybe the date of the Family Court hearing, 6th May, was a typing error, because how could I possibly be able to contest the Application if the Family Court hearing had already occurred. I was sure the 6th of May was a couple of days previous.

I was still in shock, still trying to understand how my children were gone. I read the last few paragraphs of the document again, to make sure of what I thought I had read. Yes, I had read the document correctly the first time-the Family Court hearing had been set down for the 6th May. I realised that I had not been mistaken.

But if it was true, then the Family Court had already sat, and I had missed my opportunity to contest the Application and file an Affidavit in reply, which would have detailed all the instances of Wendy's hospitalization, and her inability to consistently care for three children, let alone care for herself. The Family Court would surely never have upheld her Application for Custody if it was aware of my side of the story.

I looked at the calendar on the wall. The day was the 8th of May.

Yes, the Family Court had sat two days previously. They had read an Affidavit that was a very poor representation of the whole truth of the situation. They had not been given the opportunity to read an Affidavit from me, the accused person.

I looked again at the document to make sure I had read it correctly. I had. The Family Court hearing was set for 6th May.

I looked again at the calendar. The day was 8th May.

I still couldn't believe it. How could such a thing happen? How could it happen in Australia, the best country in the world, where you are supposed to be innocent until proven guilty?

I looked back at the document in disbelief, hoping that I would find a mistake, or that I had misread it. But it was true, the Family Court had already sat. I had not misread it. There was no mistake. I had not been able to defend myself because I didn't know the Family Court had been convened. I had not been given any opportunity to defend myself.

It wasn't my fault that I had not been given any opportunity to defend myself. It wasn't that I was an irresponsible person and had forgotten to check my mail, or that I had been out of the country and nobody had been able to give me proper notice of the sitting date of the Family Court, or that I was drunk for a few days, or that I was unconscious in hospital, or that I was out of the country.

I stared back at the document. I looked back at the calendar. My disbelief and shock slowly but steadily turning into anger.

I was angry that Wendy, working with her solicitor, had withheld from her Affidavit anything about herself that would have put a negative light on her Application.

I was angry that Wendy had said things about me in her Affidavit that I knew were not true, and she had said things about me that I knew were partly true and were therefore a deception.

I was angry that I had not been given any opportunity to defend myself.

I was angry that the Family Court system had allowed such a thing to happen.

I was angry that the Family Court had taken one person's word as being completely true, without any evidence, and without any means of testing the evidence.

I was angry that my sons had been taken from me by the Australian Government, without either my knowledge or consent.

I was angry that I was treated as guilty without proof.

I was angry that I could not do anything to prove my innocence.

My anger grew into fury.

My fury began to grow into rage.

As I sat alone in the shop holding the documents, I thought I would get even with this country Australia, with this Family Court.

But something kept me seated. Something pushed me to read the third document.

16

The third document was the Family Court Order. It was dated 6th May, two days previous. It said that every request that Wendy had applied for, was made an Order. I read it over and over, and finally accepted that there was nothing I could do.

Nobody had come into the shop during the time when I had read and re-read the documents, which was probably two or three hours.

The next day was Saturday. I knew that the solicitor that I shared the office space with, would be in the office. I could ask him what could be done. I turned the rear wall panel around ready for him. I shut the shop. I went home to the empty rented cottage.

The back door, that I had locked when I left that morning to go to the music shop, was open. A window near the door was open. Someone must have got into the house through the unlocked window and had opened the locked back door from the inside.

I went into the kitchen. My fridge/freezer was gone. In the lounge room a cabinet was gone. I thought that the most likely answer was that the Smiths had taken out of my rented house what they deemed to be was the property of their daughter. I was too tired to do anything else except have something to eat and go to bed.

Next morning, I went to the office and asked the solicitor if he would mind having a look at the documents. He read them. He said that absolutely nothing could be done about the things that the Family Court had put in place.

I asked, "What's that mean, 'ex parte?'"

"That means without you being in the court when the Application is heard," he answered. When he said that, it then made sense to me how it was that the events of the previous day had been able to take place-the Family Court had legally prevented me from knowing anything about what was going to take place; the Family Court had legally denied me any right to defend myself.

The solicitor said that only a very expensive battle with the Family Court, possibly lasting for years, could possibly sort things out.

There was no way I could think about fighting such a battle. I had no large amounts of money available, and I had a massive debt, Wendy and my private mortgage on the sixty-acre property, to handle on my own, as well as the payments for the new car that I and Wendy no longer owned. For the second time in two days I reached a point where I had no alternative other than to accept what had happened, and to get on with the rest of my life.

17

Without the boys, there was no reason for me to continue to rent the cottage in Mt Barker, so I moved back to my property. Living there alone, my only regular contact with anyone was with the people from the Bridgewater AOG outreach church, where I played guitar each Sunday.

The pastor who came up to Bridgewater from the Klemzig AOG to preach each Sunday, told me that it was likely Wendy would be planning to divorce me, and that he would be praying for a reconciliation. I told him I didn't want any reconciliation. I told him I could not cope anymore with trying to handle the situation of living with a mentally sick wife. The pastor did not say anything to try to make me change my mind, nor did he say that he understood how I felt. I guessed that he respected my decision. We did not have any further conversation about the matter.

Each Sunday, someone from the Bridgewater church came out to my property to give me a lift to the church meeting. Quite often after the meeting there was a fellowship lunch, or someone would invite me back to their home for lunch. The people appreciated my guitar playing and my singing, and I appreciated getting free feeds. I also agreed to play the guitar one evening a week at a home fellowship meeting, and on another evening for a prayer meeting, and soon after that, a weekly bible study course lasting for thirteen weeks. I also agreed to take the course. It was a big decision. Thirteen weeks was the longest continual personal commitment that I had made for a year or two.

As part of the course, the participants were given a form to fill in with personal details, including the date of their conversion to Christ. I was in the shed on the property, filling in the details on the form, and when I got to the part about the date of my conversion, I couldn't remember it. While I was thinking about it, it came to mind that a few days ago, I had discovered a hive of wild bees high up in a hollow branch in one of the old gum trees near the shed. The tree was very old and had a trunk well over a metre in diameter. I had the thought that it would be a good idea, now, to raid the hive and get the honey to eat.

I put down my pen and went out of the shed and took an extension ladder to the tree and climbed up on it to the hive. A breeze sprung up. The branch started swaying. A few bees started to buzz around my face. I got straight down from the ladder and went back to the shed and put a date of conversion on the form and signed the paper. It was a good feeling knowing that I had made a signed, written commitment to my faith. I felt better about raiding the hive. I thought that now I would do it properly.

I got gloves, hat, long sleeved shirt, long pants, and boots, and a fly net, and a bucket and a trowel, and I headed off to the tree again. It was about thirty metres from the shed.

About twenty metres from the tree, I noticed some dirt in the bucket, so I deviated slightly and went past the tree to the creek to wash the bucket. The creek was about fifty metres past the tree. At the creek, I knelt and started washing the bucket.

A very loud crashing sound, like a car going over a cliff, came from somewhere behind me.

I stood up and turned around to look, expecting to see a crumpled car lying at the bottom of the hill. There was no crumpled car. But the old tree with the beehive was lying in the paddock.

I felt the hair on the nape of my neck rise, and my neck felt cold. Only seconds before, I was about to climb the extension ladder, but instead I had changed my mind and went to the creek to wash the bucket.

I felt that God was saying to me, "You have seen my power. I saved your life just now. I caused you to walk away from the tree to wash the bucket and do things properly, now that you have made a written commitment attesting to your belief in me. Don't you ever turn away from me!"

I walked to the fallen tree. The tree had fallen straight along the line of the ladder where I had leaned it against the trunk. The ladder was smashed in pieces. The hollow branch that had the hive in was smashed. The honeycomb was smashed, and pieces lay scattered among the leaves and twigs and smashed wood. But my life was intact.

I picked up all the pieces of broken honeycomb. They were dripping with wild honey. I filled the bucket with them.

The honey was very, very sweet.

18

One day, the land agent whom I engaged to sell my property came to see me there. He told me a buyer had signed a contract to buy it, subject to the sale of his own farming property, and that he couldn't pay any deposit until he received payment from the sale at an international auction in Hong Kong of some very rare specimens of opalised lobsters that he had dug up in Coober Pedy. The land agent assured me that the man was telling the truth, and he advised me to sign the contract. He also said that the buyer requested that I let him and his son camp in his own caravan on the property. I took him at his word and signed the contract for a very good price, and I agreed to let the man stay on the block.

I was so confident that everything was going to be alright, that I signed a contract to buy a small block of land in a nearby town, subject to the sale of my property.

I went to the land agent whom I had been working for. I told him about the imminent sale of my property, and I asked him if I could stay rent free as caretaker in the abandoned house where I had cleaned all the scrap. He agreed. He said I could dismantle the shed and sell the materials for whatever I could get.

It was winter, in the Adelaide Hills. The house had no electricity, no water, no doors or windows. One day, another pastor, who was coming to the church each week from the Klemzig AOG church to lead a local home fellowship meeting, visited me. He gave me a large, fresh cabbage. I ate it that day. It was all I had to eat that day.

One very cold night, after three rainy days, with no dry firewood stored, to keep warm I fed a small fire with single sheets of paper, which I took from folders that were my lecture notes from my Wattle Park Teachers College days. As each piece burnt, I read the next one I was going to burn. On one sheet, scribbled in biro in somebody's handwriting, I found the words "Gary Atkins, Repent." A shiver went down my spine as I read the prophetic words. They must have been written by a believer, one of the college students, without my knowledge, about fifteen years previous. I thanked God that I had repented, albeit many years after the warning had been written.

One day I was walking along the main street of the town seven kilometers from my property. A policeman approached me. He said it would be a good idea if I dropped into the local courthouse. Not knowing the reason that I should be in the court, I went there. As I walked in the courtroom I heard the judge call my name. I went forward. I was ushered into the witness box. I was asked to place my hand on a bible and swear that I would tell the truth, the whole truth, and nothing but the truth.

I hesitated. Only that week at a bible study we had talked about a Christian not swearing on anything, and of not being afraid to find the right words to say when brought before the authorities, because the Holy Spirit would give the believer the right words.

I blurted out, "I'm sorry, I'm a new Christian, and I don't believe I should swear on a bible." As the words came out of my mouth I thought that in the next minute I would be arrested and thrown into jail for not obeying the judge. But instead he said, "That's OK. Just say the words 'I affirm' and then tell the truth." It was a great relief to hear him say that, because my recent experience of the Family Court had made me think that courts were dangerous places.

The judge then went on to summarise several small debts that were in Wendy and my names-a food bill for about $50, a petrol bill for about $100, and a dentist bill for about $150. He asked me when I was going to pay them. I said I wasn't sure, because I had no regular job. He said I should make a commitment to pay a regular monthly proportion of each bill, otherwise I would risk jail. I said I would pay $10 a month. He said that was OK, then he said I was free to leave the courtroom.

Being winter, the long grass around the abandoned house in which I was staying was full of hundreds of snails. I collected them and put them in a 100 litre plastic drum and fed them on old newspapers and grass. I fed the snails to three bantam hens that I kept in a small yard made of scrap material from around the yard.

Each day I collected fresh eggs. But if there were a lot of rainy days and I hadn't remembered to store some dry firewood, I could not light a fire, so I had to eat the eggs raw. The first time was the hardest. I tapped carefully on the round end of the shell, in a circle, until I had broken a piece out of the shell about the size of a five-cent piece. Then I put the egg to my lips and tipped it a bit and sucked out a bit of the white. Then I tipped the egg a bit more and sucked out a bit more of the white. Then in one quick movement, I tipped the egg right up. The rest of the white and all the yolk slipped out of the shell and into my mouth, and I swallowed the whole lot in one go, hardly tasting it, and swallowed hard to keep it all down.

Playing guitar four times a week at church meetings, my life was full, and so was my stomach, because the church people always fed me. They became my 'new' family. I did not have to buy any food, and I used any money I got from selling scrap material from the yard to keep paying off my bills.

Weeks passed, but I heard nothing from the land agent. The grazier wanted to know what was happening about the sale of the Wistow block. I told him about the contract with the opal miner.

I got paid for the shed in the yard of the abandoned house, and a guy started to demolish it and take it away.

The settlement date on the contract for the sale of my property came, but there was still no deposit and no communication from the buyer, who was apparently still camping there in his caravan. I talked to the land agent. Things looked suspicious. He made a further check on the information that the buyer had supplied him about his supposed ownership of a farm. It turned out to be false. In fact, what the buyer was doing, was deceiving several land agents with his story of signing contracts to buy a property, conditional on the sale of his bogus property. He was living rent free on every place he was supposed to be buying.

I found out that not only was he staying rent free on my property, he was also accepting money for agistment of stock, and selling my tools from my shed, to second hand dealers. He had no assets except his caravan and car, and a glib tongue.

It was my responsibility to put him off the block. I went to the block, apprehensive about confronting him in such a remote situation, seven kilometres from the town.

I knocked on the caravan door. He opened it. He was a big, strong, red headed man with a fierce countenance. I was firm, and serious, when I told him to pack his things and leave immediately. Without a word, he did exactly that. I thanked God as I saw him drive away.

I went back to the land agent who had let me stay in the abandoned house. He was not in his office. His staff said I would find him in the local hotel. I found him there in the bar, and I told him about the bogus buyer of my property. I also told him about the sale of the shed. He went into a furious rage and accused me of stealing his property. Everyone in the bar was listening. He was a long time local resident, very well known, very rich. I was not well known and about as poor as could be. It mattered little what I said in my defence, that there must have been a misunderstanding, as he shouted at me to get out of the bar, and to get off the hotel property, and to get out of the abandoned house, and to get out of the town.

I left the bar and went to the abandoned house to prepare to leave and return to my property. The guy to whom I had sold the shed was there and demanded his money back. I told him I didn't have the money. He said, "Wait here."

He soon returned with another man who said he was a former policeman, who told me that if I didn't hand over the money that I received for the shed, then I would legally have to hand over something of equal value in lieu. I could not argue with him, except to say that the materials from the dismantled shed would have to be returned to the property, otherwise I would not agree to hand over my personal property.

The two men agreed with my demand. They returned the shed materials. I handed over my electric organ. I left the abandoned house and returned to my property, to the shed at the bottom of the 250 feet valley.

19

I decided to shift up to the top of the block and live under the stars. It meant having to carry the furniture from the shed, 250 feet down in the valley, on my back, up the rough track to the top of the property. Slowly and surely, with a lot of rests partway up the track, I did it.

The most difficult thing to move was a nearly full 100-pound gas cylinder. I rolled it up a bit, put one foot under it to stop it rolling down the hill, and wedged in two stones to hold the cylinder, pulled out my foot and changed my position ready to push the cylinder another fifty centimetres further up the hill. About halfway up the hill, my two wedging stones crumbled, and the cylinder started rolling down the hill. I managed to stop it after about a metre, but the effort made me breathe heavily. I had to rest. I wondered whether I would ever get it to the top of the hill. It seemed that God spoke to me in an audible voice, saying, "Get up." I did just that, and finally pushed the cylinder to the top.

Living at the top of the valley made things a lot easier, not having to walk up and down the 250 feet hill each time I went away from the property. The only problem was, the wind was stronger than in the valley, and kept blowing my wardrobe over.

Food was still a concern for me, but I found ways to live off the land. I caught a sleepy lizard one day and cooked it on an open fire. It was tasty. Whenever I came across others, I grabbed them and kept them in a box so that I always had one handy to cook.

One of the church families had a small Angora-cross male goat that needed shearing. It was a strong animal, with very long, sharply pointed horns. A pastor who was an ex-shearer, was asked to do it, but he hadn't shorn a goat, and he didn't have any shears. He knew I could shear a sheep with a pair of shears, and he knew I had a pair. He asked me to do it. He said the owners couldn't afford to pay me, but they had an XL Ford Falcon station wagon that had been sitting around the property for years, and they were willing to give it to me if I shore their goat. I thought it was a good deal, even though the vehicle, having been used for years as a shelter for a sheep, was full of sheep dung.

I shore the goat, and took the Ford and registered it. The paint job was faded and scratched in places, but the motor ran well. I drove it home and cleaned out all the dung. With my own transport, I was more able to take on odd jobs, and got quite a few and kept paying off my bills.

Soon I had enough extra money to buy back my electric organ. I went to the guy's place to get it. There had been a lot of rain, and his house was cut off by a small, flooding creek. He said to me with a smug grin, "You can have the organ back if you can get it from the house." I guessed that he thought it was impossible for me to get to the organ because of the flooded creek. There were lots of loose rocks on the bank of the creek. I worked for about two hours and built a temporary rock ford. Then I drove across the ford, loaded up the organ, and drove back over the ford.

A few weeks later I was driving back to my property. Ahead of me, a man was carrying a car differential and axles on his shoulders. I slowed, intending to offer him a lift, but as I got close, I recognised the man to be the one who took my electric organ. Perhaps it was not the right thing for me to do as a Christian, but I drove on without stopping.

Regular bible study continued to have an importance in my life, and I continued to attend the New Christian course. One of the lessons was about a person being born a sinner, and how nobody is sinless. It helped me to understand why many people in the Methodist church find it difficult, as I had, to accept that I was not a good person really, no matter how good a life I led. All those things I did as a lad that nobody found out at the time, the stealing, the lying, were known by God and were paid for by Christ's death.

The last lesson of the course was about water baptism. As a child, I knew of other children who said they had been baptised, and I had not been baptised. I thought at the time that being baptised was when you got your name given to you, when a minister sprinkled water on your infant forehead. But the lesson taught that this form of baptism was merely a church tradition, and it did not have a scriptural base. I learnt that it was very important for me to be baptised as an adult believer, because it was a commandment from Jesus. At the next opportunity, I went down to the Klemzig AOG church and got baptised. As I came up out of the water, I felt a great relief, as though a very heavy burden had been taken from my shoulders.

Another time when I was at the Klemzig church, a preacher said that he believed God had told him that he had been given a divine gift of healing. It seemed logical to me. I was familiar with the scriptures that related to the healing powers of Jesus and his disciples. It would be good if I could have a miraculous healing of my long-term back problem-without warning, sometimes I would feel a twinge in my back while I was lifting something heavy, and then straight away and for many days after that initial twinge, I could not stand straight, and I was in pain. Sometimes the pain would last for a fortnight.

The preacher said that God had told him that there were three things that would be healed that night in the meeting. He named the three things. One of them was back problems. He asked that anyone who had any one of these three problems, and who believed that God could heal them in the meeting that evening, stand up. I stood up. In the congregation of about 400, about twenty people stood up. The preacher prayed that there would be a miraculous, instant healing of those who stood up. As he prayed, I felt a tightening all around my body around my back, as if someone was pulling the strings tight on a corset. I could not explain it. I believed that I had received a divine healing from God.

20

My mother and one of my sisters, who lived interstate, became so worried when I told them on the phone about my decision to believe in Jesus, and how I was playing guitar and singing every Sunday in a church, and they got my brother-in-law, who worked for Australia Post, to make some free interstate phone calls to check out if I had become involved in a cult.

It would be great to see them and tell them face to face about my new-found faith. But I couldn't think where on earth the money would come from for petrol. It would have to come from miraculous provision, because I certainly did not have any cash to buy petrol to get started on the interstate trip, let alone any cash to keep on traveling. All I had was a box of brand new blues harp mouth organs, and some guitar strings, that I could sell, that were left over from my music shop.

Was God really saying for me to go all that way to talk to my sister and mother, or was it just wishful thinking on my part? Sure, it would be great to do it, but how could I do something like that knowing how much it would probably cost, and knowing that I did not have the money to do it?

I wanted to be sure if it was God telling me to make the trip and to trust Him for the finance, or if I was just being stupid and making the trip without proper preparation. A story came to mind from the Old Testament, in the book of Judges, of Gideon the Israelite. An angel of the Lord came to Gideon where he was threshing wheat. Gideon was so afraid that the authorities would take his grain from him that he did the job secretly. The angel said to Gideon, "Gooday mate, God is with you. You are a mighty hero!"

Gideon said to the angel, "Give me a break, if the Lord is with me and I'm a mighty hero, how come I'm here working in secret just to get something as basic as a bit of tucker, and our whole nation is in this mess under the control of the Midianites?"

The angel said, "Simple, mate. I'm telling you that you are the one to deliver Israel from the Midianites, and that's all you need to know."

Gideon knew that he was no war hero, and he knew he didn't come from a great and wealthy, influential family. He doubted the angel. He wanted more proof than just an angel coming out of nowhere and telling him he was to be the one to save a whole nation of oppressed people. He said to the Lord, "If I put out a fleece at night time, and in the morning, there's dew on the fleece and there's no dew on the ground, I'll know that you are fair dinkum, and I really am the one to save Israel."

Gideon put out the fleece that night. Next morning, he found it was just as he said-there was dew on the fleece and no dew anywhere around on the ground. Gideon must have been the kind of guy who would have insurance policies to cover his insurance policies-he asked God to be patient with him and give him just a bit more proof. "Excuse me God, what about if I do it again and reverse the conditions? How about no dew on the fleece, but dew on the ground all around the fleece? If that happens then I'll believe the angel."

Gideon put the fleece out at night again. In the morning, he found dew on the ground all around the fleece and no dew on the fleece! Then he believed the angel. As insignificant and inexperienced as he was, Gideon trusted the Lord, and went on to lead the whole nation of Israel in a mighty victory over the Midianites.

I decided to do a similar thing to Gideon, to find out if God really wanted me to go on an interstate journey to visit my relatives and tell them about my new-found faith, even though I did not have the money to do it. Upstream from me on the creek was another parcel of land cut out of a big grazing holding. Nobody lived on it. It was jointly owned by a guy who worked on shift as a firefighter, out of a fire station down in the city, thirty kilometres away, and a woman working on shift as a nurse in a hospital in the suburbs. Very occasionally the guy would come to the block for half a day on a weekend. Sometimes the woman would come to the block. Because of their different shift rosters, it was very rare that they would both visit their block together. My first condition that I put to the Lord was that in the morning I would look and see if both my neighbours were staying on their block. The second condition was that they would agree to look after my tethered goats for about ten days while I was away interstate.

Next morning, I looked over at the next block. I saw two vehicles there. I went over to see who was there. The firefighter and the nurse were there. We got talking, and it turned out that they both had accumulated leave at the same time. They had decided to spend their break together on their block. They said it would be great fun for them to look after my tethered goats for ten days, which was something very different from their normal working life, while I went away. There were my two conditions fulfilled! Full of confidence, I packed my clothes for the interstate trip, knowing that I only had enough petrol to drive to the local store, and I had no cash at all.

I drove to the store and went inside, and I showed my mouth organs to the manager. He bought some. I bought some food and some petrol and headed off interstate. After driving for a couple of hours, the petrol gauge showed nearly empty. I stopped in a little town. I went in a store and said I didn't have any cash for petrol, but I had mouth organs to trade for petrol. The manager said that would be OK. I put in some petrol and went back in the store ready to hand over some mouth organs, but the manager said, "That's OK mate. The petrol's on us."

All I could say was, "Thanks, mate," and I walked out and drove away, thanking God.

Some hours later, having crossed the state border, I needed petrol again. The petrol station was closed. I tried selling mouth organs in the hotel bar, but nobody wanted one. I started singing gospel songs in the bar, but nobody wanted to give me any money.

I slept that night in my car. In the morning, I went to the petrol station and was able to trade mouth organs for petrol. I drove on to the next town. I couldn't find a petrol station where I could trade mouth organs for petrol. It was about lunchtime, so I drove to a park where I could sit down on a grassed area to eat some lunch. A couple there were doing the same. I tried to sell them mouth organs. They said they couldn't play a mouth organ, so they didn't want to buy one. They asked me to play something. I played,

"Jesus Loves Me." They changed their mind. They bought two mouth organs. That gave me enough money for petrol for the rest of the trip to the town where my sister lived.

I told her of my conversion to Christ. She was sympathetic, even though she did not think as I did. I stayed with her for a few days. Then I met up with an old acquaintance who gave me a couple of days' work helping him paint his house, and my sister bought some guitar strings from me, and altogether I then had more than enough money for petrol to get to my mother's house in another town.

My mother listened to my story. Like my sister, she also was sympathetic, but not believing as I did. She gave me some money after I cleaned leaves from her house gutters. I had plenty of money for petrol for the return trip. I drove back home. I had about $100 left over after paying for my trip. I took back my tethered goats from my neighbours. I thanked God for his provision.

21

One day while reading the bible, I came across a scripture that said that there is no law against love. It made me think that I should break the law and go to see my sons. About six months had passed since they were taken from me, during which time I had not heard from them, nor had I violated the conditions of restraint that the Family Court had placed on me.

I drove to the town where Wendy's parents lived, to their "comfortable, well-appointed home", that Wendy had told the Family Court she and the children would be residing. I discovered that her parents had moved to a farming property near the town. I got directions and went to the farm. There I found a comfortable, well-appointed home, in which Wendy's parents were living. But Wendy and the three boys were not living there with her parents-they were living on the farm, but in a nearby, run down, old farmhouse, that had large holes in the sheeting on the outside walls. The house had electricity, but no hot water service. The floors were bare boards.

Although I was pleased to see the boys, and although Wendy did not make any fuss about me being "in the vicinity of the place where she and the boys were residing", I was very annoyed that the house they were living in was substandard.

In the kitchen, looking out of place in its dilapidated surroundings, was my fridge/freezer that was taken from my rented cottage. In another room was the cabinet that was taken from the rented cottage. At least then I knew for sure where the items had gone.

I spent some time having fun with the boys. It was only a short visit, but thankfully it didn't develop into a situation where authorities might have been called in to arrest me

A few weeks later I received a telegram to say that Ben was in hospital with burns, received when very hot water spilt on him, from a container that Wendy had been carrying in the deserted farmhouse that had no hot water service. I phoned the Smith farmhouse and talked to Mrs Smith. She said it was true. She also said that Wendy had been committed to a psychiatric hospital again. "What have you done to her?" she said. It seemed to me that she thought that I was to blame for her daughter's mental sickness. I could only say that I had done nothing to cause it.

In the nearby town one day, I met up with a guy who lived across the road from me when I was renting the cottage. He and I had played tennis against each other. He worked for a local stock and station company. He knew that I was trying to sell my property.

"I see your block is being auctioned," he said to me. It was a bit of a shock to hear that. Surely the grazier should have told me. I told him that it was news to me. Then he told me the date and time of day of the auction, and that the auction would take place on the property.

The day of the auction came. All I had to do was wait and see who turned up at the property. I was hoping for a good price, because when Wendy and I bought the property, it was bare of grass from the three-year Adelaide Hills drought, and now, after two good winters of rains, it was well grassed, and hundreds of young gums had sprung up. And I had paid for a few hundred metres of new fencing, and for a reasonable access road that had been pushed through an adjacent paddock to the boundary fence. It would be nice to make a profit and buy something else, even a smaller vacant block, and still have somewhere to call home.

At the advertised time for auction, only two people other than me were there. I stood apart from them. One was dressed smartly. No doubt he was the auctioneer. The other was dressed casually, probably a bidder. Out in the middle of the sixty-acre paddock, seven kilometres from the town, the auctioneer looked at his watch and then made the loud announcement, as if he were addressing a large, noisy crowd, that he couldn't wait any longer to commence the auction, because his instructions were to dispose of the property no matter what.

He called for an opening bid. The casually dressed man said nothing. The auctioneer called again for an opening bid. Apart from the sound of a crow calling from a nearby tree, there was silence. He called again. Nobody said anything. The auctioneer made another loud announcement to the effect that because there had not been any opening bid, and because he was under instructions to dispose of the property immediately, he would accept any offer that was made right then and there.

The casually dressed man approached him. The two talked for a while. It looked to me as if an acceptable offer had been made, because they shook hands. The casually dressed man walked away to his car and drove off. I went forward to the auctioneer and asked him if the property had been sold. He said it had. I asked him what the purchase price was. He told me. It was a few thousand dollars less than the amount I had agreed to pay for the property nearly three years previous. It was just enough to cover the total of the remaining principle owing on the private mortgage and the outstanding interest. There was not a cent left over. I couldn't think of anything to say. All I could do was stand in the paddock and watch the auctioneer walk to his car and drive away.

That day, my life's work had been completely lost. It also meant that I was homeless, and that within a few weeks I would have to find somewhere to live.

Everybody left the property. I was left alone. But I was not lonely. The Comforter, the Spirit of God, was with me, and I knew that I could trust Him.

A few days after that, a couple from the church asked me if I would like to come to their home and stay with them and their children until I could find something else. Thankful to God and to them, I said yes.

Early in 1982, I moved from the property and went to stay in the home of the couple from the church. Some other people from the church said I ought to enrol for a year at the Klemzig Church bible college. Although I had no ambition or prompting to become a pastor, I thought I would like to make a good study of the bible so that I would have something to say to many of the churchgoers who were always able to quote me scriptures to show me how I ought to be leading my life.

The visiting pastor, the one who gave me a cabbage, took me to talk to the principal of the bible college, about enrolling. He told me how much it would cost. I said that I didn't have any regular job and I couldn't guarantee to be able to pay each week on time. He said, "I think we can find a place for you." He said that if I agreed to mop and polish the bible college lecture room floor once a week, I could have a reduced student fee. I agreed.

In February I began the forty-week course, driving down from the hills to Klemzig each morning. The course was three hours of lectures each morning, Monday to Friday, with assignments. I settled in well. Five mornings a week studying the bible, three nights a week playing guitar at my local church, Saturday night youth meetings at Klemzig, and attending the local church on Sunday, where I played guitar and sang, all had a stabilizing effect on me in the turmoil of being homeless, and restrained from seeing my sons, and not ever knowing where my next dollar was coming from. It was then that I established a daily habit of, first thing each morning, a prayer of thanks to God for the gift of faith, and for guidance for the day, and then a reading of the bible.

The Klemzig Church congregation was continually growing, with many strong believers and many outreaches. The building was not big enough to seat all the churchgoers in one Sunday morning meeting, so a second Sunday morning meeting was held. This too was always packed out. The church executive decided to sell the Klemzig Church property and buy a thirteen-acre celery farm next to a river, in a semi-rural area close to an outer suburb named Paradise, and build a new church big enough to seat everyone in one Sunday morning meeting.

Each Sunday night some of the local church members drove down to Klemzig for the night meeting. We often heard the senior pastor mention how the new building project at Paradise was progressing. He always raised a chuckle in the congregation when he said, "We'll soon be in Paradise."

One morning when I got to the bible college, a few weeks into the first semester, my local pastor, who also lectured at the college, told me that the Klemzig AOG Church Executive had decided to ask me to live in an old farmhouse on the Paradise building site, rent free, as an unpaid security man, because vandalism, after the workers had knocked off for the day, had become a big problem on the site. I told him I would do it.

Within a few days, I moved down to the city and into the old farmhouse on the thirteen-acre site of the new, one-million-dollar Paradise AOG church building. It was only a few hundred metres from where, nine years previous, I had made the deal with a car salesman to buy the new VW Transporter that Wendy and Dary and I had lived in when I started as a folksinger. It was as if God had brought me around in a big circle, ready to start again, but this time as a Christian.

There was no electricity in the farmhouse. Water was available from an outlet on the building site. It was not a problem for me to handle those conditions.

Not having to drive down each morning from my church friends' home to the bible college was a big saving of time and money. I saved money on food too, by eating off the land, from almond trees and grapevines and peach trees on the old celery farm. One day I ate nine peaches, and nothing else.

Somebody told me that because I was on such a very low income I could get some free food at the West End Baptist Mission in the Adelaide CBD. I went there and after they established that I was indeed on such a low income, they gave me some powdered milk and some Weetbix.

I made new friends at the Klemzig church, some of whom were good musicians. They invited me to their homes and we had some good times. They asked me to join their weekly home fellowship meeting, which would have been a lot of fun. A college student from the country also asked me if I would play guitar for the weekly home fellowship meeting in the house where he was a boarder. Most of the members of the home fellowship group were elderly men born in Europe. Nobody in the group had any music skills. I decided to be their musician, 'singing for my supper' again, which lowered my weekly food expenses. Cash started coming in too-I got handyman work in the suburbs; I brought my tethered goats down to the city and rented them out as grass eaters on vacant blocks of land; I sang and played Christian songs in the busiest pedestrian mall in the CBD. To entertain in the streets and be paid by the passersby I had to have a daily fifty-cent busker's permit, issued by the shop owners. Busking earnt me a steady five dollars an hour.

One day while busking, I saw walking towards me the grazier who sold me the sixty-acre property that I finished up having to forfeit about $13,000, my life's work at the time, when he auctioned it. I kept my eye on him as I sang, and I saw that he had recognised me. He came close to me. He did not say anything, but he put a five dollar note in my shirt pocket, and kept walking. Most people who gave me money only gave coins. Perhaps his relatively large individual donation to me, for busking, was his way of saying that he was sorry for the hard time that I had experienced after I failed to fulfil my mortgage contract with him. I appreciated him taking the trouble to give me a donation.

22

Busking in Rundle Mall, singing gospel songs exclusively, I soon discovered my fans and my detractors. One day a detractor snarled at me and called out across the mall, "Get out of here. We don't want those songs here!" But a little old lady standing next to him whacked him with her umbrella. In response, he flipped a five-cent coin onto the mall pavers and snarled again, "Pick that up!" I happily did so, not so much for the monetary value, but for the little battle that I and the little old lady had won.

A busker's one-day permit listed the conditions under which buskers must operate: a busker must change location every twenty minutes, must not obstruct pedestrian or vehicular traffic, must be a regulation distance from the front of the shops.

Busking for several hours a day and changing position every twenty minutes, I had many positions in the mall. The most challenging was at an intersection of the pedestrian mall and a street on which vehicles were freely allowed to be driven. Mall traders bringing in stock could drive their vehicles into the mall from this street. There was a very small section of the intersection which vehicles never drove over, because of the turning circle of their vehicles. In this area, I picked out one brick in all the pavers, and facing west, I placed my right shoe with the big toe on the south-east corner of that paver. From that position, I could comfortably busk for the regulation twenty minutes without having to move for any vehicle, and I was far enough away from the line of the buildings, and I left room for the usual pedestrian walking area. When I put my foot on that paver and stood straight and steady, I felt as if I was a boxer in a ring, shaping up to his opponent.

Working for several days a week at busking, I got to recognize the regular mall people-the traders, the office workers, the newspaper sellers, the mall traders' law enforcement officers. They in turn recognized me. One day, I braced myself in my usual position with my right shoe big toe on its paver, ready to start singing. Then a familiar mall traders' law enforcement officer, in his brown uniform and cap, approached me and said, "You've got to change the kind of songs you are singing, or else stop busking." I decided to stop busking because I was not going to sing any songs other than Christian ones. I thought that if Australia was such an unjust country that the Family Court of Australia could hear a case against me, and to make a judgment, and execute it without giving me a chance to defend myself, then it was not surprising that an Australian capital city could ban Christian singers from its streets. But, as young Christian, I felt I needed to discuss the situation with an older Christian.

I knew of a Klemzig AOG youth leader who worked in a store in the Adelaide CBD. I went and talked to him. I half expected him to pray for me to go back into Rundle Mall, and disobey the Law and continue singing gospel songs. Instead of that, he said there was nothing I could do, that I should obey the authorities. I was very disappointed as I walked back towards the car park, intending to go home.

As I walked along the main business street in the CBD, I noticed the sign "Adelaide Advertiser" on a very tall building. I thought I could possibly find someone on the staff of this major South Australian newspaper who would think my busking ban was worthy of reporting. I went in the building to reception and spoke to the woman on duty. I said, "Hello, I'm a mall busker and I have been singing Christian songs regularly for some weeks now, and this morning I was told by a mall traders' official that I am not allowed to sing Christian songs there anymore."

She said, "Hey, I know who you are. Aren't you Gary Atkins the folksinger?"

Surprised, I said, "Yes. But that was a couple of years ago now."

"That's OK," she said. "Just go up to the second floor." She told me the name of the journalist to ask to speak to. "See how you go with him," she said cheerily.

I did what she said. As soon as I finished telling the journalist my story, he said, "That's great. Hang on a tick while I grab a photographer, and we'll go down in the street and get some pics."

We did it, and he wrote the article, and it made page three in The Advertiser.

A few days later, a Letter to the Editor appeared, with a scathing criticism of the mall traders' ban on Christian songs being sung by a busker. Similar letters appeared in a couple of rural newspapers.

One morning a few days after that, at the bible college, one of the students came up to me and showed me an article in The Advertiser. It said how a spokesman for the mall traders had asked The Advertiser to publish a public apology to the gospel singing busker, that there had been a mistake, and that if the busker would personally come into their office, he would apologise to him, and issue him with a permit to continue singing Christian songs if he so desired.

It was an exciting morning at the bible college. We felt victorious because of the article. That afternoon I went into the mall traders' office, received the personal apology, paid fifty cents for a busking permit, and went straight out into the mall and started singing gospel songs.

A worried looking passer-by said, "Please, don't do this, you'll get into trouble. You're not allowed to sing gospel songs in the Mall."

I told her, "Don't worry, it's all been sorted out, I'm allowed to sing gospel songs now. The mall traders apologised to me, and they said I could continue singing gospel songs."

"Oh, that's wonderful news," she replied. "I was really upset when I heard that gospel songs had been banned." Then she went happily on her way. I resumed singing the gospel songs for a couple of hours that morning. Doing so, it always uplifted me, but that morning my faith went up many notches.

23

Despite the primitive conditions of life in the old farmhouse on the Klemzig AOG's Paradise building site, I got to become settled and comfortable. I was earning more than enough to pay my college fees, and my outstanding bills, including the hire purchase fees for the car I no longer owned. Every few days I cooked damper, a home made bread, in a frying pan on an open fire. Two guys from the church who flatted together nearby, liked to visit me and eat the damper with me, with melted butter on the hot bread; around the house, I grew purple grape hyacinth flower bulbs that I brought from the property in the hills.

Sometimes when the building site water was turned off, I had no alternative but to wash in the river, which was polluted. However, I could dive in and keep my eyes closed and get out of the water without letting any water in my mouth.

After I had lived about two months in the farmhouse, I was told by the church executive that the farmhouse was to be demolished, and a car park for the church members was to be made in its place, and I would have to find somewhere else to live.

My two flatmate friends had by this time moved out of their rented flat, and they were renting a house in another nearby suburb. I asked them if I could share the rent and move in with them. They agreed. Soon after, a fourth guy from the church moved into the house, and I shared a bedroom with him. I felt like a father to the three younger men, as though God was preparing me for eventual reunion with my three sons.

The college student from the country was heading home at the end of the first semester. He was from Coober Pedy. He offered to pay for the petrol if I drove him there in my car, and he said I could stay for the break in his parents' hostel. I drove my Ford there, and I stayed with him. I met the son of my friend's landlady, who asked me to be his gopher -'go for this, go for that'-in return for meals in his home, while he operated his tunneling machine, searching for opal. We did some tunneling but didn't find any opal. My friend and I returned to Adelaide to the bible college.

A fifth man, from another AOG church, came to live in the rented house, and we had many lively discussions. He was interested to hear about my experience with the Family Court, and how I had been told by a solicitor, albeit in a casual conversation, that I could do nothing, in the short term, about the Family Court decisions that had been made without my knowledge, and that only after a long and costly court battle would I be able to plead my case. He told me of a solicitor he knew, who attended the same church that he did, who might be willing to do work for me without me having to pay immediately. He offered to introduce me to him.

It had then been about five months since I had last seen my sons, during which time I had neither heard from them or my wife, nor had I risked visiting them again. I had almost become resigned that I may never get an opportunity to get back to a 'normal' relationship with my sons. But thanks to God, here then was my chance to do that. I agreed to meet the solicitor.

24

The solicitor told me that the first thing I must do, in my course of getting custody of my sons, was prove to the Family Court that I was not a violent man. He said that the way to do this was for him to organise a series of meetings of me and my sons, through the Family Court, and if the meetings could take place without any untoward behavior on my part, that would then be the basis for an appeal to the Family Court to consider dissolving the Restraining Order and the Injunction on me. If I was subsequentially successful in an appeal to the Family Court to dissolve the Restraining Order and the Injunction, I would then have to maintain regular contact with my sons, with Wendy's agreement, for such a period until the boys and I had re-established a normal relationship, and then, without Wendy being told that it would be going to happen, I could, conditional on me being able to demonstrate that I could properly care for the boys on a day to day basis, apply for their custody.

It was wonderful to hear from the solicitor the whole strategy, each step by step, towards achieving what I had nearly given up hope for. It was wonderful to realise that what previously had been a vague, distant, faint hope, without any clear way forward, was now a plan of substance, with a real possibility of success. My sons were now nine, seven and three years old. We had now been apart for more than a year. At last, I could see how things could be restored, even if it would take another couple of years. With much thanks to God, and to the solicitor, I agreed to cooperate with him. I handed over to him all the papers I had received from the Family

Court. He photocopied them and gave the originals back to me, and I engaged him to begin the long process.

The solicitor said I should be very specific and very strict in my requirements for the arrangements for my meetings with my sons, because, he said, the 'other party', my wife, would be sure to find any way possible to prevent me from having contact with them. He suggested that the way to set things in motion would be for him to write to my wife to tell her that he was acting for me, and tell her that I was requesting permission, in line with Family Law Act regulations, to have access to the boys several times, for a few hours each time. Having had no previous experience in these matters, I simply agreed with him, trusting in the Lord that he knew what he was doing.

In July 1982, he sent me a copy of a letter that he had received from my wife, in which she said she was prepared to give me access to the boys. I then phoned him, and we talked about the next move. He said I should request three, consecutive, fortnightly, four-hour meetings with my sons. He asked me what day of the week would be suitable for the meetings, and what time of day would be suitable, and exactly where the access should take place. I said that for me a Saturday was best; between 1 pm and 5 pm would be suitable. I told him that I wanted the access to take place in a public area, in the closest town to where they were living, somewhere which would be in full view of any local authority, to make sure there would be witnesses, in case Wendy tried to deceive someone later with a misleading statement about my conduct. I said I wanted the access to be taken in the main street of the town, right outside the local Police Station.

Fourteen days later, my solicitor told me, by phone, that my wife's mother had accepted my proposals for access, the first access to be three days hence. My solicitor did not make any comment about the situation of my wife's mother, instead of my wife herself, being the one to communicate with him about the agreement to the access proposals. I did not concern myself with that either, at the time, because I was so excited that I would soon be seeing my sons, for the first time in more than a year, with the full agreement and the authority of the law.

A friend from the bible college took me in his car to the first access meeting. I got him to park his car in the main street of the stipulated town, right outside the Police Station, a few minutes before 1 pm, the time for the access.

The street was quiet.

The nearest parked car was a couple of hundred metres away.

We waited.

Soon, a car pulled up on the same side of the street, about fifty metres behind us. We watched, from inside my friend's car. The rear passenger door opened. Three little boys got out and stood together on the footpath, looking in our direction. I looked intently at them because they were dressed in clothes that I did not recognise. They seemed a little taller than the boys I had visited illegally, some months previously. Yes! they were my sons. They kept together on the footpath, looking towards my friend's car.

I got out of my friend's car and stood on the footpath, looking at my sons. They started to walk slowly towards me. I stood still on the footpath by my friend's car, looking at the approach of the boys. I had no idea what they might have been thinking, or what they might have been told about me. I thought it must have been a strange experience for them as they walked towards me, their father whom they had seen only once in more than a year, and with whom there had been no other communication. The only things they would have been aware of concerning me in that period would have been what they were told by their mother, and that surely would not have been anything good.

They continued walking towards me together, all the way along the footpath, until we were facing each other. They looked apprehensive. I felt so happy to see them, and yet at the same time I felt so sad, because I knew that in four hours' time they would be walking away from me, along the footpath outside the Police Station again, and they would get into a car and be driven away, and I would not see them again for another fortnight.

Eventually we hugged each other on the footpath. Then we all got in my friend's motorcar and we drove off to a public reserve on the banks of a river.

I wasn't sure what to do with my three-year old, seven-year old and nine-year old sons, who had been ripped out of my life, who had not had any opportunity to know my side of why or how that had happened. I knew only one thing—it was no use in the four hours of the access to try to delve into what the boys' life had been like in the recent months, and

I saw no use to try to explain to them why I was suddenly no longer a regular part of their lives, and no use to justify anything that had recently happened, and no use to try to explain to them why I would soon disappear again from their lives for another fortnight. The four hours were to be enjoyed, and not overshadowed with the circumstances surrounding the get-together.

We ran around together on the grassy river bank. We walked along together next to the water. We kicked a rubber ball to each other. We chatted.

Just before the four hours were up, we returned to the main street in my friend's car, and he parked it outside the police station again.

A car came along the street and parked about fifty metres away, just like earlier in the day. I and the boys got out of my friend's motor car. We said goodbye, and, "See you again in a fortnight." The boys turned away from me and walked along the footpath together, towards the other motor car. When they got to the motor car, the rear passenger door opened again. The boys got in. The door shut behind them. The motor car drove away. We did not see who was driving the motor car.

I could not dwell on the sadness of the parting. I could only rejoice that we had been together, and that there had not been any conflict between me and the driver of the car that took my sons back to their home. We drove away too, back to Adelaide.

Four days later, I received an account from my solicitor for the work that he did in arranging the access -

"2 personal attendances

8 telephone attendances

5 letters

drawing and engrossing Notice of Acting

perusal of orders and copying."

The amount was about $140, but, as arranged, I did not have to pay any of the account until I had the money.

I got to access the information from the psychiatric hospital that Wendy had been committed to, that she was committed there from August 2 until August 15, which explained why her mother, instead of Wendy herself, was the one to communicate with my solicitor to say that the access proposals were agreed to.

On August 21, 1982, we did another successful access meeting, and on September 11, we did the final one of the three that had been agreed on through my solicitor's legal work.

The three access meetings, on terms mutually agreed to by me and Wendy, had taken place without any conflict, or argument, or unsatisfactory incident. They had achieved the purpose of proving that I was not 'a violent man'. Although the Injunction remained in place, and would do so until an application from my solicitor to the Family Court on my behalf, to dissolve it, was successful, a 'truce' existed. Wendy could no longer object to me contacting her or our sons, or object if I came to her place of residence. We entered a period of peaceful communication.

I continued at the bible college, earning a living by busking and doing odd jobs.

I went to see the boys again, about a fortnight later, because Wendy agreed that I could take them for a picnic for a few hours. They were not at home with her. I had to go to another house to pick them up, where they were with a man whom I had never met.

25

One of the casual jobs I got in 1982 while at the bible college was for another son of the lady in whose house I played guitar for home fellowship meetings. He had come down from Coober Pedy for some business. He had starter motor problems with his motor car while he was staying with his mother. He said to me, "What are you like with a spanner?"

I answered, "Not bad."

He asked, "Can you take off my starter motor?"

"No problems," I replied, and did it.

He gladly paid me five dollars. As an outback earthmoving contractor, it would not have been a problem to him to take off his starter motor, but in a quick trip to Adelaide and back from Coober Pedy, his time in Adelaide was important.

At the end of the next bible college semester, I drove to Coober Pedy again and did some more 'gophering' with the opal miner and his tunneling machine, with the same result as before-we did not find any opal. Then I drove back to Adelaide.

Next door to the house I shared renting, a vacant quarter-acre block was for sale. It was overgrown with weeds, on a slight slope. The asking price was $16,000. I thought it would be nice to be able to buy it and build a home there. But having no savings, and not much more cash than enough to survive each day, it was pointless to think about the possibility of buying the land, let alone paying for any development costs. I could also see that, with my earning capacity at that time, the likelihood of ever getting any place of my own was remote-I was attending the bible college lectures for fifteen hours a week; busking a few hours a week making a steady five dollars an hour; my four Anglo-Nubian cross Angora goats rented out on suburban blocks were bringing in a dollar per week per goat; the Anglo-Nubian cross nanny was supplying me with milk to drink; I got an occasional odd job for cash.

Then one night reading the bible, I came across Proverbs chapter 27, verse 26: "You can make clothes from the wool of your sheep and buy land with the money you get from selling some of your goats."

Now for me as a new Christian, reading something like that, it was obvious that one couldn't take any and every scripture and appropriate it for one's personal life. Sure, I had goats, but only about ten, and if I sold some of them I would not even get enough to pay for their transport to market and the selling costs, because sheep were bringing about ten cents each in a buyers' market and goats would no doubt bring even less.

I had heard from some Christians that you should only apply scriptures to your own life, bearing in mind the original context of the scripture. Proverbs 27:26 was in the context of an owner of thousands of goats, who would be selling only hundreds of them, in a rural area where land prices had no comparison with current suburban Adelaide prices. It would therefore be faulty logic to appropriate this scripture literally for my current situation. And it would be a miraculous thing to get $16,000 for the sale of my goats.

I also knew of some people who had been regular churchgoers all their long lives, who would say that miraculous things only happened in the time of Christ, so one shouldn't bother to expect any miracles in the present day; and besides that, they said, the bible was only a book of parables and fables and nothing actually happened as described-the bible was all stories written simply to keep kids amused.

And yet I knew of other Christians who would say that if you read a scripture and it really spoke to you and you believed it, then it would come to pass, no matter how unrealistic it may seem.

All this left me thinking, do I want to believe the scripture for myself, no matter how unrealistic, that I could buy a block of land from selling some of my goats? I decided that the best thing I could do was to get on with life in its day to day reality, and keep working as I was, to get enough money to pay my rent and food and motor car expenses, and part payments of my solicitor's account. There were also the payments for the car I no longer had. Any thoughts of getting a property for myself would have to be 'put on the back burner.'

In September 1982, I received a letter from my solicitor, asking me for instructions in relation to matters referred to in documents enclosed in the letter. Enclosed with the letter was a copy of a letter from Wendy's solicitors to him, saying that they were again acting for her, and that she had given them instructions to issue proceedings for 'dissolution of her marriage.' Also enclosed was a copy of Wendy's application for 'dissolution of marriage', in other words, divorce. The application was listed for hearing in November. I probably could have just replied straight away to my solicitor and told him that I had no objections to the divorce, but, having had the unpleasant experience of reading documents generated by Wendy about custody of our sons, more than a year previous, I knew I would have to read her application for divorce very carefully. Perhaps she would be attempting to assert that I had committed adultery, which, if I had done so, she could divorce me. Adultery was the only thing that I was aware of which would be a reason that a married couple could get divorced, and I knew that I had not ever been with any woman other than her, since we got married.

But there was nothing in the document about adultery. The first statement only said that Wendy and I had been living apart since April 1981, a period of "not less than twelve months immediately preceeding" her application for divorce. There was nothing in that statement which I disagreed with.

However, I disagreed with the next statement: "the children shall continue to reside in a house which comprises of three bedrooms and is well appointed." How anyone could describe a timber frame house which had holes in the asbestos sheet cladding of the outside walls, and had no floor coverings, and no hot water service, no curtains, no blinds, as "well appointed" I didn't know.

Not surprisingly, there was no reference in the application to her relationship with the man whose house I had recently been to, to pick up our sons and take them on a picnic. I could see on that day that there was a well-developed relationship between her and that man.

The next statement was correct if it were to be taken in isolation, but if put in the context of the complete situation, it was not correct, and in fact, was, in my opinion, deliberately misleading: "the wife attends to the supervision of the children and when appropriate is assisted by her mother." I wondered what the Family Court would say if they knew that Wendy, since leaving me about sixteen months previous, had twice been committed to a psychiatric hospital, and on both those occasions, Wendy would have been incapable of looking after the children.

The document then cited the currently operative Orders of the Family Court that were made well over a year previous-that Wendy still had custody of our children, that access was to be agreed, and that I was restrained. Strictly speaking, yes, I was still under an injunction, restraining me from contact with Wendy and the boys, or from coming near where they lived, but because of the three access visits that had taken place, the restraint was irrelevant.

Notwithstanding my objections to the misleading nature of most of the statements, I realized that there would be no point in raising them, because, basically, my sons were being cared for, and I did not have any comparable means of looking after them, when compared to the combined assets of Wendy's brother and mother and father.

I replied to my solicitor and told him that I did not want to appear in the Family Court to hear the application for dissolution of the marriage, nor did I want to contest anything, or make any submissions.

Late in November I received another letter from my solicitor to say that the Family Court of Australia had granted a 'decree nisi of dissolution of marriage,' which meant that if I wanted to make any objection, I would have to do it within one month, otherwise, the 'decree' would automatically progress from 'nisi' to 'absolute', meaning that the marriage would then be 'dissolved', and that Wendy and I would then be divorced, and that either of us would then be legally able to remarry, according to Australian law, without committing an offence of bigamy. I told my solicitor that I would not be doing anything further in the matter.

In December I received notice to say that the 'decree absolute had been posted.' I said to myself, "Thank God that is over!"

26

In December 1982, as the end of my forty-week bible college year approached, I and the other students had to make the decision either to go back into the work force, or to continue with another year of bible study.

The year had been a momentous one-I had got myself 'back to normal' after a year studying the bible and going to church seven days a week, and I had got divorced. For me, I could only do one thing-go back to work.

There were two possibilities. I had a job offer in Coober Pedy as a contractor's offsider, where I could stay in the contractor's worker's house rent free, or I could continue share renting the house in Adelaide, where I had increasing handyman work coming in, and the busking was a steady $5 an hour.

If I took the job in Coober Pedy, it would not be easy to come back to Adelaide if things didn't work out with the job, and access with my sons would be difficult at 840 kilometres distant, over 500 of which was dirt road. However, if I stayed in Adelaide, it would be a lot easier to visit my sons. I talked about the situation to a few people in the church. Most of them thought that I ought to stay in Adelaide. However, one man said, "You need to go to the country and live there for a long while." I didn't ask him why he said that, but his words stayed in my mind. He had become a valued friend of mine in 1982, a married man with teenage children, and I had meals in his home several times.

After many days of deliberations and discussions, I could not decide where to resume work. Adelaide was my preferred choice, but Coober

Pedy kept nagging me. Then the thought came to me once again about Gideon and his fleeces, just like when I was trying to decide whether to go interstate to see my sister and my mother. I thought that if I applied that method of testing to the Coober Pedy-versus-Adelaide decision, then I would find out what God wanted me to do.

The first test came to mind straight away. It was to ask for guidance from the senior pastor at the church, a very experienced and very busy man, the persom whom I thought was the most likely to guide me the best. If he thought it was a good idea for me to go to Coober Pedy, then that would be the 'dew-on-the-fleece-and-not-on-the-ground' test. I couldn't think of anything right then for the 'dew-on-the-ground-and-not-on-the-fleece' test, but that didn't bother me, because I knew it would come to me later.

I went to his secretary and asked for an appointment, thinking that I would get one in a few days. She said for me to wait. She came back in a couple of minutes and said, "Yes, you can go in straight away."

I thought, "Oh, oh, this is ominous—an immediate appointment!"

He listened while I told him about the job offer in Coober Pedy, and the opportunities I had in Adelaide, and the custody and access battles, and the distance to Coober Pedy and how that would make the access visits even more difficult. Then he prayed. While he prayed out aloud, I prayed silently to God that his prayer would be of good help. I heard him pray for God to guide me to make the right decision, and that if I chose to go to Coober Pedy I would be "mightily blessed!"

His prayer was a very wise piece of guidance. It didn't help me to make any decision right then, but it gave me confidence that whenever I made the decision, it would be the right one. And as a bonus, if I went to Coober Pedy and God was faithful-and how could he not be faithful?-I would be 'mightily blessed.' And who wouldn't want to be mightily blessed!

The second test came to mind a day later. Quite often on a Saturday night after youth meetings, people in the church would go into the city to the Teen Challenge outreach coffee shop in the city. It was a great place to meet other Christians from different churches from around the city and suburbs, and to get to talk to some of the really hopeless wanderers of the streets, people who had gone 'off the rails' in a big way. The condition that I put before God was that if I should go to the coffee shop and meet someone, for the very first time, from Coober Pedy, I would know that I was to leave Adelaide, and start my working life again in Coober Pedy. I thought that the chance of meeting anyone there from Coober Pedy, other than the two bible college students from there, was remote.

On the next Saturday night, I went to the Teen Challenge coffee lounge. I started chatting to a woman. I asked her, "What do you do for a living?"

She replied, "I'm a nurse, what about you?"

I answered, "I haven't got a job right now-I'm a student at a bible college."

She asked, "Which one?"

I thought that this was strange–it was not very likely that one would come across someone who would be aware that there would be several bible colleges in Adelaide. But then again, not so strange-after all, it was a Christian coffee lounge we were in. I replied, "Adelaide Bible College."

She said, in surprise, "Really, I have a sister there!"

I answered, also in surprise, "Yeah? What's her name?" She told me. I commented, "Wow! I know her. She sings. We both sing. We get on well together." Carrying on with our casual conversation, I asked, "Where are you nursing?"

She answered, "Coober Pedy."

I could hardly believe it. Now I had my answer. But it was a bit of a shock. I wanted to stay in Adelaide.

In mid-January 1983, while still share renting in Adelaide, I received a letter from my solicitor to say that, because I was recently divorced, any matter of property settlement would need to be dealt with by the Family Court, and I would need to issue proceedings by November 1983. My answer to him was very simple-I told him there was no property left to settle.

A week later I left Adelaide. As I drove past the northern edge of the suburbs, and kept heading north through the rural areas, I remembered the times back in 1965, '66 and '67, when I did the same thing, as a young schoolteacher. It was exciting for me back then, heading to a new job, to a new part of Australia, a new career in front of me. But this time I was heading north out of the city as a 'new creation', as a born-again Christian, with a totally new future 'career', and this time I was not doing what I wanted to do, but I was doing what I believed God wanted me to do. It was far more exciting for me.

27

As I got into the open countryside, I burst into singing the songs that I had learnt in the previous two years in the church, and I spoke and sang loudly in tongues. The further I went, the louder and more joyfully I sang, as it slowly sunk in that this new, unknown life before me was assured of success, because the Lord, the Comforter, the One who dispels all doubts, was going before me, preparing the way. My longings for life in Adelaide slipped away, as did any misgiving I had about leaving the city, and 'easy' contact with my sons.

In Coober Pedy, as a contractor's offsider, I started work at daybreak each day. January was the height of the desert summer. I worked under his direction on machinery in his yard. On one extremely hot day in the yard, we were working on bulldozer tracks, replacing pins. The tracks had to be heated with oxy, and the pins belted out with a sledgehammer. The day was so hot that a steel handled tool that had been left in the sun for only a few minutes was too hot to hold.

About half the dwellings in Coober Pedy were below ground. They were known as 'dugouts'. In summer when the outside temperature was in the forties, in an underground house it would be only in the twenties, without needing an air conditioner. My rent-free house was above ground, and had no air conditioning or fan, and was too hot to sleep in, so I slept outside. Many times, barking dogs woke me, as did screaming, drunken prisoners in the open-air jail at the police station about a hundred metres away. But I was happy to be in Coober Pedy, doing this kind of work, at age

37. It was what I wanted to leave school and do when I was a fifteen-year-old schoolboy.

Very few houses had fences. Most roads in the town were dirt, with lots of loose rocks. There were no footpaths, no street signs, very few trees, no grassed areas.

In early February I received a letter from my solicitor which said that they would wait to hear from me before they did anything more for me about me getting custody of my sons. An account was enclosed. I had no spare money to pay it. I was still paying regularly for the VW Golf that I had returned without completing the payments for the hire purchase agreement.

Early in March, as the contractor's work load slackened off, I drove to Adelaide and stayed for a day in the shared rental house to recover from the arduous journey of 500km of dirt road in high heat, before driving another 90km to the farm where Wendy and the boys were staying. They did not know I was coming. When I got there, I saw Andrew and Ben playing outside the farmhouse. It was wonderful to see them, and to see that they looked healthy and happy. They looked at my car just arrived. They must have recognised it, because, even before I got out of it, they came to me. It was such a joy to me to see that. Then Dary came out of the farmhouse. And there we were, the four of us together again. How wonderful it was. We played cricket. After about ten minutes, Wendy came out of the farmhouse. She said it was time for the boys to eat their tea. I was surprised when she asked me in too.

The inside of the house was a virtual rubbish dump. The floor and the table and shelves were cluttered with clean and dirty clothes, clean and dirty dishes, cutlery, books, dressmaking materials, empty cardboard cartons, and opened and unopened mail.

It was a strange feeling to be at table, eating quietly and peacefully, with Wendy and the boys, considering the recent times when there had been so much conflict. She looked to be going through a period of stability in between acute attacks of paranoid schizophrenia.

Part way through the meal, Wendy said I could put the boys to bed after tea, because she was off to a woodwork night class. That surprised me too. She had not been in such a stable condition in my recent memory. She left the table and went out of the house and drove away. We finished tea and went outside. I was curious to find out how Wendy's parents felt about me, because the last thing I remembered with them was their apparent attributing of blame on me for their daughter's mental sickness. I took the boys with me, over to the main farmhouse to visit them. They invited us in. We chatted for a while. They were at ease with me looking after the boys while Wendy went out for an hour or so, to night school. It was a relief to see that there was no bad feeling towards me there. I took the boys back to the farmhouse and I put them to bed. After they went to sleep, I left, and I drove back to the shared rental house in Adelaide, planning to return the next day to Coober Pedy and my offsider job.

The contractor rang me. He said not to bother to come back to Coober Pedy, because there was no more regular work available with him. He said he would contact me if he needed me. It was very disappointing to hear that I no longer had a regular job in Coober Pedy, but I told the contractor that I would be coming back, regardless of that, because the Lord had told me that I was to go Coober Pedy, and He would provide for me.

Without a regular job, I signed up for Unemployment Benefit. It hurt when I had to tick the 'Dependents' box for 'None.'

I drove back to Coober Pedy after selling some of my goats. Even though sheep were still bringing only about ten cents a head, there was an unexpected demand for export goat meat, and I got an amazing $40 for them.

I stayed in the contractor's workers' house again, rent free, in return for doing odd jobs. His brother, whom I had worked for as a gopher, was building a machine that would process dirt from abandoned opal mining claims. It was known as a 'noodling' machine, and he offered me cooked meals at his house if I helped him build it, with a promise that I would go on shares with him when the machine was finished. I accepted his offer.

Not knowing how long I would be able to stay in the contractor's workers' house, I decided to try to find somewhere else to stay, preferably where I did not have to pay any rent. Looking around the town area, I saw a few tin sheds on blocks of land. It looked like nobody had stayed in any of the sheds for a long while. I thought I could probably move into one of them, and 'squat'. The problem with living in a tin shed in the desert, was the lack of protection from the extreme summer heat. It would be much better to live underground. I found out that there were ten unoccupied blocks of land available for lease in the town, each one available on an 'Occupation Lease'. An Occupation Lease in Coober Pedy in 1983 entitled a person to live on the block of land and stay there indefinitely, if the annual licence was renewed by the paying of the lease fee. There was no Local Government in Coober Pedy, and there were no building regulations or building approval requirements, and no requirements regarding a timeframe for completing a dwelling on an Occupation Lease. The only requirement was that the occupier lived in a way that did not pose a health problem to nearby residents. If I could get an Occupation Lease, it would be virtually the same as owning my own land, and I could build a dwelling there at my own pace, as finance allowed.

I got hold of a town map. After hours of walking around the town, looking in the rocks and dust for the hardwood government survey marker pegs, I located all the blocks.

One block, Lot 1008, was about an acre, and had a small hill with a pushed dugout face and a backhoe excavation in the face. To me it looked like home. I filled in an application for an Occupation Lease on it, and I posted it. A week or so later my Occupation Lease approval came in the mail. The cost of the annual licence was $40. This was the amount I had received from selling some of my goats! Proverbs chapter 27 verse 26, that I read just over a year previous, which said that one could buy land by selling some of one's goats, as faint a hope it generated in me just over a year ago, had become a reality!

In the meantime, the contractor had hired a grader driver and gave him the rent-free workers' house, and I had to move out. I moved straight to Lot 1008 and I lived there in my Ford Falcon station wagon.

28

The first thing I built on Lot 1008 was a toilet. About ten metres away from the south-facing bulldozer bench that had been pushed into the side of the hill on the block, I dug a hole about 500 mm deep and 400 mm square, using the heavy handled, heavy head, road making pick and the spade that the bogus buyer left behind after I'd put him off my property in the Adelaide Hills. Around the hole, I put in four posts, of tree branches that were lying on the block. I put in another two posts for an entrance and privacy. I tied some old clothes together, that were lying around on the block, to the posts, for walls.

My drinking and washing water came from the public water pump three kilometres away in the town. Two twenty-litre plastic containers full usually cost me twenty cents, but if I went to the pump after a tourist bus got water, I quite often got my water free, because the bus drivers didn't know exactly how much water was needed to fill their water tank, and they put in too many coins.

I did my cooking on an open wood fire. It was hard to find firewood nearby. The nearest trees were over a kilometre away. I fashioned a frying pan out of a piece of corrugated iron lying on the block, stomping it flat with my boots.

There was hardly a blade of grass on Lot 1008. Some hardy desert bushes about half a metre high, like saltbush, grew in a shallow depression. Most of the ground was covered in stones.

The next thing I needed to build was a bedroom, underground. I thought that the best place to start digging would be in the western side of the north-south backhoe cut in the hill. There, the room would only be exposed to the sun in the mornings. I had no idea how to build an underground home. All I knew about a dugout was what I saw when I ate the cooked meals in the dugout where the noodling machine builder lived.

The backhoe cut western face was about four metres high at the highest point of the small hill. The top of the hill was covered with rocks and stones. Underneath the rocks was about 100 mm of dry, red-brown, clayey soil. From there the ground gradually faded in colour from orange to cream to white. That part was powdery. Under that, the white ground became solid, sometimes blocky, and continued for three and a half metres to the bottom of the cut. Although solid, the ground was soft enough that it could be scratched with a fingernail. It held together very well-a very hard whack with the pointed end of a pick head would only knock out a piece the size of a tennis ball. Sometimes there were fracture lines in the ground, and by 'reading' the lines, it was possible to pick out larger pieces.

I scraped out the outline of a doorway in the face. The pick handle was old and very dry. It was alright using it to dig a hole in the ground, for the toilet, but holding it high to dig into the face for the doorway, the heavy head kept slipping down and grazing my knuckles. I used a rock to bang the handle back in. The head remained in place for a few minutes and slipped down again. I banged it back in again with the rock. Soon it slipped down again. But that pick was all I had, and it had to do.

I sweated a lot in the sun, working with the pick, and had to knock off early in the afternoon and rest in the motor car. It was hot there too, but it was the only shade available. When the sun got lower, I started picking again on the doorway, in the shade. By nightfall I had picked about ten centimetres deep in the face, for the doorway.

I cooked after dark, by the firelight. I had no money for torch batteries. I had no money for candles. After eating, I slept in the motor car.

Next morning, I woke before the break of day, had breakfast in the twilight, and started picking again before sunrise. Each cubic centimetre I picked out of the wall was progress. I used the broken pieces to make a raised track on the block, starting at the backhoe cut, and going through the block to the road that went into the town, at the south end of the block.

Picking slowly like this, I learnt to 'read the ground', always looking for cracks, always changing the angle that I struck the wall, to pick out the maximum amount of ground with each strike.

I did this all day and every day, for many weeks. The only other things I did were to go shopping on Thursday mornings, when the weekly fresh food arrived in Coober Pedy by road train from Adelaide, and go to mid-week and weekend church meetings, where I played the guitar for the chorus singing, in return for meals.

Playing guitar and singing in the home church meetings, I was joined by a man who loved playing guitar and singing. He wasn't a believer. He took great delight in telling me that he had two birthdays. He said he was of Aboriginal and Mexican descent, born in a remote community, thousands of kilometres away in the north-west of Australia. As a young boy, he had birthday celebrations on what was generally regarded as his birthday, but there was no calendar in the remote community. Later he moved into a town and needed a birth certificate. A date was chosen, which then gave him a second birthday.

He and I had a strong affinity in music, and we enjoyed singing "When the Saints go Marching In" as a harmonizing duet, which everyone really enjoyed.

One day he took me to a mining field called Greek Gully, named after the many migrants from Greece who had mined in the area. He showed me how and where to noodle (search) for opal, and to use a sieve to shake out the dust, and to run my hand over the pieces in the sieve to see all sides of each piece, in bright sunlight. I went there later, on my own, and noodled, using a broken sieve that I found in the rubbish dump and repaired. I found several nice pieces of grey opal. What was known in Coober Pedy as 'grey' opal was strictly not grey in colour, it was white, and had traces of rainbow colours.

Using a rope that I found in the rubbish dump, I went down a nearby shaft (a vertical hole) on the Greek Gully field. With a borrowed torch, I checked a drive (a horizontal hole) and found some thin layers of grey opal, like a layer of jam between two slices of bread in a sandwich. It was exciting for me, as a 'new chum' on the opal field, to find it. I didn't try to dig it out, or to follow it to see if it got wider or deeper. That would be a job for another day.

One day an opal buyer came to my block and I sold him some pieces of opal that I had noodled. He gave me a couple of dollars, which I thought was not much for the effort I had put in to get it-Greek Gully was about twenty kilometres from the town. He went to drive out of my yard but couldn't get his motor car started. I worked on it for a while, checking spark plugs, points, and spark gap, and got it started. I charged him enough to make up for the low price he paid me for the opal.

One day I had a visitor, whom I met at a church meeting. Most times he was drunk. His skin exuded oil. He had a massive raised scar on his chest, high on the breastbone. He told me to wrap a piece of cloth around the pick handle before putting the head on, to keep the head in place. It worked. As I worked with the pick, he scraped the loose ground away from my feet.

Another visitor came, also from the church. He stood and watched as I used the pick. Without visitors, sometimes three days might pass before I saw anyone or spoke to anyone.

After three months, I had dug into the face far enough to lay out my bedding (swag), and sleep in the hole, instead of in the motor car. From then on, each morning I would roll up my swag and take it out, and dig some more, and at night clean out the drive, which extended straight in from the doorway, and lay my swag down again.

I carved the words, "Glory to God, 19 April 1983" in the wall, to remind me not to become proud of my achievement. I dug in for three metres. One metre in, I then dug sideways for about two metres. It gave me enough room for a kitchen, in which I cooked on Rabbit Trapper Perce's kerosene stove. It was exciting to stand in the recess and be out of sight of anyone looking in the open doorway.

I washed dishes and showered outside, in the cut. For my shower, I heated about nine litres of water in an old aluminium cooking pot from the rubbish dump, and I tipped it in to a ten-litre plastic bucket, also from the dump. Standing in another plastic bucket from the dump, I dipped a cup into the hot water and emptied it over my hair and then another cupful down my back. The third cupful was for my left arm. I stretched my arm upwards, and I tipped the cup slowly onto the back of my hand. The water ran down the back of my arm, running underneath my arm as it went down. I did the same for my right arm. Then there was one cupful each for my thighs, one for my groin, and one for my backside. My whole body had then been wetted.

I soaped up my hair and scrubbed my scalp. Any soapy froth left over, I used to wash the rest of my body. Three cups were enough to wash all the soap out of my hair, then two cups for each arm, tipped slowly on the back of my hands as before, followed by one for my back, one for my groin, one for my backside, and a final one on the back of my neck.

I noticed that water ran off the end of my penis and fell to the ground outside the bucket. Wanting to collect every drop, in future I kept my knees bent and arched my back when I tipped water over my body. Every drop then went into the bucket I stood in. I used the dirty shower water as a first rinse for my socks. I then put that water on small bushes.

Living in the dirt as I was, each time I went shopping, or to church meetings, it was like a 'culture shock' to see buildings, with carpets and window glass and furniture and water taps and electric light fittings.

In the yard, I gathered rocks and piled them up. I used some to mark out my raised track on the block, and a circular driveway in front of the dozer face. I marked out other areas for firewood, and scrap steel, and anything else that I picked up from the rubbish dump or off the roads when I went into town. An acre was over four thousand square yards, and I wanted to make the most use of every one of them, and of the rocks.

Flies were a constant problem, starting from early in the morning. One morning while I was shaving, they were buzzing at my face. I jerked my head sideways each time one was about to land, but I had to be careful not to slash my face with the razor.

If I was carrying anything, I had to leave one hand free to keep the flies off. I had no spare money to buy a fly net. One day while walking on the block to one of my designated areas, I was so besieged by flies that I stopped walking, and stood still and clapped my hands together in front of my face. I didn't have to aim, just clap my hands together, and most times I killed one fly, sometimes two.

When I stopped clapping, the flies buzzed at my face, and went up my nose, in my ears, in my eyes, in my hair. I kept clapping. As I stood there killing them, they fell to the ground in front of my feet. I noticed that one fly that I thought I had killed began to move, so I dragged my boot sole over it. I continued clapping and killing, and the more I killed, the better I felt. I was counting the dead flies. When I got to about fifty, I noticed some movement in the dust where I had dragged my boot sole over a 'dead' fly. As I watched, the movement continued. The colour of the dust became darker, about the size of a fly. Little legs appeared. A head appeared. Wings appeared. It must have been the fly I dragged over with my boot sole. It had escaped death twice. It climbed out of the little dust bowl that it was in, and it walked between some stones that were about twice as big as it was. Then I realised that when I had previously dragged my boot sole over it, it must have rolled over and over in a small amount of dust between two rolling stones, and it had thus escaped being crushed. I realized then, that when a clapped fly falls and lands in the dust, it might only be concussed, not dead, and then to drag your boot sole over it might not necessarily kill it. I knelt and put the ball of my index finger over the escaping fly and pressed down hard enough to feel that the body of the fly was crushed under my finger, and I dragged my finger through the dust. The crushed fly left a dark smear in the dust, like in a finger painting. I stood up and continued clapping. When I got to 140 clapped flies, I'd had enough. It was time to wash my bloody and stinking hands, and to try to remember what I was doing before I started clapping.

The flies attacked all the time, all day, even while I was picking underground. It was too distracting to have to put the pick down and brush away the flies-I just flicked my head from side to side to get rid of them, or else I tried to blow them away. The problem with that was, if a fly was crawling into my eye and I blew hard upwards to try to get rid of it, I blew all the fine dust off my cheekbones and into my eyes.

I phoned Wendy and asked her to let me have the boys stay with me at Coober Pedy for one week in the May school holiday. She agreed, and I drove down south, picked them up, and brought them to my new home. It was a tight fit, but the four of us slept in swags, underground on the dirt floor. I took them back as arranged.

While I was in Adelaide I did some busking. I noticed a man sitting and watching me, and when I shifted position, he was there again. He was dressed shabbily, with long, unkempt hair. He looked poor. In between songs I said to him, "Are you as poor as you look?"

"Yes," was his simple, truthful answer. I carried on busking, and he stayed listening. At the end of the twenty minutes he was still there. I introduced myself. He told me his name, and that he was from interstate. He said he liked the Christian songs. He said he was going through a rough patch in life. I offered him a free ride to Coober Pedy and to stay with me, and we would share living expenses. He agreed.

It was company for me for the long trip north, and at Coober Pedy we had many long discussions about many things. After a few weeks, he decided to go back interstate and have another go at life.

29

I was feeling very pleased that instead of having to sleep in my motor car, I could sleep in the hole in the side of the hill. Even without a door in place, it was cooler in the hole than outside.

In a small town, everybody knew everybody else's business, and if they didn't know, they could invent and imagine and come to conclusions and gossip. People criticized me for my 'primitive' working method. They said I ought to get a tunnelling machine, or else a compressor and a jackpick. They said I was stupid to be working in the eighties like they did in the sixties. But to me it was they who were stupid, because I was living within my means and making progress. And to be banging away at the hole, hour after hour, day after day, week after week, month after month, helped me to cope with my situation of being a divorced man under a Restraining Order.

Nearly all the people who met as a church were married couples. They had lived in Coober Pedy, isolated from most of society, for enough years to put them right out of touch with mainstream society and the stimulation of being in constant contact with many Christians from many places. Meeting regularly, we got to know each other. Discussions took place about many things. They were aware of my divorced status, and of my Restraining Order, just as I was aware of their positions in life, but they viewed divorced people almost with contempt, especially me, with a Restraining Order. They said that a divorce would be a permanent scar on a person's life, and they quoted the scripture, "God hates divorce."

In such a unique location like Coober Pedy, where most people were involved in opal mining, many discussions took place every day about the kind of ground where opal was found, and the methods of mining, and about the different types of ground. The ground in my little hill was typical of other ground. Even though I was new to the life, I could still contribute to discussions on 'ground', with the result that people would sometimes come to see what I was doing, partly out of the consuming interest they had in opal mining, partly out of concern that I might not be working safely as a new person 'on the field'. Somebody said that the ground I was working in was not good for an underground home-a 'dugout'. They said I should dig down lower until I got underneath a gypsum level. I had no experience to fall on, so I decided to follow their suggestion.

So that I didn't have to roll up my swag and lay it down each day, I slept in the kitchen area, and cooked outside again, and dug downwards into the part of the floor that I had been sleeping on, hoping to find a gypsum level.

Everybody called the ground 'sandstone'. There was no sand in it, and it wasn't hard, like sandstone. It was more like chalk. Sometime in the short history of Coober Pedy, someone must have used the word 'sandstone', and it stuck.

After digging downwards for about a metre, I found what everybody said I needed-a gypsum level. It was like a layer of filling in a sandwich, about three centimetres high, stretching across the half metre width of my recent diggings, composed of the white vertical crystal of gypsum. I dug under the gypsum level, and further into the hill, cutting steps in the sandstone as I went, until I was about two metres beneath the gypsum level. I carried the sandstone up the steps in a twenty litre oil drum that I found in the rubbish dump, and I tipped it into my wheelbarrow. I dumped the sandstone on the track that I drove on from the dugout to the public roadway. The wheelbarrow, which I inherited when my grandpa died, had a steel wheel.

Fourteen steps down, I dug a drive straight ahead, about three metres long. At the end of the drive I dug a doorway in the left side of the wall, about 400mm deep, and then dug to the left for about two metres, leaving a supporting wall about 400 mm thick, and then widened the little drive until I had enough room to lay out my swag, in a new bedroom. Then I cooked underground again, where I had recently been sleeping, on what was now a 'mezzanine level'.

In the wall, I banged some old nails that I had pulled out of second hand timber from the rubbish dump, and I hung up a hammer and a pair of pliers and the pick and the spade, and a shovel that I found in the rubbish dump. It felt good to have a place for the tools.

While digging out my new bedroom, I developed a working method: I would work for fifty minutes, and rest for ten. It took five shovelfuls of dug out sandstone to fill the old oil drum. I scratched a mark in the wall for every time I carried out a drum of sandstone. At the end of one day, in which I worked for eight hours, I counted ninety scratches-that meant about eleven buckets per hour picked out of the wall and carried up the steps, which meant roughly four working minutes to pick out five shovels full, that is, forty-eight seconds a shovelful.

I dug another room on the other side of the end of the bottom drive, again leaving a 400mm supporting wall. I then had two small bedrooms and a kitchen underground.

Early in September 1983, I headed off down south to visit the boys-it had been five months since I had seen them. It was very hot, and I carried plenty water. The old Ford Falcon purred along. About twenty kilometres south of Coober Pedy, I came across a car and caravan and two very distressed people. They said they had been waiting for hours for a northbound motorist to get a message to Coober Pedy that they needed a replacement wheel bearing for the caravan.

I offered my water. They grabbed it and tipped it up and over their heads, and they guzzled until it was all gone. If I had not come by just then, they might have perished of thirst within an hour or two.

I thought to continue south without any spare water, trusting the Lord that my own water had served its purpose in saving the lives of the stranded people.

After driving a few kilometres further south, I heard a sharp bang. The temperature gauge needle climbed rapidly. I stopped and popped the bonnet. I saw a circular slice in the radiator fins. One of the fan blades was bent backwards. It must have been bent by a flying rock, at just the right angle to slice the radiator fins. There was some water left in the radiator below the sliced fins, and in the bottom radiator tank. I drained it into a container. I took the bottom radiator hose off the bottom radiator tank and loosened the other end of the hose from the block, and I turned the hose upwards and tightened the hose at the block. I undid the top hose from the radiator and loosened the other end from the water pump and turned it upwards too, after tightening it at the water pump. I poured the drained water into the upturned bottom radiator hose.

Heading north this time, I got into top gear as quickly as I could, and as soon as the temperature gauge needle was dangerously high, I turned the motor off, put it into neutral, and coasted to a stop. I had gone about two kilometres.

When the needle stayed low after I turned on the ignition, I started the motor and repeated the process. Each time I did it, I went less distance. At one stop I loosened the radiator hose at the block. No water came out.

From then on, I drove in short bursts, the only coolant for the motor being the motor oil. It was enough to get me two hundred metres at a time. But each time I stopped, I had to wait about half an hour for the motor to cool down. After about twelve hours I had travelled the twenty kilometres to home.

I didn't have enough money at the time to repair or replace the radiator, so I had to abandon my attempt to visit the boys. Staying home in summer, my longest car journey would only be three kilometres at a time, so I would be able to continue to drive the old Ford without a radiator, until I got money to fix the problem.

30

In late September 1983, I received a letter from my solicitor to say that in November, the Family Court would be considering my application, that he had submitted for me, to remove the Injunction and Restraining Order that was placed on me sixteen months previous, in 1981. It was only a formality, because there had not in that time been any problems when I had visited the boys, but it was important that it be formally removed.

Two months later, my solicitor wrote to me again to say that on November 9, the Family Court of Australia discharged the Injunction and Restraining Order, meaning to say that it was no longer there. It was a great relief to read of the discharge. It had hung over my life like a dark cloud for nearly two years, during which time it could have possibly been used against me. I could also now update my friends and acquaintants at the church meetings of the discharge, which made me feel more like one of them, who had never experienced such a thing.

Enclosed with my solicitor's letter was his account for his recent work, which listed the amount still owing for his original work in 1982. He also enclosed a copy of the Family Court Order which 'dissolved' the Injunction and the Restraining Order.

31

In 1984, in my second year of living without power or water or phone in my little dugout, I was in my kitchen one morning when I heard a deep, guttural voice with a Greek accent say, "Come, I show you better place to live." I looked up into the open doorway at the top of the stairs and saw 'The Captain'. He was very tall, had a big black moustache, and wore a seaman type cap. His nickname came from his story that he had been a Greek Merchant Marine ship's captain.

I was happy in my little dugout. The peace I had with God was sufficient to keep me happy there. But I knew that my lifestyle there had plenty room for improvement. I thought that there would be no harm in going to look at something better. I knew that a person was entitled to hold only one Occupation Lease, but if what The Captain was going to show me was better, then I could cancel the lease on Lot 1008 and get a lease on a better place.

"OK," I said, and I went with him in his car. We drove through the town and headed east for a couple of kilometres, past the edge of the town and into the mining fields. He told me that he owned some land in the mining fields that was suitable for dugouts. The land was more than he needed, and he would give some of it to me if I agreed to share the development costs with him.

We stopped on a track on the east side of a two-hundred-metre-long hill that ran in a north-south direction. Halfway up the hill was a dozer face about fifty metres long and ten metres high, which was plenty of space for two or more dugouts of many big rooms.

We walked up the hill and stood at the base of the face. To the east was a valley about half a kilometre wide. Beyond that was virgin mining land, on another north-south ridge of hills. The south end of the ridge merged into the horizon. Near the north end of the ridge, about two kilometres away, some bare sandstone dumps indicated mining activity. Further north, the horizon stretched out towards Oodnadatta, a small village 190 kilometres away. In the valley were a few 'monkey' cuts, that had been dug with backhoes, and some small dozer cuts.

The Captain picked up a sandstone rock and tossed it. It landed about ten metres away at the base of the face. With a wave of his arm he said, "I give you that part, I keep this part."

Just near where the rock landed, there was a two-metre-wide hole in the face. In from the hole was a head high blasted area about seven metres in diameter. In front of the hole was a one metre diameter shaft. Next to it was an old kerosene fridge and a Massey Ferguson 35 tractor with no motor.

I agreed to go halves with him in the cost of hiring a dozer to rip half a metre deep into the floor at the base of the face and push away the dirt. I told him that I didn't have the money. "That's OK, pay when you have," he said. Then he took me back to my tiny dugout.

A few days later I went out again to the site. There were several well-established dugouts on the other side of the hill. I talked to the people living there. They had all been there for several years in their mining field dugouts. I told them about The Captain and the deal that we made. They all said that what The Captain had told me was not true-he did not own the land, nor did he have any lease on the land. They all said that nobody had lived on that site for years, and it was free for the taking. They said that anyone who wanted the land could simply move there and occupy it, just like they had done years ago, where they were now living. They all said that they had no official ownership of the land on which their dugouts were built either, because it was part of a South Australian Government Proclaimed Opal Mining Field, officially known as Potch Gully.

On hearing this, I was disappointed, realising that I had been tricked by The Captain, but then I thought that it didn't matter much, because I had not signed any papers with him, nor did I have any obligation to him-it was like the old saying, "a verbal agreement is not worth the paper it is written on."

I went back home, thinking that if I ever wanted to move to the site, I could do so at any time, and occupy it, free of charge.

32

I had many part time, short term, casual jobs in 1983, '84, '85, '86, for many different employers-supermarket shelf filling, builder's labourer, home handyman, which were everyday type jobs, no danger, easy to do, easy to get to.

There were other jobs which were not so. Some driving jobs were dangerous. On one, for the contractor who gave me my first job in Coober Pedy, I drove his short wheel base Toyota as a backup vehicle, while he drove his tipper truck. He had to put rags in the gaps at the rear of the tipper tray, to prevent spilling any of the load, which was going to be tested for diamonds. We went to a sandy creek bed somewhere on nearby Anna Creek Station, one of the largest cattle stations in Australia. We had no satellite phone or any other form of communication. The idea was, if we had a breakdown in the tipper, or an accident, I could drive the Toyota to get help.

We started at daybreak on a sizzling summer morning. In the creek bed, the contractor loaded the creek dirt onto the tipper with a frontend loader, and we carted the dirt to William Creek, a little village half a day's drive east of Coober Pedy, where he tipped the load for an exploration company to do the testing.

It was well past midday when we left William Creek for Coober Pedy. Before we left, the contractor got me to go to the hotel to buy a bottle of fruity mineral water. I copped some ribbing in the bar-everyone else was drinking beer. They didn't have any of the drink that the contractor wanted, so I bought some soda water instead.

We were stressed with the heat, and the contractor was even more stressed that I didn't get the right drink. We headed back to Coober Pedy with me driving the Toyota behind him in the tipper. The tipper got bogged in a sand dune that had recently drifted over the dirt road. I drove around to the front and we hooked on a tow chain. When the chain became taut, I gunned the Toyota motor. I could hear him gunning the tipper motor. I put my head out the window and watched my rear wheel jumping up and down in the sand, hardly moving forward at all. We turned off the engines and used shovels to clear sand away from the wheels, then we started again. While we were digging, the contractor's dog got burnt feet from walking around on the hot sand. Stinging, salty sweat ran down our brows and burnt our eyes. We were sick with exhaustion by the time we gave up trying to get the tipper free. It was late afternoon. We left the tipper behind, and the contractor drove the Toyota.

We had only about a litre of very warm water left in a container. We had to only sip from it. With about two hours driving ahead on the dune covered dirt road, I began to wonder if we would make it. I opened a quarter vent to get some breeze, but all I got was a blast of hot air. I wanted to tip the last water over my head to try to cool off. By the Grace of God, we made it back to Coober Pedy.

Later in the evening, after resting for hours, we found out that the Coober Pedy temperature maximum had been 48 degrees that day. We had been out in the full sun, in the hottest part of the day, shoveling sand away from around the bogged tipper wheels!

On another driving job, I drove the Toyota again, towing a fuel tank. We were headed for a mining exploration tenement located hundreds of kilometres away in the desert. Instead of a regular cup and ball towing connection, there was a high-tension bolt and nut that went through the hole in the Toyota draw bar and the trailer drawbar ring. It was a loose fit. Every time I accelerated, the fuel tank dragged back on the loose connection. Then the fuel sloshed backwards, pulling back the Toyota. Then the fuel sloshed forward, pushing the tank forward because of the loose connection, which pushed the Toyota forward. Every time I braked, the opposite happened. It was a very long driving day, trying to compensate for the continual surging and dragging. When I got out, I was dizzy and could not walk for a while.

We camped for the night. Next day we headed further into the desert. The track became less and less defined. Several times we came across a sand dune across the track, making it impassable. In the convoy was a prime mover and low loader, carrying a dozer. The contractor offloaded the dozer and pushed away the dune. The convoy moved through, the dozer went back on the low loader, and we kept going, until it had to be repeated at another dune.

After a few days, we finished up somewhere west of Emu Junction, near Maralinga, where the British government had tested atomic bombs in the 1950's. Here, the contractor and his brother were to put in a series of dozed tracks for drilling rigs to drive on, in an exploration program for an international mining company.

We found out later that the reason the track was duned over so badly was that it was no longer in use-in fact, there was another track that we could have taken, which would have got us to the destination two days earlier. On the positive side of that, I got two days extra work.

On a third driving job for the contractor, I had to take his backhoe/front end loader to a railway siding, about forty kilometres from Coober Pedy. The loader was on the 12-Mile opal field. The contractor drove me there in his Toyota. On the way, we stopped to do a job. One of his operators had suffered a stroke while grading a road. He had collapsed onto the steering wheel. The grader blade had dug into the side of the road, the motor had kept running, the grader blade was jammed hard into the ground. We had to dig it out.

After that we went on to 12-Mile. From there, I had to drive the backhoe cross country to the 8-Mile field, through creek beds and over rocky outcrops. From the 8-Mile, it was a 'normal' dirt road all the way to the siding. But the backhoe kingpins were worn badly, and it was difficult to control the swaying tractor.

At the siding, another employee was waiting with one of the contractor's tipper trucks. In the siding was a long line of railway trucks, full of crushed metal, that had to be carted to Coober Pedy to be used in concrete for new water tanks in the local Aboriginal Community. The gates on the trucks had been welded in, for the hundreds of kilometres train trip from the crusher. The line of trucks had been left in a position on the siding track where it was impossible to put the backhoe and the tipper close enough to offload the metal. I had to study the braking system on the trucks, and finally figured out how to free the brakes. Then we pushed the trucks along the line with the backhoe, to a better position. The other employee had to use the backhoe bucket to dig the crushed metal out of the railway trucks, backhoe bucket by backhoe bucket. I went back to Coober Pedy before it was finished. No doubt when the contractor found out what was happening at the siding, he took an oxy set there and cut off the railway truck gates, so that the crushed metal could be taken out quicker with the loader bucket instead of the backhoe bucket. Eventually the metal was carted into the contractor's batching yard, concrete was made and trucked to the water tank building site, and the new water tanks were built. I got a four-stitch gash in my leg during the construction.

Another dangerous job of driving was for the owner of a wrecking yard which was full of Holdens, Fords and Valiants dating back to the sixties. I started working there as a 'grease monkey'. My boss handed me some spanners and told me to go right through all the wrecks and take off all the starter motors, alternators and generators. I worked at that for a couple of weeks. By then it was time to take rubbish to the dump, which was a forty feet deep dozer cut at the top of a hill, two kilometres away, in an opal mining field.

The boss used an old tipper truck to carry the rubbish. A tipper tray, from another bigger tipper, simply sat unattached on the chassis, with no hydraulics attached, overlapping about a metre at the sides of the truck. There was about ten ton of scrap steel in the tipper tray. The tipper motor did not run, and there were no brakes, no windows, no windscreen, no mirrors, and no horn. My job was to steer the tipper while my boss towed me with his forklift, two kilometres to the rubbish dump at the top of the hill, using a ten-metre-long steel towing chain. When we got there, he towed me in a big U-turn so that I was facing the town, then he reversed his forklift back over the top of the towing chain, lying on the ground, until our two vehicles were touching, and then he nudged me backwards into the dozer cut.

The tipper moved very slowly down the ramp. I sat at the steering wheel, keeping the wheels in line. I couldn't look where the tipper was heading because I had to keep my eye on the towing chain. After the towing chain took up the slack, and the tipper started to roll faster, backwards, down the ramp, my boss used his forklift brakes now and then to control the descent of the tipper, until the tipper had dragged the forklift down to level ground at the bottom of the cut.

Then my boss took off the towing chain and drove the forklift around to the side of the tipper. He put the forks under the side of the oversize tipper tray, just behind the truck cabin, and started to lift it. It rose, but he was not exactly at right angles to the truck, and with a sickening squeal of metal on metal, the oversize tipper tray slid off the forks and crashed back down onto the truck chassis.

He tried it all again, and he managed to hold the front end of the tipper tray steady, about a metre higher than the chassis. Then he explained to me that my job then was to wedge two car rims between the chassis and the underside of the raised tipper tray, one on each side, to hold it up, so that he could take the forks out and then put them back under the tipper tray at a lower position, and then lift the tipper tray higher, so that the ten ton of scrap steel would start to slide off.

I understood clearly what he wanted me to do. I knew that if the rims slipped while I was still getting out from underneath the raised tipper tray, I would be crushed to death. I prayed to the Lord, "Lord, if you want to take me home today, then I am ready. I think it would be a waste if I ended my life like this, but I trust your judgment."

Then I took the two rims and wedged them as I had been told, and then got out of the way. The boss lowered the forks, and the tipper tray sat propped up on the car rims. He reversed the forklift and then drove forwards, putting the forks back under the tipper tray, closer to the rims, and lifted it again, about another metre higher. The scrap steel started to tumble down the inclined tipper tray. Amid the cloud of dust, he dropped the forks suddenly for a few centimetres, and jolted the rest of the rubbish off the tipper tray.

I took out the two rims. He lowered the empty tipper tray back on to the chassis, and then drove the forklift around to the front of the tipper. I hooked the towing chain back on and he dragged me up the dozer ramp.

At the top of the ramp, facing towards the town, he stopped. He got off the forklift and walked back to me. "Use the clutch as a brake," he said.

I put the tipper into second gear, and I held the clutch pedal down to the floor. He got back on the forklift and slowly moved forward until the towing chain took up slack again. With a shudder, the tipper started moving forward.

The track only had a gentle incline at first, and most of the time I held the clutch pedal down to the floor. A couple of times when the slope was steeper, and the towing chain became slack, I let the clutch pedal up a bit, using the clutch as a brake, until the chain became taut again. About halfway down the hill, my foot and calf muscles and thigh muscles started to ache from keeping the clutch pedal pressed to the floor. The track ahead for a few hundred metres was almost flat. The pain in my leg was too much to bear. I knocked the gearstick into neutral and let the clutch pedal up. The towing chain remained taut. After a while the pain in my leg subsided.

The track started to get a bit steeper, but still the towing chain kept taut. Ahead, the track got steeper again, and then flattened out for the last hundred metres or so. I knew that very soon I would have to depress the clutch pedal to the floor again, and knock the gearstick into second gear, and be ready to let the clutch pedal up if the towing chain got slack. I kept my eyes on the towing chain, and on the track ahead. As the track got steeper, the towing chain got a bit slack. It was time to use the clutch as a brake again. I depressed the clutch pedal to the floor and held it down. I tried to knock the gearstick into second gear, but it wouldn't budge. I looked ahead and saw that the towing chain was now so slack that it was dragging along the ground behind the forklift. I let the clutch pedal up and depressed it to the floor again, and I tried again to knock the gearstick into second gear, but it wouldn't move.

Ahead, the gap between me and my boss on the forklift was gradually decreasing. Part of the towing chain was now dragging along under the tipper. There was no horn to use to warn him. I shouted at him at the top of my voice. He kept looking straight ahead, blissfully ignorant of the impending danger. I tried to get third gear with the clutch pedal depressed to the floor. The gearstick wouldn't move.

I could see that I was catching up fast with him, and soon I would be ramming him from behind. I yelled again. He kept looking ahead, unaware of what was happening. I steered over to the left. I was drawing near to level with the back of the forklift. The towing chain was bouncing along, across the road between me and the forklift. Soon I would overtake him and maybe drag him sideways and capsize the forklift.

For some reason, he glanced to the left. His jaw dropped when he saw me about to overtake him. He changed gear and accelerated, and quickly went ahead of me. The track started to flatten out and I dropped behind him, and after a while the towing chain got taut again, and then he slowed and stopped.

"What the Hell, are you trying to kill me?" he screamed.

"Well, what do you expect; you could easily have killed me back in the rubbish dump if those rims had slipped!" I shouted back.

We went back to the wrecking yard. After he paid me, I finished up with him.

After having been a grease monkey in the wrecker's yard, I was able to see opportunity for getting part of a living from old cars. An opal miner had a yard full of them, along with a lot of other scrap. The wrecks had parts that I could use on my car, and other parts that I could sell. The opal miner wasn't in town, but his number one man was. I asked him about getting some parts. He said that the opal miner wanted the yard cleaned out, and he said that I could have all the wrecks for nothing if I cleaned out the whole yard, including all the rubbish.

I gladly agreed to do it. I started by taking some old steel frame beds. Then I took a few of the better cars. The number one man came and saw that I had not yet taken any of the rubbish. "Hah!" he said, "You ony taking good stuff, and you gunna leave rubbish." No matter what I said, he would not believe me.

"I clean out this yard. You never find where I dump cars. You not get any more from here," he said.

It was disappointing to lose the remaining vehicles, but at least I had got some profit for my time.

Of all my part time jobs, the best was for a film company. It had chosen Coober Pedy for its base camp because of its proximity to an area of distinctive natural beauty and stark desert landscape of hills of amazingly varied natural colours, known as The Breakaways. The film was "Mad Max III, Beyond Thunderdome", starring Mel Gibson and Tina Turner. The company needed hundreds of 'extras', as well as semi-skilled people. They hired nearly everybody in the town, daily, for the duration of the filming, which was several weeks. Each day they bussed hundreds of locals out to The Breakaways for location filming. Massive tented areas were set up there to cater for meals for everyone during each day of shooting.

I scored several jobs: as an extra; as an offsider for the Number One Mechanic, who had the responsibility of maintaining the 'crazy cars', which only had one-liter fuel tanks for safety because they were often involved in crashes and rollovers; as a truckdriver transporting props around on the various film sites in The Breakaways, and when the filming was over, driving the trucks onto railway flatcars at the railway siding which I had worked at previously; as overnight security guard on Mad Max's special vehicle, parked each night in the hotel car park. Each of the jobs paid many times the hourly rate of any of the other jobs I had for local companies.

The 'Outback Grapevine'-the name given to the way stories from remote areas of Australia are communicated over vast geographical areas nationally-was working well as usual, because just when I got paid up for all my Mad Max work, I received an appeal from my solicitor to settle my account, immediately, in full, for his work for me over the last few years. Gladly, I paid him.

33

One day, while standing in the main street late in 1984, I thought back to the time in 1960 when I passed through the town with a group of Boy Scouts on the way to Alice Springs, in the centre of the continent, and how when I came back home to Lameroo, I wrote a little story about my outback trip. Most people in Australia never get to experience life in remote areas, but they love to read about it. Their experience of Australia starts in the capital cities and goes as far as the edge of the suburbs, and yet Australians like to cling to the idea that the typical Australian is a sun-tanned, strong, rough and ready character. Then my mind went forward to 1973, when I again passed through Coober Pedy, as a folksinger, and I wrote some songs about what I saw then. I thought again about the idea I had in 1973 to start a newspaper in Coober Pedy, and write about life in the outback. It was impossible for me to do it then because I was only passing through. But here I was, back in Coober Pedy in 1984, and I thought that perhaps this time was the time to do it.

I was looking at the rooms above the bank, and I thought they would be a suitable premise-in the main street, with a good view of the comings and goings of the townspeople. I asked in the bank whom should I contact to inquire about renting the flat on top of the bank. The bank accountant told me to speak to the owner of the opal retailing business in one of the other offices on the ground floor, who was the manager for the owner of the building. I went to him. He told me the owner of the building lived in Adelaide. He said I would have to wait until the owner visited Coober Pedy.

One day some weeks later, I heard that the owner of the building was in Coober Pedy. I went his manager, who took me up a flight of stairs and into a gambling house, known as the Coffee Club, and he introduced me to the owner.

He was a small man, dark skinned, Greek, wearing customary heavy gold rings set with big stones. He had a heavily lined face and very serious expression. His hair was thinning and greying, but he looked to be a very strong man with a menacing presence, not one to trifle with.

He agreed to show me the flat. It had a kitchen, a bathroom with shower, a toilet, three furnished bedrooms and a large, carpeted lounge. The rooms were very dusty, and the carpet was dirty. He said I would have to make sure I didn't use too much water when I showered, because the water would leak through the floor onto the desk in the accountant's office, and he didn't want Westpac Bank, his prime tenant, to be unhappy.

The doors of the wardrobe in the main bedroom were open. The wardrobe was full of washed and ironed shirts and pants and ties, and expensive shoes. I said to him that I wanted the wardrobe cleaned out, because I thought it wouldn't be nice if I was renting the flat and someone came to collect the clothes. I said, "Whose are all these?"

He said, "Oh … don't worry about them. You can have them. They belong to the previous manager of the Coffee Club. He used to stay here when he came up from Adelaide, but he won't be coming up anymore. And the new manager is too big for the clothes, and anyway he stays in his own house in Coober Pedy."

"Oh … OK," I said, nonchalantly. But inwardly I rejoiced at the thought of a lot of nice clothes, all my size, worth hundreds of dollars, for free. I thought it would be a good idea to know the name of the owner of the clothes, just in case he turned up for some unknown reason and wanted his clothes back. It turned out that he was the man who had paid me and my folksinging partner in beer, for our singing in Coober Pedy, back in 1973. Inwardly I was now doubly rejoicing, because after fifteen years, I was getting an excellent bonus.

We agreed on a rental amount. "What about electricity?" I enquired.

"You don't have to pay for that-it's included in the rent money. There's only one metre for the electricity for the Club and the flat together."

"And water?" I asked.

"That's included in the rent too. There are some water tanks at the back of the club that supply the whole building for all the tenants. Your water for the flat comes out of them. The Club Manager will order more water when the tanks are getting low. He'll ring up the water carter and get him to cart water to the Club and fill the tanks and pay him. You don't have to do anything. If you run out of water in the flat, just go into the Club and tell them, and they'll open a valve from another tank for your water in the flat."

It all sounded simple enough. I said, "OK, I'll take it." I moved in that day.

One day I turned on the tap over the kitchen sink to get a drink, but no water came out. I knew I had to go into the Coffee Club next door to ask the manager to open a valve from another tank for water for the flat. I went out the front door of my flat and walked along the verandah towards the front door of the Coffee Club. I saw through the club windows many men seated at tables. As I walked through the doorway of the Coffee Club, the steely stare of the men watched me intensely. They were playing serious card games. Wads of paper money lay on the tables.

After what seemed a very long time, a heavily built man got up from a table and came to me. "What you want?" he said. After I explained, he said, "OK, I get you water."

He went into the kitchen and opened a door of the sink cupboard. He reached down under the sink and appeared to me to be turning something. He stood up and turned to me and said I would have water in the flat now.

I left the Club. I was glad to get out of the smoke-filled, intensely serious atmosphere. Back in my flat, I turned on a tap and, thanks to God, water came out. But I wondered what I might do in the future if I ran out of water and the Coffee Club was shut.

Several weeks after that, early on a Sunday morning, I turned on a kitchen water tap to get a drink. There was a croaking sound. No water came. I walked out of the flat and along the verandah towards the Coffee Club door. I could see through the window glass that nobody was seated at the gambling tables. Even though I thought it was a waste of time, I walked to the door, and pushed on it. It opened. I entered. I saw a man fully clothed, asleep, sprawled out on top of a billiard table. Hanging out of his pants pocket was a bunch of keys. I walked carefully and quietly to the billiard table and extracted the bunch of keys from his pocket. The man was in a sound sleep and did not stir.

I went to the Coffee Club door and tried the keys until I found the right one. Then I took it to the hardware store and got a duplicate cut.

Back at the Coffee Club I tried the new key and it fitted. I put it in my pocket. I put the bunch of keys back in the pocket of the sleeping man, and I went into the club kitchen. On the kitchen shelves were many new cartons of cigarettes, and bottles of beer and soft drink. I went to the sink and opened the cupboard door.

Underneath the sink were several valves. I opened one of them and went back to my flat and tried the kitchen tap. Water came out. I went back to the Coffee Club door and shut it and tried it. It was locked. I felt very happy and victorious and thankful to God as I walked back along the verandah and into my flat, knowing that I now had access to the Coffee Club for my water supply, without the knowledge of the owner.

For printing my newspaper, the "Coober Pedy News", I used a hand operated, second-hand duplicator that I bought in Adelaide. The typewriter I used on the printing stencils was an Olivetti that my parents had bought me in 1969.

I managed to get small advertising sponsorships from various local businesses. An old business acquaintance and WPTC fellow student, now an opal buyer, signed up for and paid in advance for one year of advertising.

Around the same time, some local school teachers started up the "Coober Pedy Times", a community run paper. It was a better production standard than my publication, and far more widely supported. Many of the businesses that advertised with me thought they were both the same.

The manager of the Coffee Club; visited me one day. He said that things in the Coffee Club were not going too well. He said that he couldn't afford to continue renting the room between my flat and the Club, and he wanted me to rent it. I went with him to look at it. There was an air conditioner in the west wall.

"Does that work?" I asked.

"Yes," he said, and he walked across the room and turned it on. The room started to cool down immediately.

The main electrical switchboard for the Club was inside the room. There was carpet on the floor.

"OK," I said, "I'll take it."

"Thanks, man," he said, and handed me the key for the door. I was pleased with the thought of having a room with an air conditioner. It would be good to work on my newspaper in the cool.

As soon as the club manager's rent week was finished, I started paying the rent for the room. It was separated from the Club by a concertina door which was locked on my side. I could see into the Club between the panels of the concertina door. In the afternoons, the hardened, gaunt faced miners and gamblers watched the children's TV program, "ABC Playschool", to learn the English language.

One night I couldn't sleep. There was a lot of loud talking in the Club. I went into the new room and I looked through the concertina door. The manager was talking loudly, with a cigarette in his lips. As he spoke, the cigarette flapped up and down. He was wearing white leather shoes. His jacket collar was turned upwards. His narrow brim hat was pulled down over his eyes. He looked exactly like a 'crim' in a Batman comic.

I picked up from the broken English that there had been a visit by local police, who regularly checked the Club, knowing that most of the Club had connections who 'were of interest'. The club patrons, mostly uneducated Greek migrants, were trying to pronounce the word 'harassment', in relation to the police visit. I went back to bed and slept.

Some days after that, I got all the newspaper things together, ready to move them into the new room. I put them down on the floor outside the door of the new room. I opened the door and moved the things into the room. It was not a very hot morning, but the electricity for the air conditioner wasn't going to cost me anything, because all electricity costs were included in the rent, so I decided to turn it on.

But when I looked, instead of an air conditioner in the wall, there was a big hole. Someone had taken the air conditioner. I went straight to the club manager. "Do you know anything about the air conditioner in the new room? It's gone; there's a big hole in the wall instead," I said.

"That's OK," he said. "I took it. I needed it in another room."

"What! You can't do that. It was in the wall when I agreed to rent the room," I said, very annoyed.

"Yes, I can. It doesn't belong to you. It belongs to the Club, and I am the Manager of the Club," he said. I walked out in disgust.

Back in the room, I shut the door behind me and sat down and tried to think what to do. I thought of nailing a sheet of plywood over the hole in the wall. I thought to phone the owner of the building and complain. Then I remembered that the main electrical switchboard for the Club was inside my new room, and I had the key to the door. I got up, went to the switchboard, turned off the power to the Club, and waited to see what would happen.

Soon there was a knock on the door. I opened it. A little boy, about twelve years old, stood there. I didn't know who he was. "Turn the power on, mister," he said.

"What!" I said.

"Turn the power on!" he said, with a mean look on his face.

"Well, who are you?" I said.

He put his hands on his hips and glared at me. "Don't get smart with me mister. Just turn on the power!" he yelled.

"Get lost, kid. Run away," I said.

"If ya don't turn on the power, I'll get my Dad to come and sort ya!" he retorted.

"You do that, boy," I said.

He stormed off along the verandah to the Club. I shut the door. Very soon there was another knock on the door. "Who is it?" I said.

"Open the door," the voice said, loudly.

"Who's this?" I called out. I knew it was the club manager.

"Turn on the power or there's gunna be trouble," he said.

"What are you going to do, call the Police?" I said. There was silence. Then I said, "OK, you bring me back the air conditioner and fit it back in the wall. Then you can have your power back on."

I heard him walk away. Later he came back, and said, "We've got your air conditioner."

I opened the door. He came in, with two men carrying the air conditioner. They fitted it back in the wall. I turned the Club power back on.

Some carpet cleaners came to town. I spent several hundred dollars to have the flat carpets cleaned. Soon after that, I happened to meet an employee of the Commonwealth Education Department who was visiting Coober Pedy. The purpose of his visit was to set up a guitar teaching program for disadvantaged Aboriginal children. He signed me up to be the teacher. I started teaching about ten local boys. I had to write regular reports on their progress. Many of the parents of the boys were habitual drunkards, and often the boys were hungry when they came for guitar lessons, so I made sandwiches for them. As time went by, other Aboriginals came into my studio and wanted food. I started making and selling sandwiches.

Feeding the boys with sandwiches made me think of my own sons. About 15 months had passed since the time the three of them came to Coober Pedy, during which time I received no news about them, or from them. All I ever got was excuses as to why they were not allowed to visit again, so I went to the Coober Pedy Department of Community Welfare boss for advice. He said that he could not undertake to advise me unless he was aware of the current situation regarding the Family Court and me and Wendy and our sons.

To that end, he asked me if there was any Family Court Injunction currently in force. I said, "No. There had been one in 1981, but it was dissolved in 1983."

The DCW boss asked me for proof of that, so I showed them the letter from my solicitor to me, advising me that the Family Court Injunction that had been imposed in 1981 had indeed been dissolved. The DCW boss then asked me for a copy of the Injunction. I searched through my files and found it and gave it to him. He read it, and said, "Well, we have a problem here."

When he said that, I started to wonder if I had made a mistake in thinking that the 1984 Family Court Order, which dissolved the 1981 Family Court Injunction, had been made. I said, "What do you mean, a problem? I'm sure the Injunction was dissolved."

"Oh yes, it definitely was dissolved. But the problem is, the letter that you showed me from your solicitor says that the date of the Family Court Injunction was 28th May 1981, but the Family Court Injunction that you showed me has the date of 6th May 1981. Now, which is the correct date? Or were there two Family Court Injunctions? Have another look through your papers and see if you can find the Family Court Injunction dated 28th May 1981."

I looked through my papers but did not find any Family Court Injunction with a date of 28th May 1981. The DCW boss offered to write to the Family Court Registrar for me, to request for a copy of the Family Court Order which imposed an Injunction dated 28th May 1981. I accepted his offer.

A week later, his request being granted, he showed me a copy of the Family Court Order which dissolved an Injunction dated 28th May 1981.

"What!" I said, furiously. "Nobody ever told me that there was going to be a second hearing! If I'd have known that, I could have put my side of the story, and maybe the Family Court would have changed its mind about giving custody of our sons to my ex-wife, and instead, given it to me!"

"Well, it's all too late for that," said the DCW boss. "Obviously, for some reason, you were never informed about a second hearing—either someone didn't do what they should have done, or else they forgot. It wouldn't surprise me if they neglected to tell you on purpose."

"Anyway," he continued, "there's no way the DCW can force your ex-wife to let the children visit you. You'd have to go back to the Family Court for that. In the meantime, I suggest you start writing to the children, and build up a steady relationship with them, and then they will maybe put pressure on your ex-wife to let them come to visit you."

I had no choice but to accept the situation, like I did in 1981, when the boys were taken from me, and to try what the DCW boss suggested.

Once, the man who told me about wrapping rags around the pick handle to stop the pick head from sliding down the handle, came for some sandwiches. He was very drunk. I fed him. He wanted to sleep. I helped him onto a bed and took off his boots. When he woke, he told me that he liked my sandwiches, but he liked better the hot, take-away food from the shop across the street. He said he had been booking up take-away food there for a while, and they told him he could not have any more credit until he paid his bill. Thinking it would only be a few dollars, I told him I would pay it.

We went to the shop. I asked how much his bill was, for take-away food. I was shocked when they told me about five hundred dollars. I said I didn't think it was so big an amount, and I couldn't afford to pay it after all. The wife came in, saw me, and shrieked, "That's the newspaper guy!"

The shop owner grabbed me by my shirt and rammed me up against the wall. He was about to swing a punch when his son burst into the room, raced across to his father, knocked him down, and said, "Quick, get out of the shop."

I did not hesitate to take his advice.

After sixteen weekly papers, I realized that my supporters were dropping off, so I printed one more edition and quit. I contacted the man who had paid a yearly subscription in advance, without whose support I could not have got the business started, and told him I was quitting, and sent him a refund cheque. I still had enough income from guitar teaching to continue to pay rent for the flat. However, some of the guitar students came only once or twice and never again, even though they were receiving payment to attend. I reported this. The Commonwealth officer said to change my report to read that the boys were attending, and to make fictitious reports on the progress of the missing students. That way, he said, the funding for my wages would continue. I told him I could not do that. He sacked me.

I went to the owner of the building next time he was in Coober Pedy and told him I wanted to move out. "OK, you owe me for one month rent in advance," he snarled.

"What about the cost of cleaning your carpets that I paid for, and what about the times when I had no water?" I complained. He let me go without having to pay.

In the time when I was renting the flat, from the profits of the newspaper, I was able to buy a washing machine and a wardrobe and some kitchen appliances, and I had all the clothing left behind from the previous club manager. There was not enough room for these things in my little dugout. I decided to go instead to the dugout site in Potch Gully that The Captain showed me. There was plenty of underground room there for those things, as well as for furniture from my little dugout. It would not take me long to close off the two-metre wide opening in the face, and put in a door and a window, to give protection from the weather.

I used saved money to pay for help to move everything. I decided to keep paying for the lease on my little dugout. I had come out of the newspaper venture very well-a long-time resident told me that I was the only person who had ever made a profit from renting rooms at the Coffee Club building.

34

At the Potch Gully dugout site, the edge of the platform in front of the top face was broken in places, and there was nothing to stop anyone from falling over the edge to the bottom of the lower face, about twenty feet down, so I gathered up some scrap and put up a temporary barrier. I made a toilet enclosure from scrap timber and corrugated iron, and I put it over the three-feet diameter drill shaft near the opening of the 'room'. I used some boards to cover the whole of the top of the shaft, except for a hole for the toilet waste to fall through. For a seat, I cut out the top and bottom from an old oil drum, and I put a toilet seat and lid that I found in a dump, on top of the oil drum. I swapped a team mate from the local football club where I played, a pair of my white nylon football shorts, for a galvanised, 44-gallon drum, and with another one that I found on the field, I could fetch a two-week supply of water in my trailer from the town pump. It was about three kilometres to the town, the same distance as my leased dugout block. I cooked on Rabbit Trapper Perce's stove. On the side of the highway one day I found an enamel cooking pot. It was burnt inside, but some stiff work with steel wool from the dump brought it back to new.

Some people who visited me were very concerned about the safety of the 'room'. They said I ought to get some opinions from 'old-timers'. I got two to check it out. Both had worked with tunneling machines for many years on the field. Surprisingly their assessments conflicted-one miner said the ground was no good, it was too blocky, it was not safe, and said I ought to get out. The other also said the ground was blocky, but if I domed it, the room would be safe. I decided to dome it. That meant a ceiling of about fourteen feet high, and all I had was the old road making pick, a shovel from the dump, and Grandpa's steel wheeled wheelbarrow. That being all I had, that was what I worked with.

As time passed, with daily use, the barrow was starting to wear out. Dust and small pieces of sandstone fell through the holes. The more I used it, the bigger the holes got, and bigger rocks fell through. But I found a piece of carpet to lay in the barrow. I just had to remember to hold on to it when I tipped the barrow out over the edge of the platform. I used some wedge shaped blocky pieces of sandstone to fill in the broken edges of the platform.

When I saw that free government adult education courses were offered for people on low incomes, I took the night time oxy and arc welding courses. At the workshop, I used free scrap flat steel and bronzing rods to patch the wheelbarrow holes. I was still using the heavy road making pick.

On one of my walks around Potch Gully, I found an opal mining pick, which is a much lighter pick. I could understand why it had been thrown away-the handle was broken, and so was the chisel end on the head. I also found a broken steel file. I cut the broken handle back to about 300 millimetres. With one foot holding the pick head down on an axle of the old Massey Ferguson tractor, I worked a long time with the steel file until I had made a new chisel end, and I sharpened the point end.

In the room, I stood on a chair and started picking into the ceiling with my new pick, next to the entrance. The blocky ground sometimes came down in large sections, which sped up the progress.

One day while picking, I heard a dozer working nearby. It was a worrying noise because on Potch Gully field, being a mining field, anyone could put mining pegs over the top of my 'residence', and I could at any time lose any 'ownership' of the work that I had done. But to my relief, the dozer was only passing by.

I went to the Mines Department to find out about getting a lease on the land. The Mines Inspector asked me where I was talking about. I told him. He said he knew the place. He said if he found out I was living there, illegally on a mining field, he would come out with gelignite and blow the place up. I said nothing. It seemed ridiculous for him to threaten me like that, because he must have been aware of the people who lived in the well-established dugouts on the other side of my hill, who had no lease on the land. I left his office, deciding not to pursue the matter with him, and take my chances on continuing to occupy the land.

One day while picking at the ceiling, I heard a crashing sound, like vehicles falling over a cliff. I went outside. I saw a tipper, about one hundred metres away, tipping cars into a cut. I recognised some of the vehicles. They were from the yard of the opal miner whose number one man had dismissed me from my cleanup job, and who told me I would never find out where he was going to dump the cars. I couldn't help smiling for the rest of that afternoon, thinking of the irony of the situation. The number one man would not have had any idea that I was watching the dumping of the cars just walking distance from where I was living.

After a few months of picking, sandstone piled up inside the dugout. Much of it I had earlier used to patch up the track into the site, and the holes in the platform and at the edge. I continued doming, starting at the side and working towards the centre, taking out about a metre, in height, from the ceiling as I went.

In one part of the ceiling there was a crack running horizontally for about three metres. I picked at the ceiling, sideways for about two metres on either side of where the crack stopped, and straight ahead for a metre, and then behind. This left a mass of sandstone of several cubic metres hanging in the ceiling. I figured that one day it would drop, and that would save me a lot of picking.

The sandstone pile covered most of the floor, with only enough room for cooking and showering and sleeping. To get some more floor space for sandstone, I carried my bed up to the top of the pile, and set it up, just underneath the ceiling, away from the hanging piece. At night after showering, I would put on my boots to climb the sandstone pile to the bed.

One day I was sitting at the top of the sandstone pile, resting from picking the ceiling. I heard a 'ffffft' sound, and a few minutes later, another. I didn't know what it was. I looked to the hanging piece. There were a few more 'ffffft' sounds. Each time a 'ffffft' went off, little spurts of powdery sandstone burst out, all along the crack above the hanging piece. Suddenly the whole piece, probably weighing over a tonne, dropped on to the top of the pile, about a metre away from where I was sitting. It was a narrow escape. It also saved me a few days of picking at the ceiling.

After about 15 months of letter writing, as suggested by the DCW boss, my second son Andrew, came for visit. We stayed in the Potch Gully room. It was arranged entirely between him and me, through our letters, with no input from Wendy. One day, he said he had been told by his mother that he was going to get a new father, and that I would not be his father any more. He was about nine years old then. Judging from the casual way in which he told me that, I guessed that it would have been explained to him as just an everyday kind of situation, that a boy would be getting a new father. I thought it best to say nothing about it. That way it would not cause any conflict between us.

About five months later, Andrew and Ben came and stayed with me at Potch Gully, again the result of many letters between us, independent of any involvement of Wendy. They said they were going to get some money soon, because the man who they had been told was going to be their new father had just died. I asked them, and they told me his name. I managed to find out the name of one of the deceased man's survivors, and I phoned her. She told me that Wendy and her parents were contesting the deceased man's will, on the basis that Wendy and he had been planning to marry. She said she and her siblings were very upset, because in their opinion, Wendy had "moved in" on their father in his time of grief and loneliness after his wife had died, and Wendy had known him for a matter of months only. I told them that I thought Wendy was wrong to do this, and I told them that she and I had only been recently divorced. Then I told Andrew and Ben that I didn't think it was right for them to expect money from the man's will. I said nothing about them getting a new father. The boys went back down south after the holiday.

35

In Potch Gully, without television or radio, going for walks was my entertainment, and it was at virtually no cost, because my footwear was free, from the rubbish dump. To say 'the rubbish dump' is misleading, because although there was a designated area for the town refuse, all the mining fields in a radius of about two kilometres from the town centre were used as rubbish dumps. There was no local government to impose fines for illegal dumping. Abandoned dozer cuts were used for dumping old car bodies, car parts, household refuse, workshop and building waste, and washing machines and fridges, TV sets, radios, tools, furniture and clothes, and building materials. I got a lot of things just for the taking.

My next-door neighbor walked a lot too. He used all the cuts within a few hundred metres of his home as toilets. To say 'next-door' neighbour is also misleading, because his dwelling had no door and neither did mine—we both lived in holes in the side of the same hill.

Every few days, I went for a walk, eventually covering the whole Potch Gully field of several square kilometres. I picked up many beer bottles and aluminium cans. From a recycle centre I could get twenty cents a dozen for beer bottles, including Victorian screw top stubbies, on any weekday. They also bought scrap iron and non-ferrous scrap. At the rear of one of the local supermarket on any Wednesday afternoon, I could get five cents each for the aluminium cans that had '5c deposit' stamped on the lid. The recycle centre also bought aluminium cans that were manufactured before the government brought in the five-cent deposit law. Because they were bought by the kilo, each can had to be free of dirt. I had to shake them until the dirt came out. If the dirt had got wet from some rare fall of rain and later become hard clay, I had to tear them open and scrape them clean. One can was only worth about one quarter of a cent, so it was a lot of work for very little money, but at least it was an income source.

The many backhoe and dozer cuts on the field provided a sheltered area that the rare rain washed the thin topsoil into. Windblown seeds collected there. Wind damage was less in the cuts, and sunlight exposure was less than on flat, open ground. Native wattle trees, bushes and grasses got a good chance to get established there. One day in a small backhoe cut I found a watermelon bush with one ripe melon about 30 centimetres long. It tasted sweet.

There was a small backhoe cut about 60 metres away from my dugout, at the bottom of the hill. Years of accumulated washed topsoil had built up a reasonably fertile area in it, possibly enough, I thought, to grow flower bulbs. I had some purple grape hyacinth bulbs left over from the church building block at Paradise.

On the edge of the platform in front of the dugout, I set a forty-litre plastic bucket with an outlet tap. I used ten-centimetre-long copper pipe offcuts and twitched wire to join enough scraps of garden hose to run from the bucket to the cut. The hose scraps were cracked and no longer good for pressured water, but were still suitable as a low pressure, gravity fed, water conduit.

Everything I used came from rubbish dumps, even the pliers for twitching the wire and the hacksaw for cutting the pipe.

After each time that I showered or washed dishes or clothes, I carried the waste water to the plastic bucket and tipped it in. Every few days I could turn on the tap, and water half the bulbs. By the time I had run down to the cut, it was time to shift the hose and water the other half. The bulbs grew well and flowered. I sold a few bunches of flowers. After the leaves had died off following the flowering, I dug the bulbs up. I sold all the large bulbs for twenty dollars, to the person who ran a Thursday morning garden nursery on the footpath in front of the post office. Then I bought a forty-kilogram bag of feed wheat. I set up a gate and enclosure, out of netting and wood, across the opening of one of the holes in the side of the lower cut. I bought a few laying hens and set them up in the enclosure. For a while, I was eating fresh eggs.

But one afternoon when I went to check the fowls, I found two feral dogs there. One had a fowl in its jaws. There were bloodied feathers everywhere. All the other fowls were lying on the ground, slaughtered. When they saw me, the dogs bolted along the cut and up the slope. They disappeared over the top of the cut. I was furious. I set off after them. After tracking them for about two hundred metres up and down dumps, I arrived at a dugout. The tracks went right up to a bowl of water outside the dugout door, and from there, led away on to stony ground, where I lost them.

I went back to the dugout that I had tracked the dogs to. I knocked on the door. Nobody came. I tried again on other days, at different times of day, and finally, late one afternoon, a man came to the door.

"Do you have a couple of dogs?" I asked, describing the dogs.

He answered, "Yes, they are my dogs," to which I replied, "Well, your dogs came to my place and killed all my chooks. I caught them in the act and tracked them back to your dugout, so you'd better compensate me for the loss."

When he answered, "Well, they're not really my dogs," I got annoyed. I said, "What do you mean, not your dogs-you just said they are your dogs, and I told you I tracked them to your dugout, to the water bowl outside your door!"

"What I mean is," he explained, "the dogs don't belong to me. I don't know who they belong to. I just keep a bowl of water there for them to drink, and they come and go whenever they like. I'm not responsible for them and I'm not going to compensate you for your chooks that you said the dogs killed."

Reluctantly, I agreed with him. I went back to my dugout feeling sorry for myself, and wild with the dogs.

A few days later, a man from the church came around and told me how I could get a paid, regular job as a dog catcher, employed by the Coober Pedy Progress and Miners Association. He said he was already doing it with his own vehicle, and he used the Progress Association dog trap, and if he had to shoot any dogs, he used his own gun and bullets. He was doing it not so much for the wages, but to get rid of feral dogs which roamed the town and sometimes menaced his children when they walked to school. He said he would drive me about in his ute and he would train me. I guess he assumed I had no shooting experience.

I agreed, and we set off to work. In a street in the town there were some wandering dogs. "Shoot them!" he said.

"What, in the street!"

"Yes, it doesn't matter, shoot them!"

"But you can't discharge firearms in a town area!"

"Don't worry about that, just shoot them. Nobody will worry about that here."

There are times when one should submit to one's Christian brother. This was not one of them.

"No, I won't shoot in the town area," I said.

We drove on. At the edge of town, we could see a dog wandering in the fields.

"Shoot that one if you can." He sounded a bit sarcastic. I told him to drive closer to the dog. He drove forward and stopped. I shot the dog fair between the eyes, and it dropped dead in its tracks. I had been on trial, and I had passed.

Then he took me to the Progress and Miners Association Hall, and he told the Chief Executive Officer that I was going to take over as the dogcatcher. The CEO looked pleased. He photographed me for my Authorised Dog Control Officer ID card. He gave me the keys for the Progress Association dogcatcher ute, and he told me I could drive it home. He said the job was funded for ten hours work a week. He handed me a small booklet and said, "Here, study this." It was a copy of the South Australian Government "Dog Control Act."

At home, I spent some time studying the Dog Control Act. Having a good education, including a study of English at university level, it was not a problem for me to understand the Act. In one sense, it was a very boring publication, made up of numbered Divisions, Parts, Sections and Subsections, detailing the duties and responsibilities of an Authorised Dog Control Officer, and the authority which the officer had, and how I would have to work in cooperation with other government authorities. But I found it quite exciting reading, because I began to understand how Australian society was ordered, how the concept of the Rule of Law operated. At last, I finally had an answer to the question I wanted to ask my parents when I was sixteen, "What is the Law?"

My first assignment was to go to a dugout where a miner had reported five strange dogs hanging around his area. When I got there, he had the five dogs held in his yard. I recognised two of them as the ones that got my chooks. With great pleasure, I coaxed them into the canopy on the back of the ute. The canopy had four doors, each one leading into a steel mesh compartment. The dogs had no collars, so I did not have to impound them. It was up to my discretion as Authorised Dog Control Officer as to what to do with them.

The miner said, "Shoot them!"

"What with?" I said.

"Didn't they give you a gun?" he exclaimed.

"No, they're waiting to get one up from Adelaide."

"Here, I'll loan you mine. I haven't used it for a long while. There's no sight, and you have to push the trigger instead of pulling it, but it should work."

I took it. Now was my chance to kill the dogs that got my chooks.

I drove away with the rifle and dogs to the dozer cut out of town that was the current designated rubbish dump. Each afternoon in the dump, the contractor had to burn everything so that people could not scavenge food scraps. As dogcatcher, I had to drag any dead dogs onto a pile of combustible material ready to be burnt.

But I had no dead dogs-only a ute full of lively ones, very lively ones. I had been told that a previous dogcatcher had taken live dogs to the dump, and let them out to shoot them, but they ran away before he could shoot. Being new, I wanted to get it right. The only way was to shoot them through the hole in the ute canopy, at the back, where you put your hand in to pull up the tailgate release lever.

With a bullet in the borrowed, single shot, bolt action breech, I pointed the barrel at a dog's head and squeezed the trigger. Nothing moved except the dog. Then I remembered that the trigger was meant to be pushed, not squeezed. I tried again. By the time I had killed four dogs, using six bullets, one of which went through the ute floor, the fifth dog was not very happy, and was very interested in protesting and making evasive movements. I was not happy either, but the job had to be done. These dogs were only a small percentage of local feral dogs that roamed in packs that sometimes set upon people, and each night they tipped over street rubbish bins, trying to get a feed.

The last dog jumped around frantically in the ute canopy. It took me another seven shots to kill it. After that I dragged the bloody bodies out on to a pile of cardboard boxes, and drove to the Progress Association works yard, and washed out all the blood and hair and faeces. Then I drove home and wrote up the day's deeds in a diary.

The next time I was in town, I got a message to go to the police station and report to one of the detectives. He was a big man, with a big voice, and we were in a small room. I was a small man with a small voice. He loudly accused me of shooting dogs in the town area. I thought that if I didn't stand up to him, he would bully me into inadvertently admitting guilt for what he was accusing me of, so I raised my voice to match his, and denied his accusations. My response quietened him. He backed off his intimidatory approach. He accepted my statements. But he made me understand that I should make myself familiar with another two South Australian Government parliamentary acts, the Firearms Act and the Cruelty to Animals Act. Later, the Progress Association supplied me with copies of both Acts, and I did some more homework. I learnt from them the laws about the discharge of firearms, and about the humane killing of feral and other animals by an authorised person.

Once again, the man from church came to me to talk about getting rid of feral dogs, a subject about which, in my opinion, he had an almost unhealthy interest. He told me he had arranged a time and a place and wanted me, as dog catcher, to help him get rid of some dogs. I agreed to go with him. I drove my dogcatcher ute. We went to the edge of the town, to a big open area.

Several Aboriginal families lived there, in three very basic, identical dwellings in a row, with no fences in between. Adults were sitting around talking, children were playing. About twenty dogs and puppies wandered around, or else lay sleepily in the dust. None of these dogs were registered, nor had collars, nor were any Aboriginal owners ever put under any pressure, because of a 'dual culture policy' to register their dogs.

A police car turned up. In it was a rookie officer who was new to the area.

My church acquaintance held out his gun for me. Knowing the laws about such a situation, I refused to take hold of it. He was annoyed with me. He turned away and immediately shot dead the closest dog. Then he shot dead another, and another, and still another. By this time dogs, children, men and women and dust were scattering everywhere. Dogs yelped, children and adults screamed. Every living thing was trying to escape death, running around corners, through open doorways, and in between the three houses. He kept shooting until there were no living dogs in sight. Then the police car left.

As the dust settled, dead dogs could be seen all over the place. An old man wandered around the now deserted houses, dazed, clutching a teddy bear to his chest. It was left to me to gather up the dead dogs and take them to the rubbish dump to be burnt.

Next day I visited a member of the local Rifle Club, and I showed him the rifle that had been loaned to me to shoot my first five dogs. We stood together outside his house. He put the rifle to his shoulder and looked along the barrel. "It's amazing you shot anything-this barrel is crooked!" he exclaimed.

While we both laughed about the crooked barrel, his dog came to us. It weed on my boot.

"That means you are really the dogcatcher," he said, and we laughed again.

36

One day while I was in the Progress office to hand in a report, a small woman in her late thirties, dressed like she was going to a society ball, came to me and said, "You have taken my puppy, haven't you! What have you done with it? You've put it in the fire in the rubbish dump!"

She must have known that was what happened to stray dogs that had been killed by the dogcatcher. No matter what I tried to say, she continued in her anguished state, and began to pummel me with her dainty fists. I continued to protest my innocence.

She said, "I'm going to find my puppy in the rubbish dump. You are a terrible, terrible man," and left the office.

"Wow, what can you do with someone like that?" I said to the Progress office worker behind the counter, who said, "There's nothing, nothing. She's just like that, don't worry; she'll be OK later. Anyway, there's been a call from someone about some abandoned puppies."

"OK, I'll go and see," I said, and I left. I found the puppies and picked them up, and put them in the cabin, and later in the day, on my way home, I decided to go to the rubbish dump to scavenge. Spirals of smoke were coming out of the rubbish dump cut-the contractor had already lit the combustible rubbish.

As I drove down into the cut I saw someone poking around amongst the burning rubbish. You would have to be very desperate to be looking for food or deposit cans in the smoky, stinking refuse, but some people in Coober Pedy were just that. Closer, I saw it was the finely dressed little lady. Her hair was awry, her dress was sooty, and pieces of burnt plastic were stuck on her nice shoes.

Then I had a brilliant idea-I would get one of the little puppies and take it to her. She would be overcome with gratitude that I had found her a replacement puppy. As I walked towards her with the puppy cradled in my arms, I called out, "Hello, I've got you a lovely little puppy dog," offering her the puppy in my outstretched arms.

"Oh, you terrible man, how can you put a little puppy in the fire! You cruel, cruel man," she screamed as she rushed at me. She pummelled me with her dainty fists again. I retreated with the puppy and got into the dogcatcher ute and drove away.

The Progress CEO told me one day to concentrate on one open area location in the town, early in the morning. He said packs of dogs had been seen there. He handed over my new rifle that had arrived from Adelaide. It was a .22 calibre semi-automatic with a ten-round magazine. He also gave me my firearms licence that the Progress Association had paid for.

Early one morning, I went to the area. I parked the dogcatcher ute on the side of the road and walked into the old opal mining dumps there, carrying my new rifle, fully loaded and cocked, ready for any pack of dogs that I might encounter.

Ahead on top of a dozer ramp I saw a lone dog, sitting, looking intently down into the cut. It would have been an easy shot, but probably there was a mob of dogs in the cut, so I didn't shoot the lone dog. Instead I made a wide arc and came up near the top of the other side of the ramp, without the lone dog seeing me. Then in one movement, I shouldered the rifle and stepped to the top of the ramp, and pointed my rifle down at the bottom of the cut, finger lightly on the trigger, ready if necessary to discharge ten bullets against a mob of feral dogs.

"Don't shoot!" cried out a man who was squatting in the bottom of the cut doing a poo. He jumped to his feet with his hands raised and his pants hanging halfway down his legs.

I lowered the rifle.

"Sorry man, I thought there was a mob of dogs in the cut," I said, and turned and walked away.

On further visits that area, I shot several feral dogs, but sometimes my assignment was to trap dogs on private property in the town, and then take them away, and shoot them. I got a message one day about such an assignment, from the local butcher. He was built like several sides of prime beef carcass glued together. It was said that he was a former champion weightlifter. He left a message for me one day and asked me to come to his butcher shop.

"I have trouble with town dogs in the yard behind the butcher shop. They come for meat scraps. Go and bring your trap," he said, when I got there.

I got the trap, and we baited it with a big bone, and overnight we caught a very big Alsatian-cross male with a massive scar on its nose. It took the ex-champion weight lifter and me together to lift 'Scarface', in the trap, into the back of the ute. I was explaining to him about how I saved money buying meat at the supermarket butcher, only ever buying stewing steak instead of cuts of steak, and bacon pieces-shredded bacon-instead of slices of bacon.

"Next week I have cheap bacon pieces for you. Come," he said.

"No worries," I agreed.

I drove home and parked the ute with Scarface still in the trap. I managed to get him out of the trap, without getting mauled. It was getting late, so I left him loose in the ute canopy and made tea and went to bed. Next morning, I went to the ute, intending to take Scarface to the rubbish dump and shoot him. But he was gone!

There were teeth marks and blood and hair all around a gaping hole in the tin that covered the ute canopy. All the ripped pieces of tin were pointed inwards. It must have taken Scarface hours to painstakingly and gradually, with his large teeth, enlarge the hole in the canopy above the ute tailgate release lever, to a point where he could rip open large pieces of tin at a time, and escape. I never saw Scarface again.

The workers in the Progress works yard could hardly believe their eyes when I showed them the repair job they had to do.

The following week I went to the butcher shop to buy the cheap bacon pieces. They were cheaper per kilogram, but not shredded; they were huge pieces about forty millimetres wide and thick, and four hundred millimetres long. I kept my word and bought them. I stored them in a fridge cabinet at the rear of the room at Potch Gully. It took me months to eat them, the last pieces just getting a tinge of green, but when the green was scraped off, they tasted fine. Butter also kept for weeks in the fridge cabinet, even at the height of the desert summer. It got quite soft, but never rancid.

One day I was driving home in the ute after destroying some dogs. I had not yet washed out the faeces and blood and hair. I passed a group of tourists walking along the road. They called out to me to stop. I turned around and went back, wondering what they would want with a dogcatcher and his ute.

"Can we have a ride in the back of the ute?" one said.

"It's filthy, blood and guts and poop everywhere," I replied.

"No matter, we want the experience, please let us?" they pleaded.

"OK, it's up to you," I said.

I opened the four doors and all the tourists got in, except one, who took photos of the others in the back of the ute. Then he said for me to wait till he got in, and then to shut them all in, and drive down the road a little way. I did it. As I drove slowly along, all the tourists started making dog noises-some deep, strong, menacing barks, some high-pitched yelps, some friendly yaps, some annoying small dog barks, some mournful moans and howls. Then they knocked on the back of the cabin and asked to be let out. I stopped and opened the canopy doors and they scrambled out, 'happy as Larry', not at all concerned about the filth from the floor of the ute on their clothes. As I drove away I could still hear them laughing.

One day when I was in town with the dogcatcher ute, I had collected my mail and was walking back to the ute. An old man, who was often in the street and nearly always drunk, came to me in his bedraggled, torn clothes. He was so thin he would have hardly got wet in a shower of rain.

"Shoot me," he said, "I'm just a dog." He was disappointed when I refused to put him out of the misery of his earthly life.

If I trapped or caught a dog that had no collar, I was permitted to destroy it. If I apprehended a dog wearing a collar, even if it did not have a registration disc, I had to impound it, and keep it locked up in the dog pound for 72 hours, and to put up notices in public places with a description of the dog. The dog pound was the toilets at the old drive-in theatre. The wooden doors had been replaced with heavy steel mesh gates with huge padlocks. This was effective for keeping impounded dogs in.

But sometimes I would go there to feed a dog, and it would be gone. The steel mesh had been cut with an angle grinder, or with an oxy torch. Opal miners' dogs were precious to their owners.

The four doors of the dogcatcher ute canopy were all padlocked and all opened with the same key. Sometimes, I found that when I returned to the ute, all the locks had been picked or broken, and all the dogs were gone. The CEO was amazed when I asked him for four separate, large padlocks for the ute.

One evening I was in the ute, parked near the Lions Club Wishing Well, waiting to catch dogs that raided street rubbish bins. A man approached slowly, with a drunken gait. He came right up to my open car door window.

"You killed my dog," he slurred. Then he raised his arm, and I saw a large rock in his fist.

"You killed my dog," he accused again. Then he said, "I gunna smash yor win'screen."

And he did. The laminated glass pieces cascaded into the ute cabin. I started the motor quickly and sped away, before further damage could be done.

Another unhappy dog owner accosted me in a service station one day. In front of the staff, he said, "If I find out you killed my dog, I'm gunna kill you!"

Yet another murder threat was made inside the Progress office, in the presence of Progress staff. I reported these instances in writing in my diary, which I had to present each week before I was paid. Nothing ever came of it.

Once I impounded a wandering dog with a collar and a registration disc. I checked through the Progress books and found it was owned by a well-known local man who had, according to opal fields scuttlebutt, shot and killed a man on the field in an opal claim dispute. The CEO was amused when he saw the infringement notice I had written out for him.

"Wait and see," he said, expecting trouble when the dog owner turned up to claim his dog. Fortunately for me, the man later came into the Progress office, and simply paid his fine, and collected his dog.

After ten eventful weeks as Authorised Dog Control Officer for the Coober Pedy Progress and Miners Association, during which time I killed fifty dogs, survived two personal physical attacks and two murder threats, I thought it was time to quit while I was ahead, and I handed back the rifle and bullets and ute and the copies of the Acts of Parliament, thinking my stressful life of a remote opal mining town dogcatcher was over.

But for many months after that, I received further murder threats. One time, as I was going into a cafe, a man accused me of killing his dog. I continued walking into the café and had something to eat. Outside in the street, the man who accused me had begun to talk with two other men, and they looked menacingly into the café at me. Inside the café were two guys I knew. I told them what was happening. They agreed to walk out of the café with me when I left. Later, the three of us walked out of the café together. I got safely into my car and drove away.

I went to the police and told them the situation, and asked them what I could do. They said to make detailed notes if such a thing happened again–time, place, who said what, witnesses-and do it for three times. Then they would act. Twice after that, I had reason to make detailed notes. But a third situation never ever happened, and my life became threat free, for which I thanked God.

The only other time anything happened about my dog killing was about ten years later. I was in a queue in the bank waiting to be served. Another waiting bank customer came up to me and said in a quiet voice, "Hey, brother, you remember me?"

I turned to him. "Yeah, maybe, but I can't remember your name," I replied. I expected to be asked for some money next, but instead, he said, "Sorry, brother, I was the one who smashed your windscreen a long time ago when you were the dog catcher. Sorry."

37

There were several blocks in one area of the town that were designated as 'Industrial', available for an annual rent of sixty dollars. About a month after I finished my dogcatcher job, I took up one, to use as a wrecking yard, because I had been offered free cars if I towed them out of the owners' yards. To the owners, the cars were a liability, but to me they were a possible source of income, and I was interested to learn about them too.

A friend agreed to tow wrecks to my yard for free, in return for free parts. Most of the roads in Coober Pedy at the time were dirt, so nobody worried much if skid marks were gouged into the surface by a vehicle being dragged with only rims and no rubber tyres. We towed about fifteen wrecks there.

One day I was on the block using my hand pump to inflate a tyre. When I took the connection off the valve, a piece of grit lodged itself in the valve stem and kept the valve open. Air shot out. Squatting by the wheel, I reached down to try to find a piece of a stick to use to dislodge the piece of grit. There was nothing but rocks and dust. I looked around and there was nothing there within eyesight. Coober Pedy was in a very dry spell. There had not been any rain for about two years.

One day a man with a formidable reputation for violence, earned from the time he attacked someone with a crowbar, came to my wrecking yard. "I have two EH Holden utes you can have for fifty dollars," he said.

"I don't want to buy them," I said.

"You're operating a wrecking yard, aren't you?" he said menacingly.

"Yes, but I'm looking to tow away vehicles for free," I said.

"You've got to buy if you want to be in business. Are you serious or not? You got to buy them!" He was getting angry.

"Ok, Ok, I'll buy them," I said, to keep the peace.

Both the utes were 'rust buckets'-no windows or windscreens, every panel severely damaged, motors only, oily, covered in dust, with no distributors or starter motors or alternators, no radiators, with broken seats and huge rust holes in the floors. They had probably been standing out in the open in his yard for twenty years. They were only worth scrap metal price, about twenty dollars worth for the two of them. I had made a loss.

Some days after that, I decided to clean them up, hoping to find a few coins or some tools underneath the seats. Underneath one seat was an old plastic bag, so dirty I couldn't see inside it. I pulled it out from under the seat and was going to throw it in a rubbish bin, but there was something solid in it.

I opened it. It was full of blue-green crystal opal. About one third was chips, but the rest was good, sound, cuttable opal. If I wanted to sell it, I probably would have easily got quite a few hundred dollars, but I was not that desperate to sell. I had made a nice profit after all, from buying the utes, for which I thanked God, but I didn't bother to thank the man who sold them to me.

But I was desperate for another coil spring for my HD Holden station wagon front end. The vehicle lurched so badly it was dangerous to drive. I remembered an EH ute on a vacant block of land across the street from the yard where I had worked for the contractor, three years ago. The coil springs for EH utes would fit my HD model. The ute had sat untouched there for years, so it was reasonable to assume that anyone could help themselves to parts.

I walked into town to check if it had a spring, and I was pleased to find it was still there. I walked in another day with tools. It was summer. I started early in the day and worked under the ute until it was too hot. I walked home again, planning to go back the next day and finish the job.

The next day I woke a bit later than usual, had my breakfast and set off walking to the ute. It was another very hot day. For three days, I had not eaten any meat. I knew from the bible that one should not crave meat, and Daniel in the Old Testament lived on a meat free diet, and because of his superior health, was selected as the emperor's top adviser. I felt very healthy on my recent meat free diet. But I thought it would be very nice to have a meal of grilled, tender, lamb chops.

As I walked, my mouth was watering with the thought of the tender, grilled, lamb chops. About fifty metres from the ute I noticed something on the ute bonnet. My first thought was that someone had been keeping watch on me working under the ute, had gone to it after I had left, had finished off my work and taken the front-end spring, and left their tools on the bonnet and forgotten to take them.

Then I thought, at least I would get their tools, so all my effort would not have been for nothing. Sweat was running down my face already in the heat as I was walking. I thought that if it was true that someone had taken the front-end spring, then I wouldn't have to work on the ute. I would grab the other person's tools and walk home and stay in the dugout in the cool.

As I got closer to the ute I saw that whatever was on the bonnet was wrapped in plastic. It seemed a strange thing to do, to wrap your tools in plastic. Maybe they did it to try to keep the sun off them. I came closer. Inside the plastic wrapping was something reddish, which I thought was a strange colour for tools. But when I got right to the ute, at mid-morning on that hot summer day in Coober Pedy, I could see what was wrapped in the plastic. It was frozen lamb chops!

I didn't bother right then to try to understand how such a thing could have happened. I put the frozen packet of lamb chops in the shade under the ute, finished off taking out the front spring, walked home with it and my tools and the lamb chops, and grilled the chops and ate them, with many thanks to God.

Resting in the cool dugout that afternoon, I reasoned how the frozen packet of chops might have come to be sitting on the bonnet of the ute. The ute was next to a well-worn walking path that was used by Aboriginal people who lived on the 'Reserve'. Most likely one of them had got their pension money, bought frozen lamb chops and some grog, got drunk on the grog in the street, walked past the ute on the way back to the reserve, put the chops on the bonnet and lay down and slept, woken up and got up again and walked on to the Reserve, leaving the chops behind.

One day out scavenging in the field, I saw two five-cent-deposit cans at the bottom of a twenty-five-foot-deep cut. It was a long walk just to get ten cents value, but I was so much in need of cash that I went down and got them.

As I started to walk up the ramp, I noticed on the ground some bright red, crystal opal chips. Red crystal opal being the most valuable opal, I picked up every one of them. They were pieces of broken, opalized seashells, locally known as 'skin shells'. The further up the ramp I went, the more chips I found. By the time I got to the top of the ramp, I had what I estimated to be about forty dollars worth.

I looked around the ground at the top of the ramp. In a dozer windrow I spied a large piece of opal, about 40 centimetres across. It was good, sound opal, nearly two centimetres thick, and it had broad red, green, blue and yellow flash. I sold it later to an opal dealer for one hundred dollars.

I reasoned that it had either been in the wall or in the floor of the cut next to the cut I found the cans in, and it had been pushed up the ramp of this cut by a dozer. I went down that cut to check. At the bottom, about a metre up from the lowest part of the cut, was a gouged-out area in the face where someone had been working with a pick. I scraped in the dust on the ledge. I found some very small red crystal chips. Looking closely at the wall where the pick had been gouging, I found a ten-centimetre long trace of red crystal opal as thin as a piece of paper. I decided to peg the cut, with the usual fifty-metre sided, square opal claim, and start mining it, even though all I had to mine with were hand tools.

I hadn't taken much notice of the location when I first saw the two cans at the bottom of the first cut, but after I climbed to the top of the second cut, I saw that I was only about sixty metres from the bitumenised Stuart Highway, that ran all the way through the continent of Australia, from Adelaide in the south to Darwin in the north.

From where I stood, to the south, and to the north, and to the west, were many kilometres of opal fields. But to the east, just forty metres away, on the other side of the bitumen road that ran along the western border of the Town Area, above-ground houses lined the town streets for about one kilometre, reaching right through to the Central Business Area.

Thinking about the demand for new dugout ground, and current moves to extend the town area eastwards, to incorporate Potch Gully, where I was 'squatting', I realised that the area of the Big Flat field where I intended to peg my claim, just outside the western edge of the Town Area, could very likely soon be considered as another expansion area for the town. Already there were a few quite well-established dugouts in parts of the Big Flat.

I also realized that as soon as my claim was registered, and people noticed my pegs near the town boundary, many get-rich-quick local 'entrepreneurs' would want to be a part of any possible new real estate development, and they would try to 'peg me out' of a corner position at the junction of the two bitumen roads. I went home immediately and got my four mining pegs, and my prismatic compass and tape measure, and pen and paper, and returned.

Knowing that a mining claim was normally expected to be square, and fifty metres on each side, I pegged a fifty-metre sided square, at an angle of about forty-five degrees to each of the bitumen roads, not leaving enough room for anyone to peg between me and the bitumen roads. Then I looked around and found the nearest Mines Department survey marker peg and measured the distance to my claim, and the compass direction from the marker peg to the claim, and the compass directions of each side of my claim. I put all the information on paper and went straight into the Mines Department office, and said I wanted to 'Notify', which has to be done within twenty-four hours of pegging.

The office worker asked me for my PSPP (Precious Stones Prospecting Permit) number.

"Double nine, double three I think it is," I said.

"Ah, yes, here it is. Your second claim, I see," he said after finding my record.

"No, this is my first. I've never pegged a claim before," I contradicted.

"Well, here it is on this card. You pegged a claim on the Black Flag field about two years ago," he said.

Then I remembered loaning my pegs to someone. They must have been the ones who pegged the claim that he was talking about. "That wasn't me, that was someone I loaned my pegs to," I blurted out.

"You what!" he almost shouted at me. Then he calmed down and told me off, and said not to ever do that again. He filed my application to

'Notify', together with my piece of paper with my diagram for the location of my claim on Big Flat.

A day or so later I went back into the Mines Department and found out that my diagram had been accepted as being accurate enough. My next step was to pay the regulation fee and register the claim. I didn't have to, by Mining Regulation, register it straight away, but to make sure that there was no chance of losing my opportunity to secure a hold on potential real estate, I paid the fee there and then. That afternoon, I started working on the claim with my pick, in the cut, where I had found the paper-thin trace of red crystal. It was hot work in the full summer sun. The wall faced north. The sun reflected brightly off the white ground. I built a temporary dry wall of sandstone to provide shade, and I continued with the pick. Disappointingly, the red crystal trace disappeared after about 300 millimetres.

I told a Greek friend from church, who had the wonderfully typical Greek name of Taxiharsis Gyftopulous, about the trace on my claim. He was interested enough to come and have a look. He had been involved in mining at Coober Pedy for several years, as a non-financial partner on percentage. He had no tools or equipment or plant, but he was experienced in using gelignite. He lived nearby on the Big Flat field, in a hole in the ground with a shed above it, no electricity or water, like me at Potch Gully. His only furniture was his bed. He said his name meant 'Brigadier General of the Gypsies.'

"Gary, you buy hand drill and auger, and I get geli and fuse and dets, and we set off bomb," he said, after I showed him the chips that I had dug out of the red crystal trace.

I bought a hand drill and auger from a local engineer, who constructed every single part of it. The hand drill was just like a carpenter's brace. He also made augers by twisting hot flat steel, and brazing on one end two tungsten cutting tips, and welding to the other end some steel rod which fitted the brace jaws. I also bought detonator crimp pliers.

Tax and I met at the claim. He took my pick and gauged out a small hole about one hundred and fifty millimetres underneath where the trace ran out. He clamped the auger in the hand drill, poked the auger cutting tips in the hole and began drilling. It was slow going with the hand auger.

After he had drilled for about four hundred millimetres, he stopped and pulled the auger out. He crimped a one-metre length of fuse in the detonator, poked the detonator into a stick of geli, and pushed the stick into the hole with a piece of wood. Then he packed the hole with sandstone. He struck a match, lit a sparkler, and touched off the end of the fuse.

We walked to the top of the cut and waited. The bomb went off. We went down and had a look. There was a hole blasted underneath the level of the trace. We picked out the loose dirt. There was a bit of grey trace. We set off a few more bombs, and then I set one off. We found some more grey trace, nothing to sell, but for me it was a valuable experience.

I found some strong rope about fifty feet long in the dump. I laid a steel pipe over the top of one of the three-feet diameter Calweld shafts on the claim and tied the rope to it. I took some candles and my pick and climbed down the rope. At the bottom of the shaft was a head-high drive about forty feet long and eight feet wide. A 'level' (a pronounced change in the ground) went the whole length of the drive, but I could not find any trace or material (opal) in it.

In a rubbish dump one day I found eight old steel mining ladders. I told an old miner about them. He said they were probably thrown away because they were rusty and not safe to use.

"Let me look at them first," he said. I showed them to him. He got a hammer and belted each rung and each side of each of the eight ladders.

"You can't use four of them-they're too badly rusted. One is partly rusted. Sandstone has got inside the pipe, and then when a bit of moisture gets in, they're finished." He cut out the rusted piece and welded some good, sound pipe in its place.

That evening, talking to another old miner, I told him about my use of a rope to go up and down the shaft, and that I had since got some ladders. He offered to give me his old, wooden hand-made winch to use to lower the ladders in the shaft. He said he was too old for that sort of work anymore. The winch barrel shaft had no bearings to run in. It sat in a tin lined groove, which was nearly as friction free as a greased bearing. The winch had no ratchet. I took it gratefully.

I set it up at the claim on the Calweld shaft where I had been going down on a rope. I hooked one ladder on to the steel pipe at the top of the shaft. I hooked a second ladder on the hook end of the winch cable and lowered it down the shaft to near the bottom of the first ladder, and then tied the winch handle. I climbed down the first ladder and unhooked the second ladder off the winch cable, and then hooked the top of the second ladder on the last rung of the first ladder. I climbed to the top of the shaft, up the ladder, untied the winch handle, attached a third ladder to the cable, wound it down, tied the winch handle, climbed down two ladders, and attached the third ladder. I let down the fourth ladder till it hit the bottom of the 35-foot shaft.

I got down into the old workings a lot easier, and checked again by candlelight for trace, but I found none.

It was cool in the drive, thirty-five feet down, away from the bottom of the shaft. I cleaned up the floor for a place to rest. There was a lot of household rubbish there. If I could get a partner, it would be easier to work the claim. In the meantime, I had plenty other things to do.

38

It was 1986. Nearly two years had passed since I had moved to Potch Gully. During that time, I had not been to my old dugout. A friend and I were chatting one day. He said to me, "Gary, have you sold your little dugout?"

"No, mate, why do you say that?" I replied.

"Well I heard that a Yankee guy has got it and is making plans to put shade cloth over the cut and grow a garden."

"He can't do that, I hold the current Occupation Lease on it."

"Are you sure Gary? He said he made enquiries in the Department of Lands and was told that the lease had expired."

"I can't believe they would do that. Sure, I'm not living there, but I still hold the lease."

"Maybe you should go and talk to him. But be careful, he's a Vietnam veteran with a Purple Heart!"

"OK, I will," I said.

A day or so after that conversation, after making enquiries, I found the Yankee's place. He was living in a tin shed on a level block. And yes, it was true that he had served in Vietnam and was wounded on the face by shellfire and now had grown a moustache to cover the scar. He said he was from Nevada, and in pre-Vietnam days had been involved in small scale silver mining there. He said he was passionate about mining. He showed me various books on stoping, which was rarely done in Coober Pedy opal mines, because of a lack of trees for timber, and rare rain to saturate the soil and make it unstable, and some books about Nevada silver mining. He told me a story of how some companies with registered silver mines in Nevada had managed to convince naive investors to buy shares in the mine at a time when the shares were soaring. Then the owners sold out, the shares plummeted, and the shareholders were left with a worthless pile of paper.

The Yankee's heritage was Irish with a trace of French, like mine. He had a great collection of videos which he offered to loan me. He had quite a few power tools and ladders and lights, a generator, and a drill that he had brought from USA that he said would revolutionise Coober Pedy opal mining. It would drill an exploration hole of about 70mm in diameter, and so the exploration expenses would be only a fraction of that of a nine-inch diameter hole made with a Proline drill, or a three-foot diameter hole made by a Calweld drill.

He told me he had been walking around the town and had come across my block and had seen that nobody had been living there for quite a while, so he made enquiries, telling the Government that. He said the Government man had searched the details of the block and told him he could apply for a new lease, which he did, and it was granted to him.

I told him that I held the current lease, and there is no way it had expired, and the Government man must have made a mistake when he said the block was available. I showed him my lease paper. He agreed that the Government man had made a mistake. He apologized to me and I said it was OK, it was the Government mistake. Then we got to talking about opal mining. He said, "You're a local; you should know where to find opal. I wouldn't know where on earth to look in this vast field. What about it?"

I told him about the old workings at Greek Gully next to where I had noodled some grey from the dumps up top, and that I could show him trace in the wall in a drive down below. He was interested. I told him I had no money for expenses, so he agreed to pay everything. We agreed we would go 50 per cent each in the opal.

Some days after that we went out to Greek Gully in his ute. We took his ladders, lights and generator. I found the old shaft amongst all the dumps. It looked like some activity had taken place-some of the dumps had been shifted, and the ground in general showed someone had been there with a backhoe. But there were no pegs, so we were free to work anywhere in the area. We set up the ladders and generator and we went down the shaft and made our way along the drive to the place where I remembered the trace was.

The wall had changed. Someone else had been there since me. The Yankee was quite excited to be using his battery powered, head lamp hard hat attachment with the belt mounted battery pack. He seemed more excited in the search than I thought a man ought to be.

We kept searching, scraping the wall with picks. Soon we uncovered some grey trace, about 2mm thick and 100mm long, but with very little colour. I was happy that at least I was able to show him some trace, even though it was worthless. But he nearly exploded with excitement: "Wow, man, we're on opal, we're on opal!"

I thought, "This man is a bit crazy! There's nothing to get excited about here!" But then again, the saying is that most people who come to Coober Pedy are a bit crazy. We kept digging into the wall that day until his excitement had subsided and he started to rest more often. We went home, and returned and worked there for a few more days, finding more material, but nothing worth selling. It seemed he tired easily. I was thinking about asking him to join me on my claim, because we got on well, and that is very important for opal mining partners. With opal mining, there's always a chance of a big find, if you persevere.

However, he developed ulcers in his stomach, which probably explained why he got tired easily. He had to leave Coober Pedy for an operation on his stomach, which developed complications, and rendered him unable to continue in the physically demanding opal mining work. We had to quit our agreement. It had been a typical opal mining venture, one in which very little outlay of money was required. Coober Pedy thrived on stories of miners who worked very hard physically, and had minimum expenses, and who eventually got a lot of money.

The thing about opal mining is, to be able to pay as you go, and always leave enough money for living expenses. There were lots of stories of people who invested heavily in opal mining and got big returns, only to find that the returns were not enough to cover their expenses, meaning that they had a net loss, but usually they still had enough left over to go back to a farm, or to a business, or to a paid job.

The worst opal mining economic disaster stories were of those where people, with dreams of finding a fortune in opals, borrowed money on the security of private property, invested it in opal mining, did not find any opal, couldn't pay their mortgage, forfeited their property, and had to live in rental accommodation.

Probably only about 10 per cent of all opal miners are successful.

Perhaps the best thing about opal mining is that, if you find opal, you don't have to either, declare how much you found, or declare what you found as an income unless you sell it. And if you trade it, for real estate, or for furniture, or for anything at all, the thing that you trade it for is not regarded as an income. But if you sell that asset, the amount of the sale is regarded as income.

For me, the plan was to only invest in opal mining if, when it came time to stop, I still had money to live, and I hadn't borrowed money to do the mining.

There was yet another method-to get into a partnership in which you did not have to pay any of the mining expenses, and you agreed to take a much lower percentage of any opal sales that eventuated.

It was only a matter of a couple of weeks after I ceased with the Yankee that I got that sort of opportunity. One man in a two-man opal mining partnership had to cease involvement in that partnership for a certain amount of time because he also had another business involvement, one which required him to work away from Coober Pedy. His opal mining partner could not afford to wait for him to return to Coober Pedy and start up again, but at the same time, he himself did not want the mining to proceed in his absence. That's where I came in. Although I did not have a fraction of the experience that either of the two partners had, I was strong, I had a sharp eye for opal, and I had the reputation of being a trusted and reliable man. The partner who had to go away got his partner to agree to letting me take his place, on the basis that I was to provide labour only, and if opal came during the temporary partnership, I would get 5 per cent of the sales. We all agreed to start immediately the first partner went away, which was the day after the temporary partnership was sealed with a shake of hands.

Each day I would drive my vehicle to the second partner's dugout, and then we would go to the claim in his vehicle. Even though I regarded him as my boss, rather than as my opal mining partner, I was the more positive one, and insisted we take a sack each day to put opal in.

After a few days, we found some opal. According to my instructions from the partner who went away, I was never to let any of the opal out of my sight, except when it was locked in the safe in the boss's dugout, and I was the only one to hold a key to the safe.

Together, we put the day's opal in the sack and took it back to the boss's dugout to sort into grades of value. The boss did the sorting, as I watched carefully to make sure no opal went out of my sight, before he put the different value grades, which were weighed by the ounce, into separate, marked, plastic bags, which remained on the sorting table until sorting was finished for the day. After sorting, I watched him put all the plastic bags of graded opal in the sack and put the sack in the locked safe. The safe stayed at his house, but I took home the key.

On the claim, he showed me how to use the Makita drill and to put in the shot holes. Although handheld, it was very powerful, and heavy, and had to be controlled, which was a difficult thing to do because pressure had to be made on the drill to keep the drilling auger forced against the face, and the auger was more than a metre long, and was flexible. He showed me how to operate the machine known on the Coober Pedy mining field as a 'blower', that sucked dust and smaller rocks from below ground and sent it up top, through pipes.

One day he generously allowed me to light the shots. I struck a match and ignited a sparkler. I touched the first fuse with the sparkler and it burst into life. Fuses burn at one foot every forty-five seconds. I had nine fuses to light. I had some trouble lighting the sixth one. The boss said, "You're not lighting it in the right place. That's the trouble with you, you think you can learn everything that us old fellas know real quick, and then you think you know everything."

The sixth fuse sputtered into life. "Well I can only try. I'm not perfect you know," I reasoned.

"I don't know why I bothered to let you have a go in the first place. It would have been a lot quicker to do it myself," he continued. "Next time I'm gunna do it and you can watch. I can't sit around here doing nothin' while you muck around. Why do fellas like you come to Coober Pedy in the first place? You know nothing at all about opal mining."

I was yet to light the seventh fuse, listening to him sounding off at me. Suddenly we both realized that while we had been talking away, six fuses had been slowly and steadily burning their way to the bombs. Our eyes met. "Quick-light the other ones," he said urgently.

I did it without a word, and we moved smartly back the drive and around a corner, and I pulled the cord that was attached up top to the throttle on the blower. No sooner had the blower motor surged into high revs, the first bomb went off. We looked at each other and said nothing. But we both knew we had narrowly escaped serious injury, even death.

We counted five explosions. Then there was a long silence, except for the blower motor. We looked at each other, and again said nothing. Soon the sixth bomb went off, then another anxious wait, and then the next three followed in normal intervals. After about half an hour, when the fumes had been cleared by the blower, we checked the newly blasted wall. There was a nice thick trace of grey showing!

It was late in the day. Normally we would have dug out the trace before we went home, but we were too tired. Instead, we pelted handfuls of sandstone on the trace until it didn't show, and we went up top, locked the weldmesh grid over the shaft, and went home.

Next day on the claim, we found fresh boot marks at the shaft, and the weldmesh cover had been cut. Below, we saw where someone had been picking at the wall, but fortunately they hadn't uncovered the trace. We set to and picked it all out. It ran for a few metres and in some places was half a metre deep, and sometimes it was three centimetres high. We put it all in a sack, took it to the absent partner's house, and put it, and the opal from the other day, through a tumbler with water, to knock off the water-softened sandstone. Then the tumbled, rough opal was put in the safe.

Next day, we spent several hours with opal snips, snipping off the edges of some of the rough opal pieces, to better show the colour. There were so many pieces to snip that we finished up with several hundred ounces of chips. There was one individual piece of rough opal that weighed seven-and-a-quarter ounces. We classed everything as best we could, and then took the parcel to an opal classer for a final appraisal. He re-classed it, fine tuning our effort, and re-bagged it, weighing each bag, and then marking each bag with its weight and his estimate of how much per ounce we could expect it might sell for. He advised us the maximum we should ask for, and the lowest we should accept.

Then the absent partner returned. He and my boss sold the parcel of opal that the boss and I had found. I received my share of several hundred dollars. It was the most cash I had held in my hand at the one time for a few years.

39

Life as a single man doing opal mining by himself is very monotonous, and tourists love to go out on the field with a miner. One day at the church I met a woman who said she was a nurse, on holidays, passing through Coober Pedy. She was maybe in her thirties, bright-eyed, small, but strongly built. I offered to take her out on the field and show her my claim. She was excited to accept my offer.

On the way to my claim, I noticed her looking from side to side out the car windows. She seemed to be looking for landmarks in case she needed to find her way back to town on her own. When we got to the claim I said, "Do you think you could find your way back?"

"I don't think so," she said.

On my claim, I took her to the edge of the shaft and told her it was thirty-five feet to the bottom. I pointed out the steel bar across the opening, the top ladder hanging off the bar, and the winch.

I said, "What about I go down the ladders and fill up a bucket of dirt and you see if you can wind it up?"

"OK," she said. "That's sounds like a bit of fun."

I hooked an empty bucket on the cable and wound it down till it sat on the bottom. I turned to her and said, "The only trouble is, there's no ratchet on this winch, so once you start winding up the bucket, you'll have to bring it right to the top without any rest, and hold it up, and then grab the cable and swing the bucket across till it's suspended over the ground at the side of the shaft, and then let the bucket down on to the ground."

She looked at me the whole time as I gave the instructions. After I finished, she was still looking at me as if waiting for more instructions. I said, "If you let go the handle before the bucket is set down on the ground, the bucket will fall at top speed, and the handle will fly round real fast, and it could break your arm if it hits you."

She said confidently, "OK, down you go, don't worry about me, I'll be right."

I climbed down and half-filled the bucket and set it in the middle of the shaft. I put the cable hook in the bucket handle and lifted the cable until the handle was standing straight up. "OK, you can start winding," I yelled up the shaft.

"OK," she said.

When the cable became taut as she started winding, I let it go. The bucket lifted off the ground and slowly disappeared up the shaft. I stepped back into the drive, in case some rocks got dislodged from the side of the shaft by the swinging bucket.

Soon I heard her call out, "The bucket's getting heavy."

It seemed that she was not as strong as I thought.

"Keep going don't give up now," I called out.

"It's getting very heavy, I can't do it."

"Keep going, you'll soon be at the top," I called out. I thought that all this time, the bucket had been going steadily up the shaft.

"Oohh I can't. Ooohh!"

There was a sound like metal hitting something. Then the bucket crashed to the floor in a cloud of dust and rocks, only centimetres in front of me. Then there was silence.

When the dust cleared, I saw on the floor, with the bucket, not one ladder as before, but three! I called out, "Are you alright?"

"Yes, but I feel a bit sick. But I'm OK. What about you?"

"Yes, I'm OK too. But now I'm stuck down here."

"Ooh, what are you going to do? I don't know what to do. What are we going to do?"

She sounded helpless. She might have been able to find her way back to town to get help, but I was sure she would not have been able to find her way back to my claim with helpers. I knew what I would do if I was at the top. But I was at the bottom, and my mate for the day, with a bit of shock happening, was at the top, and was new to everything on the field. I would have fished up one of the fallen ladders with the hook at the end of the cable, and then winched it up till it was about three rungs past the bottom of the first ladder. Then I would have tied the winch handle to keep the hanging ladder in place, climbed down to the bottom of the first ladder, which was still hooked to the steel bar at the top of the shaft, grabbed the hanging ladder and hooked it onto the bottom of the first ladder. After repeating the process with the other ladder that had fallen, I would have had four ladders to climb out of the shaft.

The shaft was thirty-five feet deep. Each ladder was ten feet long. The top ladder was still in place, hanging down from the steel pipe across the top of the shaft. When the four ladders were in place, the bottom ladder was hooked on about halfway up the third ladder. I could get nearly ten feet up on the ladder resting on the bottom of the shaft. Then I could wedge myself, shoulders pressed into one side of the shaft and feet pressed into the other side, and go up like that, inch by inch, for fifteen feet, until I could get a handhold on the bottom rung of the top ladder, and I could then pull myself up, rung by rung, until I was able to climb the top ladder and get out of the shaft.

I shouted up the shaft and told my new chum mate what I was going to do. She agreed.

The "wedge climbing" was a strain on my muscles for the first couple of feet, and after that it became progressively more painful. Having my two feet pressed into the shaft wall was alright, but when I lifted one shoulder to inch my way upwards, the other shoulder bore the full load. Again, when I pressed in with the higher shoulder in preparation to bring my other shoulder up to the same height, it too bore the full weight. I had to "rest" each time I had brought both feet up higher. But there was no real rest, because I had to keep up the pressure into the wall, otherwise I would fall.

Most of the wall of the shaft for the first ten feet above the bottom ladder was relatively smooth, having been bored out in good ground by the Calweld drill bucket. But then the wall belled out, in bad ground. Instead of a three-feet diameter Calweld shaft, I now had to negotiate a four or sometimes five-feet diameter shaft. The wall was uneven, and rocks jutted out. They got dislodged easily as I climbed. The higher I went, the more abrasions I got on my shoulder blades, and the further I would have to fall if I couldn't complete the climb. In the widest parts of the shaft, my body was stretched out fully, horizontally, and the pain in my belly muscles was extreme.

Finally, I got high enough to grab the bottom rung of the top ladder, and I hauled myself up until I could put my feet on a rung. Then, for the first time, half a ladder from the top, I relaxed.

"You made it," said the nurse.

"Yes. I'll get out in a couple of minutes," I replied.

When I got out of the shaft, I was feeling sick and dizzy. My whole body ached. My shirt was bloodied at the shoulders. I staggered towards my car.

"Sit down, and put your head between your knees," said the nurse.

I did what she said and I closed my eyes. After a while I felt better. With my head still between my knees, I opened my eyes. I had sat down right next to an old nine-inch diameter drill hole. The first thing I saw was chips of opal with colour on the collar of the drill hole.

"Wow, look at this," I said.

"Ooh, that's opal," she replied.

"Yes. It means one of two things-either opal was drilled up when the drill hole was put down, or else someone dumped stuff down the hole that they couldn't be bothered sorting, so nobody else would get it."

"What can you do?" she said.

"Nothing much. Maybe one day I'll put in a shaft there, but I don't have any money for that right now."

I took her back into the town and she thanked me for a very interesting time.

For me, it was a lot more than interesting-it was painful and dangerous, and I resolved to never take tourists out on the field again and expect them to do anything other than watch.

40

After living alone, in the dirt, with no power or water, for about three years, I was getting depressed, and thinking I would never be able to get back to 'normal' living. But the Lord gave me the strength to persevere, and He provided me with some relief for about two months, in two other houses with utilities.

An elderly couple from the church asked me to come for an evening meal. After tea I was trying very hard to teach the husband to play the guitar. He was serious and thought he was doing well, but his wife realized he was only dreaming. His fingers were stiff, and he had no sense of rhythm. But he wanted to play for the Lord in the church. They asked me if I would like to stay for the night. I said yes. The next night, I ate tea there again, and I gave some more guitar lessons. They said I was welcome to stay for as long as I liked. I could not refuse, even though in summer my dugout was a lot cooler than their above ground house that had no air conditioning. I had to sleep naked on the lino floor there, to keep reasonably cool.

The husband and I talked after tea each night. In his first language, Greek, he was well educated, but his English was broken and heavily accented. Mid-sentence, when he couldn't think of the right English word to use, he stared at me until the right word came to him. His stare was intense. His face was heavily lined and set like a flint.

While staying with the Greek couple, I needed to replace the muffler box on my car. There was a wreck on the Big Flat that had one. I went there and worked on it and nearly finished it by sundown. Next day I went to it again. I lay down on my back on the ground and felt underneath for the nut that I was undoing the previous day. There was something underneath the wreck. It felt like plastic. I looked underneath. It was a radio/cassette player. I pulled it out. It was clean. I put it in my car, and continued working on the muffler box, and got it off.

That night at the Greek couple's house, I tried the radio. It worked. I tried an old cassette and it worked too. It seemed a crazy thought, but I reckon someone saw me working on the wreck on my first day there, and put the radio underneath that night for me, knowing that I did not own one.

Another day I did the 'rounds' of all the dumps that I knew of near the town. There were about twenty, and I always got something that made it worthwhile-tools, furniture and household appliances (even if they needed repair), clothes, car parts, building materials, crockery, cutlery, and even cash. One day I found about twenty khaki shirts, long and short sleeved, in a neat pile, all washed and ironed. I thought someone must have put them there, just for me.

After about a week of very hot weather, the wife said she was not young anymore, and was having trouble coping, and she asked me to leave. That day, talking with the man who sold me the two EH Holden utes, I told him about having to leave the Greek couple.

"You can stay on my property. I have a spare house. You can be my caretaker," he offered. I was glad to accept. I moved some furniture and bedding and kitchen things to his spare house, and I stayed there for a few weeks. During that time, I helped him do some concreting work.

One afternoon he came to the house and stood at the door and asked me to use my old HR Holden station wagon to give him a tow start for his ready-mix concrete truck. I said that I couldn't do it because it was too much of a risk with my old car, towing his heavy truck-either I would burn out my clutch or damage my 'diff' or suspension.

He got angry. "Alright, you get out of this house right now!" was his response.

"What, I can't get out right now-I've been here for weeks and I have a lot of my stuff here," I complained.

"OK, you can stay, but you must pay $100 a week, one month in advance, today," was his ultimatum.

He walked away from the door. I sat and thought for a while what I would do. He was known to be a dangerous man. Then I went to some people from the church and told them about the situation. I thought they would be sympathetic, but they just laughed.

"That's him," they said, which was not any help to me.

I went back to the house and started to pack some things. He came to the door. I opened it. He came right into the kitchen where I was. "What are you going to do?" he said menacingly.

"You can't force me out today. You have to give me a week to pack up," I said calmly and firmly, and I stared straight into his eyes.

I didn't know how he would react. I thought he might produce another crowbar. He stood still, just looking at me. "Alright, you can have a week to get out," he said rather slowly. Then, thanks to God, he turned and walked out.

One week later I was back at my Potch Gully dugout.

I drove down south to see the boys. It was late in the afternoon, way past school time, when I went to their house and knocked on the door. Nobody answered. I thought that Wendy might have taken them with her and gone shopping. I went across to ask her parents. They told me that she had been committed to a psychiatric hospital again, and the boys had been fostered out. They said if I wanted to see them I would have to get permission from the Department for Community Welfare, who had arranged foster parents for them.

It was extremely disappointing to hear this. It made me feel like giving up continuing to try to make the effort to be a father, because nobody ever told me what was going on with my son's lives. I even wondered if I would be given permission to see them.

I resolved my doubts in the same way that I had done many times before: I prayed to God for strength to carry on, and then I went to the DCW. They gave me permission and told me the address to go to. I went there. The parents invited me into their house. It was an uncomfortable first few minutes facing my sons. I had the impression that they were looking at me as just another adult drifting in and out of their lives.

The boys and I spent about an hour together, chatting, occasionally laughing. They were in good health, and comfortable in their temporary home. It was hard to do, but I had to be satisfied with that knowledge, and leave them there and to go back to Coober Pedy.

41

Now and then in Potch Gully there was talk of getting a SWER (Single Wire Earth Return) line put there for a general household electricity supply. People would get together in their dugouts and discuss it. Usually it came down to a lack of numbers of people who could afford to pay the cost. Associated with a supply of electricity was a water supply, and telephone, all of which required the surveying of roads. There was also talk of incorporating Potch Gully and further out areas into the town area.

The discussions went on for over a year. Many dugout 'owners' were cautious about committing to an unknown amount of money for the supply of the services. Eventually enough dugout 'owners' agreed to commit to paying.

The rumours of Potch Gully coming into the town area ran hot. Across the valley from me, the hills were untouched. The area had a poor reputation for opal. But as rumours of town area got stronger, those hills gradually became completely pegged out, as if for mining. However, the motivation was not to mine for opal-it was to prepare sites for dugout construction.

The Mines Department was strict on dozers not pushing material outside the borders of a claim. Normally, fifty metres was wide enough to push a small face, ready to put in an opal exploration tunneling machine drive, without having to push dirt past the borders of the claim. But, as usual in a remote, frontier situation, people found ways to profit from the law in ways the city legislators had not foreseen. Two miners would peg adjoining claims, giving them a one-hundred-metre wide side, which was plenty of room to push a face suitable for several tunneling machine drives, as would be suitable for a dugout. The claim owners then pulled their pegs off their adjoining claims, and then registered a single claim right in the middle of where the two claims were. Then it was a matter of bluffing the Mines Inspector that the claim was bona fide, until someone came along and bought the 'claim' for a dugout site in the soon-to-be-proclaimed new town area. After that, the two miners would split the money from selling the 'claim' and then go somewhere else and do it again. At least that was not as blatant an abuse of the law as when a miner, who saw a tractor left unattended on land in a mining area, put his pegs on the land around the tractor, and claimed the tractor.

The isolated life I was leading in Potch Gully gradually made me progressively less dependent on 'keeping up with the times' via newspaper or radio or television, and more dependent on real life and people around me. But there was one time in the many months living on the field, when I was visiting someone, that I glanced at a newspaper lying on a coffee table, and a name I was familiar with caught my eye. It was the name of the farmer who, many years ago, had pulled the school bus off the railway line. When I read the newspaper story, I reflected on how my choice of friends as a Christian was so much different, and better, from my choice of friends before I become a Christian-the newspaper report related how the farmer had been sent to prison for murdering his wife!

Another 'relief' from isolated life in primitive conditions happened. My guitar playing and singing friend from the church managed a tourist mine and museum in the main street. He lived in the dugout at the rear of the business. He needed someone to stay in the dugout at night while he went interstate for a couple of weeks to promote the business and he asked me. I agreed. It was a welcome break for a few weeks to have electricity and not have to cart water.

The time came, after nearly two years of working by hand with a pick, when I finished doming the ceiling of the room in the side of the hill on the Potch Gully mining field. Then it was time to clean out all the sandstone with my grandpa's steel-wheeled wheelbarrow.

I took my bed down from the top of the pile of sandstone and put it outside, and I slept under the stars for about two months, until I finished the job. By that time the winter was finished. There were times during that winter when I went to bed wearing two pairs of socks, a singlet, shirt, two jumpers, two trousers, gloves and a balaclava. One morning I woke with slivers of ice, from my frozen breath, in the woollen balaklava.

In return for work I did for a building contractor, assisting him to rebuild the chassis of one of his trucks, he supplied me with a load of ready-mix concrete. A friend with whom I had many conversations about the Bible helped me put a concrete floor in the room. In return for some work I did for another contractor, assisting him to repair his dozer, he pushed a nice track for me to access the platform in front of the dugout. I put in a second hand window and door. Then I put my bed back inside.

Each day, flakes of sandstone fell from the ceiling on to the bed. Each day I swept them off. The opposite of the expression, 'make the bed and sweep the floor,' my Potch Gully experience taught me to 'make the floor and sweep the bed.' I also learnt, through working on the cars, that Holden parts fit Fords, and vice versa. I also learnt to make my own tools to fit unusual motor mechanic jobs, when I had no money to buy the tool.

There was always the terrible possibility, living on my unofficial block on the Potch Gully mining field, that some unscrupulous person who knew the law would put mining pegs over my development and take it just for the cost to them of the registration fee of an opal claim. I thought of how I could do something on the land that would be a deterrant, and such an opportunity came up from an unexpected source.

One day I received a notice from the Department of Environment and Heritage in Adelaide. It said, "It has come to our attention that you are developing …" It was about my collection of cars on land I had been using as a wrecking yard. It said that if I did not immediately supply plans for the fencing of the yard, and access and egress proposals, I would be liable for a fine of Ten Thousand Dollars. It was a shock to read the amount of the fine. I showed the letter to a few people. They all said that someone living near my wrecking yard didn't want a wrecking yard across the road from them, and must have known someone in the government, who knew of a way to put pressure on me. They said the expression, 'it has come to our attention', was another way of saying, "someone, we won't say exactly who, in case you want to get nasty, has dobbed you in and wants to get rid of you."

Whatever the background to the letter, the fact was that I did not have a cent to spend on fencing, let alone pay the fine, so I got a friend to help me remove the cars. Some we took to Lot 1008, and the rest to the Potch Gully land. I figured that anyone who wanted to put mining pegs over my dugout development there would be deterred by having to remove all the cars.

My dugout had become quite comfortable to live in, having a door and a window and a concrete floor. I did not think of it as a saleable piece of real estate, but some visitors to the town did. I met them at a church meeting. An old-time town resident at the church usually got to dominate the conversations with visitors after the services, but one day he said to me in, front of the visitors, "Gary, you've been in Coober Pedy for a while now, you can show our visitors around Coober Pedy."

I showed them around some of the mining fields, and then we went to my Potch Gully dugout. I gave them coffee. The next Sunday they came again. On the third Sunday, again in my Potch Gully dugout, the man said, "Gary, we want to buy your dugout. How much do you want for it?"

Straight away I thought to sell the place, because I could move back to my little dugout and use the money to put on electricity and water there, and work with power tools, and make progress a lot quicker than by hand, and not have to cart water, and not have to worry anymore about someone stealing my dugout by pegging it as a mining claim.

I made a quick assessment of my labour and materials. "Five thousand," I answered.

"Done," he said. "Here's five hundred as a deposit, and we'll go to the bank next week and get you the balance. Now you can put some money into that claim of yours and see if you get a good return."

I then explained to them about my pending application for a lease on the Potch Gully land, and that all we had to do was contact the Lands Department in Adelaide and tell them to take my name off the application and replace it with theirs. We agreed that I would remove the cars, in my own time. That was it-the following week, they gave me four and a half thousand dollars cash and I walked out, they walked in.

42

Of the total of five thousand dollars from the sale of my home, which meant it was tax free, I gave five hundred dollars to the church as a tithe. The remaining four and a half thousand dollars I could spend on anything I liked, because I was debt free. I thought the best thing to spend it on was developing the little dugout on my leased block. It was exhilarating, after many years of being in survival only mode, to contemplate spending money on other things. When one comes to appreciate that hot water and soap are luxuries, anything more than those is close to heaven. Now I could anticipate a change of lifestyle into how most people lived, because I had the strength and skills to bring it to pass-all I had to do was spend the money on tools and materials and provision of utilities.

I was tempted to get straight away into a 'normal' lifestyle by renting a nice place, but, after having lived for four years without power or water, what would it matter if I 'roughed it' back at my little dugout for a bit longer, until I had developed it to a standard of what I was financially capable of paying in rent, and live in 'luxury' while I effected the development.

I moved back to my little dugout. It was mid autumn, very mild weather in the desert, so I slept under the stars again, and cooked and ate and washed outside, so that I could continue enlarging the rooms without having to move things around during the development.

My spending spree got me a 3Kva petrol generator, a Hitachi H45SA electric jackpick, an opal mining pick, a dumpy hammer, a hard hat, earmuffs, a home welder and some rods, welding mask, chipping hammer, safety goggles, a Makita electric hand drill, a four-inch angle grinder and a geli auger, mainly for my mining, but also for dugout development.

I paid the first annual instalment of $250 on a ten-year contract to get town electricity, and $50 for instalment of a water meter. After the water meter was in place, I added some new pipes and a tap that I had found in the dump. I thought of myself then as a 'one-tap man'. I used etcher and glue for the pipes, because they had to be strong enough for the 150-kilopascal town pressure.

I paid for an electrician to put a meter box, that I found in the dump, on the pole that the Progress Association erected next to my dugout entrance, and to connect electricity from the meter box to a new double power/light point in the kitchen, and a new fluorescent tube light. I also had a new double power point outlet put in the meter box. Using scraps of electric cable from the dump, I put in temporary power points and light fittings, also from the dump, in the other rooms.

I paid for a phone connection.

I bought some new PVC water pipe and fittings, and took water, from the T-piece under the first tap next to the water meter, to a second tap near the house, so that I didn't have to climb the cut to fetch water from the tap next to the water meter, and so I became a 'two-tap man'.

Using an electric jackpick did not mean easier work-instead, it meant that, for the same hard work that I had been doing with a pick, for the previous four years, I got a far greater amount of ground dug.

I started on the south face with another doorway entrance to the hill, and about two metres in, I dug to the left and made a small room which I used as a kitchen and a bathroom and a bedroom. My old bedroom then became my office.

I bought a second-hand door with a frosted glass panel, and I used second-hand timber from the dump for a door frame, and I hung the door at the kitchen entrance.

I bought cement, and carted sand from 16-Mile Creek where it crossed the old highway, and I mortared in the holes around the door frame. I put in a window frame with glass, from the dump, in the kitchen.

I paid for a sixty-foot Calweld shaft to be drilled, as a toilet shaft, about five metres away from the kitchen door. I got a dunny for free in return for removing it from a site, and I set it up over the shaft.

As winter approached, I wanted some slippers. I could have bought some, but I was so used to relying on finding most things that I needed, in the rubbish on the field, that I decided to go to the field to look for some. After checking my usual twenty dumps I did not find any, but I found some scrap aluminium worth enough to buy some. But the very next time I went out, I found a pair of moccasins that would do. They had a lot of paint splashed on them, but after an hour or so scraping with a knife, I got them clean.

Having plenty money to go opal mining using explosives rather than working with my electric jackpick, I went to the Mines Department office and said I wanted a Permit to Purchase explosives. They asked me who I had been working with. I told them. They had not heard of Taxiharsis Gyftopolous, but the name of the miner who I had worked with at Twelve-Mile was good enough recommendation.

"Just go and get a Police Clearance from the police station," the office worker said.

After I got the Police Clearance, I got a Permit to Purchase. I gave my car registration details, and I got a Licence to Carry. I also got a Permit to Mix, even though I did not intend to use nitro, only gelignite.

I went to a local supermarket and paid for a case of geli and a roll of fuse and a packet of detonators. Then I drove out past the Black Flag opal field on the south road, to the magazine, with my Explosives sign set on my car, and handed over my receipts and got my gear.

Back at the claim, down the shaft, I set off some bombs under the opal level in the old drive. I checked the wall, and found some grey, but there was still not enough to make a parcel worth taking the time to sell it.

In February 1987, I went to the principal of the Coober Pedy school to ask how I could go about sending money, for my sons' schoolbooks, to the school where they were attending. He told me that on contacting the principal of the school, he was told that the boys were no longer attending there. They were now attending at the school in a town on an island off the coast of Adelaide. There seemed to be no end of problems to be overcome in my battle to maintain contact with my sons, but Psalm 94 verse 15 inspired me: "Justice will again be found in the courts, and all righteous people will support it."

I continued writing letters to Dary and Andrew and Ben in their new town, sending stamped, self-addressed envelopes. Quite often they asked me for money to buy bike parts or fishing tackle, which I sent.

I got permission for the three boys to come to Coober Pedy for one week, on the condition that I travel with them. Dary was 14 then. It was, to me, an almost impossible condition. Living in Coober Pedy by then for four years, to make travel arrangements on southern public transport, while in Coober Pedy, was a big task. I had no idea what was available. Eventually I synchronised my bus to Adelaide, my Adelaide accommodation, then my bus from Adelaide to the dock to catch the ferry to the island, my bus from the island dock to the town where the boys lived, my accommodation in the town, bus tickets for me and three boys from that town to the island ferry dock, ferry for me and three boys to the mainland ferry dock, bus tickets for three boys and me from there to Adelaide, accommodation in Adelaide for three boys and me, bus from Adelaide to Coober Pedy for me and three boys (a twelve-hour trip), and then all the return tickets for me and the three boys to their town, the tickets for ferry and bus for me from that town to Coober Pedy, and all was to take place within one week, all done by long distance telephone calls.

I went to the town, and to the house to pick up the boys. To be told then, that Dary was not allowed to come, was crushing. Only Andrew and Ben came with me from their island town to Coober Pedy, and back in one week.

The man who liked listening to me sing Christian songs when I was busking, sent me a letter saying he would like to come to Coober Pedy again, on the same basis as his first visit. I wrote back and said it was OK. His reply was quick, and he said he would meet me in Coober Pedy in about a week.

A week later we met up again. His situation had not changed, but mine, because of the Potch Gully land sale, was a lot different. He was very pleased to take up my offer of a mining partnership, me to pay all expenses, equal sharing of labour, him on 10 per cent.

We started blasting in the cut, where the first trace was. There was no problem with having to clear away the blasted material-it shot across the cut and whacked into the opposite face and dropped to the ground. We kept blasting until we had an opening in the face about four metres wide and three metres deep. Every now and then, we found some grey opal, and some opalised mussel shells with varying amounts of nice colour.

The opening provided shade where we could rest between shifts. I asked him to help me close it off from the cut with a timber frame and sheet tin wall, and to put in a door and a window. The work was not part of our 'contract', and I didn't offer to pay him. He agreed to do the work for free. I think he was appreciative of the amount of time I took to listen to his problems and offer him ways to solve them, but I knew he was aware of the future potential value of the mine if the town expanded, because he said, "Atkins, I can see you in twenty years' time with some valuable real estate here."

"Yes, mate, you could be right," I replied, and added, "but that's a long way off, and who knows if I will still be here then."

"Well, I certainly won't," he said with a laugh.

It seemed this level, the twenty-five-feet, was not very productive. Others working nearby in Big Flat said the next level down was better. But I only had the ratchet-less hand winch that the old miner gave me, to bring up the dirt, and I could not afford to buy a motor driven Yorke Hoist. I managed to convince my partner that we should blast a drive from the back of our current workings, at a slope of about one in five, to the bottom of the shaft in the old workings. Then we could use my wheelbarrow to take the dirt up the drive and tip it in the cut. He agreed.

The drive had to be about fifty feet long, starting from the south-west corner of the new room. But from in the room, we could only guess roughly which direction to go, to be able to hit the shaft. We needed to establish, up top, a position directly above the south-west corner of the room. Once we knew that, we could measure the bearing and distance from there to the shaft, and then use those calculations to put in the drive from the room to the shaft.

Up top, it was difficult to guess where that position was, but we thought of a way. Above the door, the wall of the cut sloped away a lot. We got a long piece of timber and hung a plumb bob from the end, and then pushed the timber past the edge of the wall at the top, until the plumb bob hung in the middle of the doorway below. Then we went down into the room and measured the distance and compass bearing of the point in the room where we would start the drive, in relation to the middle of the doorway.

Then we went up top again. We laid another piece of timber on the ground with one end touching the overhanging end of the first piece. Then we moved the other end of the second piece around, until the piece was at the compass bearing of where we would start the drive in relation to the middle of the doorway. Measuring along this piece, we established a point up top which was directly above where we would start the drive. From that point, we got a compass bearing of the shaft, and the length that the drive would need to be. Using these figures, we went below again and knocked two nails in the floor to give us a compass bearing for the shaft.

We drilled seven holes for geli in the wall in the south-west corner, and we set the geli and blasted. Part of the blasted dirt shot into the opposite sandstone wall, and part whacked into the door and the tin cladding on the wall that we built to close off the room. We had to nail some of the tin back on to the timber frame.

We used the jackpick to trim up the walls and floor of the drive. After about a fortnight, we got about ten feet down the drive, at a slope of one in five. It was too difficult to continue at that slope, so we flattened it out to about one in ten.

To save time, we only made the drive just a bit wider than the wheelbarrow handles. Even then, we turned our hands inside out when holding the handles, to avoid skinning our knuckles on the wall of the drive.

We didn't work all day, every day. I had a policy that a safe day's mining was worth more than any opal, and not even one joint of a finger was replaceable by any amount of opal. And using explosives was dangerous. If we felt a bit tired or lacked confidence, we knocked off and either rested or did something else.

Many weeks later, we hit the shaft about ten feet above the floor of the old mine. We did not find any opal along the way.

We broke through and got inside the old mine, and then started blasting our way back under the new drive, to complete the one-in-five slope suitable for barrowing out the dirt.

It was then that we hit opal in the wall. We found quite a few ounces of good and medium grey, and more opalized cockle and mussel shells and skin shells. Some of the shells were in a solid clump. Most of the individual shells had varying percentages of sandstone in with the opal ('sand-shot' shells), but some were full crystal, worth hundreds of dollars each.

The next thing to do was to clean up the rough opal and get it classed, and to sell it and take our share. But my partner didn't think his share was worth waiting for, and he had had enough of the dust and the danger, and he wanted a break from the very hard work. He left and went back to his home interstate. I cleaned the opal and put it in some Milo tins, and then put the tins aside in the dugout at Lot 1008.

Sometime later I showed the opal to an opal miner friend from the church, and he got interested in mining with me. He agreed to me paying all expenses, sharing the labour equally, and him getting 40 per cent.

We worked around the area at the bottom of the shaft. We got more opal-some grey, and some green-orange crystal and blue-green crystal, and more shells. A classer put a value of about three or four thousand dollars on the parcel. My new partner wanted to stop mining and take his share, but I didn't want to sell, so I paid him cash for his share. I knew that I could 'value add' on rough opal by cutting it into gems. If I could survive without selling the rough opal until I learnt opal cutting and polishing, I would be much better off than selling rough.

Soon after, an adult education course in cutting and polishing opal, and basic silversmithing and setting opal gems in silver, opened in Coober Pedy. Being on Unemployment Benefit, I could do the courses for free. The courses were run by locals who had many years experience in the industry. I gladly took the courses.

We learnt to cut solids, and cutting for, and making, doublets, and slicing and making triplets. We made Sterling silver rings and pendants, and we set solids and doublets and triplets in them. I made some doublets out of the blue-green opal from the EH ute. I cut some of the opal that I found with my recent partners, and I cut a stone out of the first piece of opal that I noodled at Greek Gully four years previously.

After I finished the course, I realized that I would never want to be a cutter or a jeweler. I didn't like being confined to a small workshop doing such accurate and delicate work. But it was of great value to me, because it made me appreciate the value of the opal that I had, and to appreciate greatly the value of opal in the wall. Most times when I was mining, I didn't find any opal, and the work was hard, dirty and dangerous. I was always in a mode of full strength, hard work. When I found some opal, I tended to continue in that mode, and sometimes damaged the opal. But doing the opal cutting course made me able to change mode when I found opal, and go carefully and slowly, and not be in a rush to get the opal out. Instead of looking at opal in the wall and seeing ounces, I saw carats, (a carat being about the weight of five grains of wheat).

Having done opal cutting was helpful too, when buying rough opal. I could assess its value much better. Aboriginal noodlers sold rough opal and chips in spice bottles, in the main street. I could look at a bottle of chips, and if I saw some pieces that would cut well, I was happy to pay two dollars or whatever the asking price was, and know that I would make a good profit from cutting just a couple of those pieces. Previously, I bought bottles of chips and kept them, without really knowing the worth.

And the worth of opal is whatever a person will pay, notwithstanding that there are current, acceptable prices that vary from time to time. An Aboriginal noodler held out a bottle of chips for me to see once. He didn't want to sell it to me, he asked me to sell it for him.

"Why don't you sell it yourself?" I asked.

"Cos you're a white man, you get a better price than me," was his answer.

Other random factors can affect the price of opal at the wholesale level. A Chinese opal buyer looking for a certain class and weight of rough opal to complete his requirements for his factory, in the last few days before being due to fly to Hong Kong, would pay a higher price. The reverse happens when he has just returned to Coober Pedy from Hong Kong. And an opal miner who needed money at Christmas would sell for less. An opal miner who is cashed up won't accept a lower price. It comes down to this: opal is worth what you get for it.

43

Remembering the opal chips that I found on the collar of a Proline drill hole, when the nurse visited my claim, I decided to put in a thirty-foot drive from the old workings to the bottom of that hole, to find out if the chips had been dumped down the hole, or if they had been drilled up. To save on costs, I used a five-hole drill pattern that would do me a drive less than a metre high, and even less in width, even allowing for trimming up with the jackpick.

Up top, I lined up a stick with the middle of the shaft and the middle of the Proline hole and measured the compass bearing. Down below, I put nails in the floor to line up along the same bearing as the stick up top. Then I started blasting and then backfilling the old mine with the sandstone.

After I got about ten feet along the drive I hit a Proline hole, which was very convenient for ventilation in such a low and narrow drive. Another ten feet in and I hit another Proline hole. By this time there was always a lot of sandstone to clean up after each blast, because it didn't get thrown all the way along the low and narrow drive. It was getting very tiring, dragging a bucket of dirt backwards along the rough floor while in a virtual squatting position. So I devised a better way. I got a pedestal fan in the dump, and took the column and fan off the base, which had four revolving wheels. I cleaned the floor of the drive, and lay down strips of tin from the dump, to make an easy path for me to drag backwards a bucket of dirt which sat on the fan base with wheels.

At about twenty-seven feet I hit some dark potch. It started as a trace but soon became as thick as my fist, but it had absolutely no colour at all. As I knocked big chunks out of the wall I was nearly crying, thinking how strong it was, because if it had colour, I would have had a fortune.

I reached thirty feet, the distance up top between the Calwell shaft and the Proline hole, but I had a solid wall in front of me. I went up top and checked the bearing and distance, and then I checked them down below. According to my calculations, I should have reached the Proline hole.

I sat down near the bottom of the shaft, wondering what had gone wrong. Then I happened to look up the shaft. I saw that the winch cable, hanging straight down about ten feet, didn't line up with the wall of the shaft.

I went up top and let the cable down nearly to the floor, then I went down below and saw that the shaft was nowhere near vertical. From the top to the bottom there was a difference of nearly two feet. At last I had found the answer. All I had to do was make a right turn for two feet at the end of the thirty-foot drive, and I should hit the Proline hole.

In the confined working space, it was very hard to dig to the right, at the end of the drive, but eventually I reached a drill hole. I had expected to see light, but there was none, so I dug into the hole for the full diameter. Still there was no light. I saw the marks where the Proline drill bit had cut, and a nice neat round hole, so I knew I was in the right place.

Craning my neck, I looked up the hole. Not far up, I saw some material blocking it. I put the light up the hole. There were sandstone rocks, small and large, and what looked like opal chips with some colour. I poked up the hole at the blockage. After I dislodged some larger rocks, the blockage fell apart and all the dirt showered down, and light came through. Amongst all the rubbish were many opal chips with colour.

I had solved the mystery of the opal chips on the Proline collar. It was disappointing to discover that there hadn't been a level of opal drilled up. However, the material that had been dumped down the hole had value. I took it all out, and at my leisure at home for something to do at night, I sorted it. I worked by the light of a car-battery-powered, twelve-volt, transistorised neon fluoro tube. I sorted the bigger pieces by hand, that I thought were cuttable into gemstones. I used tweezers to pick out the chips that were too small to cut. I divided the chips into four piles-one pile was chips without colour or sandstone, the next was chips that had colour and a little sandstone, the third was chips that had some colour and no sandstone, and the fourth, having the most value, chips without any sandstone that always showed colour no matter from which angle they were viewed from. This last group would be good for filling tiny glass tubes, about twenty millimetres long and four millimetres internal diameter, which I could sell for ten dollars each.

I decided to do a trip down south to see my youngest son Ben play football.

At the football match, standing in the crowd, I was unknown, but everybody knew my son Ben. He was virtually a household name as far as the supporters of the team went. I could see why-he starred in the game, amassing many kicks and marks. At one stage of the match, just after Ben had run with the ball and dodged and weaved and kicked a goal, I got so excited that I called out, "Hey, that's my son!"

People in the crowd turned to see who said the words, and they had a good long stare at me. It was obvious to me that nobody had any idea that their hero had a father.

I stayed for another week and took Ben to another town, about fifty kilometres further south, to play an away match. He starred again. He was positioned in the back lines. When the opposition team surged forward, Ben left his direct opponent and intercepted the ball in the opposition forward lines, and then ran and bounced and kicked the ball deep into his team's forward pocket. It was thrilling to see.

It was a very long drive back to Coober Pedy after the match, but the memories of Ben's football prowess kept me going.

44

As the 1987-1988 Christmas school holidays approached, I contacted Wendy about the boys coming to Coober Pedy to visit me, all expenses of which I said I would be happy to pay. She refused permission for any of the boys to stay with me. It depressed me greatly. I thought back on all the intricate processes that had taken place through the meticulous work done by my solicitor, and the three arranged accesses that took place outside the country town police station to prove that I was not a violent person, to give me the legal right to see my sons, and to prepare to make an application to dissolve the Injunction on me. I remembered the eventual dissolving of the Injunction on me, and the relief, when the Injunction was dissolved, thinking that things would be 'normal'. The Family Court had at first, on my wife's statements, treated me as at fault, and made orders on me. Years later it exonerated me.

Now I thought that, seeing the boys had been refused permission to visit me, the only thing left to do was to go back to the Family Court, and try to get the Family Court to make Orders on my ex-wife, that she allow our sons to visit me.

I rang my solicitor. I was surprised when he said he could not help me, and that he couldn't tell me on the phone why. He said if I came to see him in Adelaide he would tell me.

I drove to Adelaide and went to his office. He said, "Recently I was asked by an elderly couple to arrange their will. They said one of their sons had died but they had another son who was married, and a daughter who was divorced. The daughter's ex-husband lived in a hole in the ground in Coober Pedy. Their names are Roy and Rosalie Smith. I hadn't heard from you for quite a while, so I took their instructions. So now I can't do anything for you."

I sat and stared ahead in amazement. I didn't understand how he could do all that work against my ex-wife on my behalf, and then 'change sides'. I thought it was a disgusting thing for him to do.

"Well who can I get?" I eventually asked.

"Are you on Unemployment Benefit?" he said.

I said that I was. Then he told me the name of a solicitor who did work for people on pensions.

There was nothing I could do other than try with the other solicitor. I got up and walked out of his office and walked straight to the address that he gave me. I asked to see the solicitor, and I was shown into his office. I told him my story. He made many notes. When I told him that I was on Unemployment Benefit, he gave me paperwork, that I filled in.

Then he said, "Now, I will submit this information to the Legal Services Commission of South Australia. It is jointly funded by both the South Australian and the Commonwealth Governments, to increase access to legal services for those people such as yourself, who cannot afford to pay for private legal representation. They will consider two things: first, if you qualify for Legal Aid, which would pay for any work that I do for you; second, if you do qualify, if you would be likely to have success in any application you might make for access to your children. You just wait for them to contact you, and we will take it from there."

It was great to realise that, after all, I had made a successful start, this time with a new solicitor. I thanked him and said I would contact him after I heard from the Legal Services Commission.

My purpose in going to Adelaide completed, I headed off back to Coober Pedy. On the way, I had an experience which taught me to 'listen to the small, quiet voice of the Lord', as the prophet Elijah did, in 1 Kings 19:12, and to 'Trust in the LORD with all thine heart; and lean not unto thine own understanding', as in Proverbs 3:5.

In Pt Augusta, I filled my car tank and three jerry cans with petrol. The full car petrol tank was enough to get back to Coober Pedy, and petrol was a lot cheaper in Pt Augusta than in Coober Pedy.

About one hundred and thirty kilometres south of Coober Pedy, I saw ahead of me a ute parked on the right-hand side of the highway, facing south. As I got close, someone jumped out from the side of the road, next to the ute, and waved at me, looking like he wanted me to stop.

I slowed, intending to stop. I had gone about fifty metres past the ute and was about to turn around, but, in my rear-vision mirror I saw three or four other people jump out onto the highway from near the ute. That looked suspicious to me, so I changed my mind and kept on driving.

Soon, however, I felt that the Lord was saying to me to turn around and go back to the ute, despite my fears. I decided to trust the Lord and not my own judgment. I turned around and went back to the ute.

The group of five people was very pleased that I stopped for them. They were all traveling south together from the north coast of Australia, after finishing the prawn trawler season. They had been paid off for the season. They had paid cash for a second-hand ute, and they were all going to their respective homes in the south of the continent, for a few months break. They had plenty of cash for expenses for the trip south, but the petrol gauge turned out to be faulty, and they had run out of fuel.

The back of the ute was packed with eskies and polystyrene containers, full of tiger prawns, fresh fish, lobsters, and shellfish, all packed in ice. To buy that amount of fresh food would cost thousands of dollars, but they had got it free, as part of their season's work payment. They intended to have a lot of parties down south with plenty of expensive fish. But if they had stayed a half day waiting for help in the desert in the summer heat, all the ice would have melted, and the fresh fish would have spoiled.

From my spare jerry cans, I gave them enough petrol to go south to the next petrol pump, one hundred and twenty kilometres away. They were so grateful to me for stopping and giving them petrol that they gave me several polystyrene containers of tiger prawns and lobsters and shellfish packed in ice. We went our separate ways.

When I got back to Coober Pedy I stacked my fridge freezer with the fish and bought more ice for the leftover fish. Locally, lobsters and prawns were selling for $25 a kilo. That meant that my gift of about one hundred kilograms of fish was worth $2,500, which I ate joyfully over the next few weeks, with great thanks to the Lord.

That experience reminded me of when a similar thing happened to me once before, when I listened to the 'small, quiet voice' of the Lord. An elderly couple came to the church meeting one Sunday. After the meeting, everyone was drinking coffee together, and I got to talking to them. They told me they were from a rural city interstate. I thought it would be nice and hospitable of me to offer to take them for a drive in my car and show them some opal fields and my claim. But the petrol in my car was only enough to do just that, with nothing left for the next day, and I had no cash left to buy any more petrol. Also, my claim was due to be registered and I didn't have any money for that. I felt the Lord say to offer to take them anyway, despite my financial situation, so I offered, and they accepted.

After a couple of hours acting as a tour guide, I took them back to town. They were staying in a caravan park. They invited me into their rig for a coffee. Over coffee, while we were chatting, the woman was doing some writing. She said, "How do you spell your name?"

I told her. I thought she was writing a letter to some family back home, and saying that she had met a nice man who had been very hospitable, and she wanted to spell my name correctly. Then she stopped writing. We chatted more, and ate some biscuits. Then she said, "This is for you."

She handed me a piece of paper. It was a cheque, made out to me, for two hundred dollars! She said, "I'm not asking you to pay me back, but one day, if you have some spare money, you can send me some." She gave me her mailing address.

A couple of years later I had some spare money and I paid her back.

45

On 28th December 1987, I received a letter from the Legal Services Commission of South Australia which said that they had assessed that I qualified for Legal Aid–that they would pay all my legal fees if my solicitor thought I had a good chance of success in getting what I wanted from the Family Court. They said that they had asked him to provide them with a report on my case, and that I should contact him.

Then in mid-January 1988, I received a letter from my solicitor, saying that the Legal Services Commission had told him that they would pay for his time to get instructions from me as to what I wanted from the Family Court, and for him to tell them if he thought I would have a good chance of getting what I wanted.

It seemed to me that the Legal Service Commission had already decided that I had a good case, and all that was left for me to do was provide my solicitor with all the information I could muster about events of the years 1981 to 1988, concerning me and Wendy and our sons. I wrote back to my solicitor to tell him I would give him my account of events as soon as possible.

I began to write a report, checking old documents, collating letters, rounding up notes that I had made on scraps of paper and in notebooks, over the seven-year period. It was a formidable task and a great tax on my memory. I would write something, and that would remind me of other circumstances that should be included, so I would leave what I had already written and start writing about the new event. That would remind me of something else, and I would have to leave that one and concentrate on the 'new', new event. It took me three months to complete.

On 18th April 1988, I sent my solicitor a letter of nearly 3000 words, detailing the following:

- a description of the events of 8th May 1981, the day when government officials took my sons away from me without my permission;
- the objections I had concerning the truthfulness of the statements made by Wendy in support of her application to the Family Court for custody of our sons, in May 1981;
- the Family Court Order of May 1981 which was an Injunction on me to be restrained from contact with Wendy or the boys;
- how I engaged a solicitor to arrange for me to have legal access to my sons, in 1982, and that the reason Wendy was unable to accept my proposals for that access, when her mother did it on her behalf, was that she had been committed into a psychiatric hospital for acute paranoid schizophrenia;
- the 1983 dissolving by the Family Court of their Injunction and Restraining Order on me, that was ordered in 1981;
- how, despite Wendy telling the Family Court that she and our sons were going to live with her parents in their comfortable, well appointed, four bedroomed home with adequate room and facilities for the children, she and the children only stayed there for a few months, and then they moved to a farm, and lived in a house that was timber frame, asbestos clad, with holes in the walls and ceilings, no carpets, no hot water service, no blinds, no curtains, and generally dirty and run down;
- how they soon moved from there to a Housing Trust house in a nearby town, and from there to a house in another town on an island off the coast of South Australia, and from there to another place in that town-Wendy and the three boys, in a period of three years, lived in five different houses in two different towns, and our eldest son had been to two different high schools;
- how, at various times, Wendy had been unable to care for the boys when she was committed to a psychiatric hospital; how, on one of those occasions her mother was not able to care for the boys, and they had to be placed in a foster home until Wendy was released from hospital;

how only once in the years 1984 to 1988 was permission given for the three boys to visit me together, and on that one time, after I had driven 840 kilometres to Adelaide and then travelled by ferry to an island where the boys were living, to pick them up, one of the boys, at the last minute, was not given permission and only two came to stay with me for a holiday.

I also said in my letter that, over the last seven years, I had tried to keep up regular correspondence with the boys and had sent them money at various times when they asked me, for them to buy bike parts or fishing tackle etc. During that time, however, there had never been any encouragement from Wendy for the boys to write to me. In fact, I had to send stamped, self-addressed envelopes to them.

I said in my letter that at no time in the previous seven years was I ever told of any move to a different house, or to a different town, or that the boys had been fostered out. I sent, with my letter, copies of various letters from government authorities to me, that verified my information.

I explained in my letter that the reason why I did not, in 1981, contest the Family Court Order of 1981, was that it was not until 1984 that I became aware that it would have been possible for me to do so. I described how this information came to me purely by chance in 1984.

It was a great relief to complete the letter, and to post it. I could only then wait to find out if my solicitor thought my letter was good enough to do the job of providing him with enough information to present an argument to the Legal Services Commission that my case should be funded, that it had a good chance of being accepted by the Family Court.

46

Barely two weeks after I sent my 3000-word letter to my solicitor, the Legal Services Commission of South Australia advised me that my application for funding to pursue applications for access and custody had been granted. A week after that, my solicitor wrote to me confirming the grant of funds by the Legal Services Commission for my applications. Included with his letter were a draft affidavit form, and an application form for me to fill in and return to him, which I did.

Following that, for the next four months in 1988, a series of letters were exchanged between my solicitor and my ex-wife's solicitor. My solicitor supplied me with a copy of every one of the letters that he sent, and a copy of every letter of reply that he received from my ex-wife's solicitor. Reading the letters, I saw that my solicitor had attended many sittings of the Family Court on my behalf. No doubt that, if I had to pay my solicitor for all his work, it would have cost me many, many thousands of dollars.

Finally, in September 1988, my solicitor sent me a copy of a Family Court Order that had ordered my ex-wife to cooperate with me and not frustrate me any more in my efforts to have the children visit me. The Order set out specific dates when the visits were to take place, and the duration of the visits, as I had requested.

When I saw the copy of that Family Court Order, I thanked the Lord, and I also thanked the Lord for the encouragement that the scripture gave me, that I read some time ago, Psalm 94:15, to continue my battle with the Family Court: "Justice will again be found in the courts, and all righteous people will support it."

That feeling of justice was heightened even further one day in the Family Court, when I was present, but my ex-wife was not, and the Judge said, "Where is the wife?"

"She's not here, Your Honour," someone said.

The Judge then said, "She's probably out and about somewhere, flying around on her broomstick."

47

The Family Court Order of September 1988, made in my favour, contained three main Orders.

The first Order was for my ex-wife to give permission for Dary to visit me from the 24th day of September 1988, until the 9th day of October 1988. My ex-wife complied with that Order, and Dary came for that time. He was fifteen. At first, because we had not spent much time together in the previous few years, it was a time of holiday and getting to know each other better, and I did not try to get him to help in the house, but as the days went by, I asked him to help a little bit, but he refused to do anything, not even dry the dishes after a meal. I was not happy about that, and so, for a while, I tried to encourage him to help, but that didn't work either. The next thing I did in this regard was to try to explain to him that he was required to help, that it was the normal thing for a child to learn to help in the house, that I was not his servant, that a son should obey his father, but it was all to no avail. All he wanted to do was be fed, and to watch TV. Then I started to insist that he be helpful, and he complied with my requests, but he did not do so happily. He seemed to have the attitude that he did not have to do anything that he didn't want to. By the end of the visit, he became resentful and would not cooperate with me. It became an unpleasant time. I was glad when the end of the visit came, and no doubt so was he.

The second Order was for my ex-wife to give permission for all three boys to come to Coober Pedy for the Christmas holidays, from the 21st day of December 1988 until the 21st day of January 1989. My ex-wife complied with that order. Ben and Andrew came, but Dary did not. He wrote a letter to me to say he didn't want to come to Coober Pedy for the Christmas holidays, and said he didn't want to come to Coober Pedy at all, and he said that 'the lawyers' knew that he didn't want to come. I was disappointed, especially as Wendy also wrote to me to say that she was unable to make Dary do anything he didn't want to do. Ben and Andrew and I had a good time together. I thought it best not to go to the Family Court to get them to enforce Dary's visit to me.

The third Order was for my ex-wife to give permission for all three boys to come to Coober Pedy for half of the July 1989 school holiday, and for all subsequent holiday time visits. The dates were to be arranged by mutual consent of my ex-wife and me.

Despite the third Family Court Order, my ex-wife refused to give permission for the three boys to come to me, and continued to refuse to let the boys come, for any of the school holidays, for the next two years.

It was during that two-year period that I had another amazing experience of trusting in the Lord for the means to take a long trip for which I did not have cash to do, in late 1989.

In a church meeting, the pastor said that there was going to be a very big gathering of Christian musicians in Adelaide, to minister to the youth of South Australia. He said that he and his wife would be taking their three daughters there. I really wanted to go to the youth meeting too, even though I was forty-four years old, but I knew my 24-year-old HD Holden panel van was probably not reliable enough for the 1700 kilometre round trip, so I asked the pastor if I could go with them, but he said there was not enough room for me in his car.

I was disappointed, when he told me. I reluctantly concluded that going to a youth meeting was not for me at my age. However, a day or so later, I happened to be reading the bible, the book of Joel, and came across verse twenty-five in chapter two: "I'll give you back what you lost in the years when swarms of locusts ate your crops." It came to mind that my Christian conversion at age thirty-five, was twenty years after I decided, at age fifteen while attending the Lameroo Methodist Church, not to believe in Jesus, and I reasoned that the Lord was able to give me back those twenty lost years, thereby 'reducing' my age from forty-four to twenty-four, and so it was reasonable, after all, to want to attend a youth meeting.

I phoned the pastor in Adelaide who brought me a cabbage, asking him if he would let me stay at his house while I was in Adelaide for the concert. He said I was welcome to do that. I told him I would be there about the Tuesday before the Saturday concert.

Next, I thought about the finances required for the trip to Adelaide and back. I only had about fifty dollars cash, but I had five old twenty-litre jerry cans that I could fill with petrol on my account at my local service station, and I had some cut stones to sell, and a couple of hundred kilograms of old truck and car radiators to sell as scrap metal.

My tyres were very low on tread, but in my yard and over at the claim, I had plenty of thirteen-inch Holden rims with tyres and tubes on, albeit low on tread and still on the vehicles. I started packing about 9 pm, using a trouble lamp. Many mosquitoes were attracted to me and the light. I took a wheel off a car in my yard and put it in the panel van, and I put a pile of radiators on top of it. To the side I put the five full jerry cans.

I had to go to the claim next, to load up some more radiators and get two more spare wheels off vehicles, planning to put them right at the top of the radiators for easy access if I got a puncture. The old car was already weighed down low on the suspension. I put my suitcase in, and went to drive out of the yard, but before I got to the roadway, I had a puncture. I had to unpack all the radiators to get at the spare wheel.

I drove over to the claim, loaded up some more radiators, took another two wheels off cars there, and put them in the panel van. A few hours later at 4 am, I finished loading. There was just enough room for me and my suitcase. I checked the water and oil and drove away. I knew the oil pressure warning light did not work.

For the next few hours, the mosquitoes that were attracted to the trouble lamp while I was loading, came out from underneath the seat and bit me. About 160 kilometres down the highway, the temperature warning light came on. I slowed right down, intending to stop and check the water, but the warning light went off and stayed off, so I kept on driving.

Soon, knocking noises came from the engine. I could hear the motor running at a constant speed, but the car kept getting slower and slower. I turned off the ignition and coasted to a stop. I got out and popped the bonnet. The motor was very, very hot. I waited for a while but still the radiator cap was too hot, so I checked the oil level on the dipstick. It was bone dry. I reasoned that the motor had got too hot and had seized.

After everything had cooled, I put in some oil and water and tried to start the motor, but the battery couldn't turn the seized motor fast enough.

I stopped a passing vehicle and got a tow, ninety kilometres to the next petrol stop, for twenty dollars. From the public phone box outside a roadhouse, I called the Royal Automobile Association. They said they could not do anything for me.

Accommodation there was seventy dollars a night. I walked back to the car from the phone box. There was another flat tyre. I changed the wheel.

Doubt took over. I thought, "Come on man, you're forty-four years old, you shouldn't be going 840 kilometres in an old car to a church youth meeting!"

Thinking that going on the trip was not, after all, something that God wanted me to do, I gave up the idea of going to the meeting. I decided to phone a transport company in Coober Pedy and ask them to pick up my car and take it back to Coober Pedy. I walked back to the phone box. It was out of action, so I walked to the hotel, to use the red phone in the lounge.

Walking through the bar to the lounge, I overheard two very drunk guys trying to talk the barman into loaning them a hundred dollars on the security of their motorbike, until their pension cheque came.

In the lounge, I rang the transport company. They said they would ring back the hotel to say when they could pick up my car.

The two drunks were still haggling with the barman when I walked back through the bar. I walked around the streets trying to get some work, and to sell some cut stones, but to no avail. I went back to the hotel to see if there was a message for me from the transport company.

On the lawn in front of the hotel the two drunks asked me for money. I told them about my seized Holden motor, and that I needed all my money to put my car on a truck back to Coober Pedy. One of the guys said he knew about fixing cars, and wanted to know what the motor sounded like, and maybe he would swap me his motorbike for my panel van. He insisted on checking it. I agreed.

After a quick look, staggering drunk, he blustered into the roadhouse workshop and demanded heavy duty jumper leads and a big battery. The boy gave them to him. He hooked them up to my vehicle. The engine turned over and started. I gave him ten dollars and some hard-boiled eggs, and then drove over to the other roadhouse and sold a cut stone for twenty dollars, bought some engine oil, put it in, and headed south, thinking that the reason the transport company hadn't been able to give me a time when they could pick up my car was because the Lord wanted me to continue my trip.

After a while the petrol gauge showed empty for long time. I had heard of God making cars go on no petrol, and thought this was also happening to me, but it soon ran out of petrol and stopped. I put in a full jerry can. After that, the motor wouldn't turn fast enough to start.

An elderly man in a small sedan stopped for me. We tried starting the motor with jumper leads, but his battery wasn't strong enough. We tried tow starting, in which the elderly man towed me while I held my clutch pedal down while my motor was in gear, and my ignition was switched on, and when we got fast enough, I let the clutch up suddenly. Twice his tow rope broke. The third time was successful. I thanked him and drove on.

About 5.30 pm I got flat tyre number three, the passenger front wheel again. I pulled out all the radiators to get a spare wheel, changed the wheel, and put back the radiators. One kilometre further on, I got a fourth flat tyre, the passenger front again, twenty kilometres from Port Augusta, and my last spare tyre.

At 6 pm, a guy stopped for me. He agreed to contact the RAA in Pt Augusta for me. But by 7.30 nobody had got back to me, and a big rainstorm came. I accepted a lift offer from somebody else who stopped, and I left the panel van and got a lift to Pt Augusta. I had to borrow a coin from the petrol station attendant to ring the RAA because I had forgotten to bring my money. A recorded message gave me another number. I had to borrow another coin to ring the RAA again. The RAA guy said they'd be there at the petrol station in twenty minutes.

The storm broke, cutting power to the petrol pumps. People in nice, clean, late model sedans were queued at the petrol pumps waiting for the power to come on, while in my old van, twenty kilometres out of town, I had over one hundred litres.

About 9.30 pm the RAA guy arrived. He said his boss couldn't find any old Holden wheel for my 24-year-old car, and he couldn't do a flat tow on my old, heavily laden vehicle. The tow had to be done with a special recovery vehicle. The alternative was to give me a lift out to the panel van and take off the wheel with the flat tyre, and bring it back to Pt Augusta to be repaired, but by the time we would get back, it would be too late to find anyone to repair the puncture. Even if it could be done, he couldn't return to the job a second time on the one callout.

The RAA guy said he might have a wheel of his own at his home that he could loan me, but with the storm raging there were several emergency calls to attend to first. He said the insurance would be OK to do the job with the loaned wheel, and I could go with him and stay with him while he did the Pt Augusta callouts.

At about 10.30 pm, he finished the callouts, and we got his spare wheel and went out to my panel van. He discovered a seized passenger front wheel bearing, and that was why the last two flats happened.

We changed the wheel and returned to Pt Augusta to find that the special recovery vehicle was ready, which I assumed was part of the RAA service. We headed out again. When we were nearly at my panel van, the driver explained that there was an eighty dollar call out fee for the special recovery vehicle, and a one dollar per kilometre fee. I was not happy that I wasn't told this before we left Pt Augusta. We had such a loud argument that he pulled over to the side of the road and stopped the vehicle. Someone stopped to ask if we were OK. After they drove on, the RAA driver said, "Do you want to call the job off?"

I said, "No."

We went to the panel van and he winched it onto the special recovery vehicle.

We were nearly back to Pt Augusta when he asked me where I would be staying for the night. I told him I would sleep in my panel van. He said, "No, you won't. This vehicle is going to the wreckers. You can't stay in the wrecker's yard overnight."

After twenty hours on the road, with four flat tyres and three breakdowns, I was too exhausted to object, too exhausted even to decide where I would sleep.

He offered to take me to the caravan park on the north side of town and drop me off there. I nodded my agreement. It was midnight when I woke up the caravan park caretaker, who put me, at such short notice and at such a late hour, in a caravan with a bed but with no bedding. I flopped down on the bare mattress and slept instantly.

Early next morning, I took a bus into the city, and happened to meet some friends from Pt Augusta who recently visited Coober Pedy. They showed me where the bank was. I used the last of my credit limit to get cash for a taxi to the wrecking yard where the panel van was stored. The wrecker said I would have to pay $120 for my tow, which I knew was around about the value of my vehicle. It was like I was buying back my own car.

The wrecker agreed I could pay for the tow after I sold the radiators. I got them to fit a second-hand wheel bearing. Then I drove to the scrap metal dealer. After I waited for over an hour, the owner turned up. He gave me a cheque for $120 for the radiators. I had to take it back into the city to cash it. Then I went back to the wreckers and paid the $120.

I drove to a tyre fitter to get a second hand tyre and tube fitted to one of my spare rims. They said they wouldn't fit a tyre on to any of my rims because they were all damaged, and they couldn't get hold of another rim to fit, because my car was too old. I said, "Can I borrow a ball pein hammer?" They loaned me one. I cold dent knocked all the bumps and hollows out of one of my rims to their satisfaction, and they fitted a tyre and tube. I headed off to Adelaide, over three hundred kilometres away.

About 8.30 pm, the engine started knocking. Then the oil warning light, that I thought was not working, came on in a bright flash. I turned off the ignition immediately and coasted to a stop. I checked the dipstick. There was no oil on it. I put in some oil and started up and continued southwards. Soon after, the engine knocking noise got louder, and suddenly there was a big bang. I was at the top of a hill. I turned off the ignition and put the engine in neutral, and coasted downhill, to a town, and stopped outside a building with lights on. It was the local hotel. It was 9.30 pm. I dreaded to look at my engine to see what the big bang was about. Without even looking, I guessed that my engine was only good for scrap metal, and my trip was over. I went straight into the hotel bar and had a lemon squash. Everyone was friendly. I sold enough opal gemstones in the bar to pay to sleep the night in a very comfortable, four-poster bed.

After breakfast, on the morning of the third day of my trip from Coober Pedy to Adelaide, I discovered a big hole in the side of my engine block. I guessed that the engine knocking noise had been a loose crankshaft bearing, worn thin from friction from low engine oil, causing the conrod to drive the piston at an angle instead of straight up and down, and the piston had punched the hole in the block, with a big bang. I walked to the local Royal Automobile Association accredited workshop and told him what had happened to my engine. He rang around the Adelaide wreckers, and got a quote of $400 for a replacement motor. I had no cash left. I decided that my best place to raise some cash from selling opal gemstones and rough opal would be Adelaide.

The daily Adelaide bus had already left the town. I hitched a lift in a truck. In Adelaide, after I tried all day, I did not make a single sale of opal. People said the political unrest caused by a massive strike made things too uncertain for investing in opal. There was only one thing left for me to do-I would have to go back to the little town and try to sell gemstones door-to-door, and sleep in my panel van.

I decided to catch a bus to the outskirts of the suburbs and then hitchhike. At a bus stop, I sat down and waited. A dusty gust of wind sprang up. I said to a guy sitting next to me, "This is just like where I live."

"Where's that?" he said.

"Coober Pedy," I answered.

He said the name of someone who was his relative at Coober Pedy, and he asked me if I knew him. I said I did. Then I told him about my trip. He said I should rather catch a train from a station near the bus stop, to a town out in the nearby country area, and start hitchhiking from there. Then he stopped a woman who was walking past whom he said he knew, and that she used to live in this country town where the train would stop. She also said that's what I should do.

I took their advice, and about 8.30 pm I got out of the train at the country railway station and started walking through the town, carrying my suitcase. I stopped at a pub and tried to sell opal in the bar, but I didn't like the way people were crowding around me when I showed my gem cases of opal, so I left and started walking again.

Out of the town area, on the highway, rain started pouring down. Cars kept going past me. I walked six kilometres, in pouring rain, to the next town. The rain was unseasonal. I could see by the colour of the ripe heads of wheat in the roadside paddocks that the pouring rain would ruin the crop.

I went into the bar of the local hotel and bought a lemon squash. It was nearly closing time. A guy next to me opened his wallet and I saw a wad of fifty-dollar notes.

"You look rich mate. Wanna buy some opal?" I said brashly.

He answered, "No," and then he turned to his two mates and told them they'd better get going.

I asked, "Are you going north?"

He replied, "Yes, but you'll have to ride in the back of the ute."

As we went out to the ute they offered me a can of beer, but I said I didn't want any. They insisted. I insisted. They insisted. I insisted. They gave up insisting, urinated all over the footpath outside the hotel, and got in the ute, and we drove off at great speed.

In the open back of the ute, the cold night air was chilling me in my damp clothes. In the warm cabin they were drinking cans of beer and throwing the empty cans out the window. The cans flew past my ears and into the back of the ute and bounced out on to the road. They threw out cigarette butts too, that flew past my ears, landed in the back of the ute, and sent sparks cascading all around me.

Rain started again. I was getting soaked. They drove like lunatics through the hills, cans and cigarette butts whizzing everywhere. At midnight, I got out at my little town and walked to the workshop, planning to sleep in my panel van which I had left in the workshop yard, but it had been put inside the locked workshop. In the yard was a horse float, with an open cabin window, so I got in and tried to sleep under a horse rug in my wet clothes. I got up after a while and walked to the hotel which was still open, but they had no beds left, so I went back under the horse rug in the cabin of the horse float.

Next day I went selling opal door-to-door. By mid-afternoon I had received twenty dollars, a cup of coffee, and lots of sympathy. I changed my plan. I rang a garage in Coober Pedy to see if they could get me a motor, which I would pay for when I got back. They said they could get a rebuilt one for $1300 if I would send the money. I told them I didn't have that amount of money. They said, "Try a bank loan."

I found that there was no Westpac bank in this town, or the next one, so I rang Westpac toll free to Sydney. They said to try Westpac at Coober Pedy. I rang them. They said to try for a Visa card at the National Bank in the next town. I hitchhiked there but the National Bank manager refused my application.

It seemed that whatever I tried was destined to fail, but, looking back on the difficulties I had overcome so far on this trip, I knew that the trip was a test of my faith, and that if I persevered, I would eventually succeed. I hitchhiked back to the little town and slept the night in my panel van, in the workshop yard.

Next morning, I borrowed the garage tools and took out my old motor, then hitchhiked to the nearest big town, and sold $120 of opal door-to-door.

That night I went back to the hotel bar in the little town to sell opal, but I couldn't sell any, and I had drunk so many lemon squashes it felt like it would spill out of my ears. Again, I gave up hope of getting to the concert in Adelaide, which was on the following night. "Oh, well," I thought, "what do you expect when you are forty-four years old? Maybe sometime next week I'll be able to get back to Coober Pedy and put it all down to experience."

But in the very next minute, I sold a cut stone for $230, and then a guy came up to me and said, "Are you looking for a red six?"

He was very drunk, so I didn't believe him, but he insisted: "I took one out of my old car. It's been sitting in my yard at home for months, but it was going when I took it out. The earliest I can get it here is Monday, and you can have it for nothing. If you think it's worthwhile, when you get back home to Coober Pedy, you can send me a cheque for fifty dollars, care of this hotel."

I answered, "Thanks, mate, that's great. I'll take it." I thanked God too, for once again giving me the strength to persevere, even though I had almost given up.

I walked back to the garage and slept in the panel van, and got up about daybreak, washed in a creek, packed my case for Adelaide and the youth concert, and stood on the road waiting for a lift. I had left a note for the garage owner telling him about the red six motor that would be coming on Monday, and the phone number of the pastor in Adelaide who I was going to stay with.

A car went past. The brake lights come on, then off, then on again, and the car went out of sight around a corner. Then it came back, went past me, turned around, came back towards me, and stopped at my feet as though it was being driven by my chauffeur.

I got in. We talked, and I discovered that the driver's wife was a grade three student of mine when I was her grade three teacher, twenty-one years previous. She remembered me playing the guitar back then.

By 10 am, I was in the biggest department store in Adelaide, on the fifth floor, arranging a credit card for a $200 weekend limit for clothes. I got $180 worth and then rang the pastor's number. His wife said they were putting someone else up instead, because they were unsure if I was still coming, but to come anyway and see what her husband said.

I went there, unshaven or showered for three days. They welcomed me. I had a good soak in a hot bath for about half an hour. That night they gave me a lift to the concert, with their sons. It was a great concert.

On Monday morning I went by bus from the pastor's outer suburban home to Adelaide, then again, by train to the nearest country town, and then hitchhiked to the little town where my panel van was. The red six was at the garage as promised. It was bigger than my old one-a 173 instead of a 161. I borrowed tools again and worked the rest of the day on putting in the motor. At 5.30 pm they shut the garage, so I continued working outside in the garage yard. By sunset I had finished. The owner of the motor arrived. I gave him fifty dollars.

On the return trip to Coober Pedy, I stopped every hour to check the oil and water. Not once did I need to top up. The trip was completely trouble-free. I thanked God for his faithfulness.

48

In early January 1991, I concluded that it was a waste of time to deal with Wendy regarding arranging for our sons to visit me, and I decided to do what I did a couple of years previous-deal directly with my sons instead. That way I could maintain contact with them, and not have to wait for another lengthy Family Court appeal process to reinforce the third Family Court Order of September 1988. And this time I could do it by phone, instead of letter writing as previously.

The first time I rang, Ben answered the phone. We had a good chat. He was eleven years old. I told him I would ring again in a couple of days. When I rang next, Ben again answered the phone and we chatted again. In the next two weeks I rang several times, and Ben was the only one who ever answered. Once, I asked him to ask Andrew to speak. Andrew came to the phone and we spoke, but it was a strained conversation. Another time, I asked Ben to ask Dary to speak. I heard him ask, but soon he said that Dary didn't want to speak to me.

Then one day, Wendy answered. She said she did not want me to ring so often, and at various times of an evening. She said she wanted me to ring at 8 pm on a Sunday evening only. So, I waited until the next Sunday at 8 pm before I rang again. Nobody answered.

The next week I rang again, and I was told that nobody answered on the previous Sunday at 8 pm because they had all gone out.

So, I started ringing again, every couple of days, at various times. Once again, it was always Ben who answered. I asked him how he was going at school and he said he was getting on well. Then I rang the junior school where Ben attended, and got to speak to his teacher, who told me that, on the contrary, Ben was not getting on well. He said that Ben was rowdy, and he was a disruptive student. Next time I spoke to Ben, I had to tell him off for letting me think he was getting on well at school. But we continued to keep talking often. It was starting to feel like a normal father/son relationship. But Dary would still refuse to come to the phone, and Andrew would only come occasionally.

Finding it impossible for Ben to be able, on my request, to get Dary to come to the phone, I instead asked Ben to ask his mother to come to the phone. When she did, I asked her to ask Dary to come to the phone. I heard her ask him, and I heard him refuse. I asked her to order him to come. She said he would refuse to obey her if he chose to. I asked her to try. She refused to try.

I decided that, as I was having success with Ben, I would not give up on Dary and Andrew. But I realized I could not have any success through my ex-wife, so I decided to try through Dary and Andrew's teachers at their senior school, a different school from Ben. I realized that I was up against a lot of opposition, to do this, and that I would have to be very careful in my efforts, and that I would have to keep detailed notes on dates, people, and times, because it was likely that I would, in the near future, have to present all the information to my solicitor, for another appeal to the Family Court.

On 7 February 1991, the receptionist at Dary and Andrew's school stalled me for twenty-one minutes with my request to speak to the principal to get permission to talk to Dary and Andrew's teachers. I was not able to speak to the principal. The call cost me eleven dollars. It seemed to me very likely that my ex-wife had successfully convinced the school, when she had enrolled Dary and Andrew there, that I was not a person worthy of consideration as a father.

On 14 February, I tried again, and this time, I got to talk to the principal. He explained that he could not allow me to talk to Dary and Andrew's teachers, because, as a new principal, he had been told by office staff that I was a parent whom the Family Court had placed an Injunction on, and so he could not take the risk of letting me make contact with my son's teachers, in case he and the school became involved in my possible breach of a Family Court Order, through my contact. It was very frustrating to continually be treated as a 'bad' father, but, through praying to God,

I got the strength to persevere. At least I understood what the situation was, that the authorities had only ever heard one side of the story. Then I asked him if he personally had seen the Family Court Orders that he was referring to. He said he had not. I asked him if he would mind checking it out. He said he did not mind. Then he left the phone, and soon came back, and said he was holding a copy of the Family Court Order. I asked him the date of the Order. He said it was May 1981.

I told him that the Order he was holding was not a current Order, and that there had been another Order since that one, in September 1988, that ordered my ex-wife to provide access to me, and that I have access, to our sons, for specific periods as stated in the Order. I told him I could send him a copy, to prove that I was telling the truth. He said that wouldn't be acceptable, because he could only accept official documents from my ex-wife, as the custodial parent. He said he coud not accept official documents from me as a non-custodial parent. I said I would contact my ex-wife and ask her to send him a copy of that Order. He said he would wait until he had heard from her before he would change his mind and let me contact the teachers. I was satisfied with that.

I phoned my ex-wife straight away and asked her to send a copy of the September 1988 Family Court Order to the principal of Dary and Andrew's school. She said she would do it. I rang the principal straight back, and I told him that I had my ex-wife's assurance that she would send him a copy of the Order.

On 18 February, I rang my ex-wife to ask her if she had sent the copy to the principal. She said she had not done it yet.

On 20 February, I rang my ex-wife again. She said she had changed her mind, and she would not send anything to the principal.

On 21 February, I rang the principal and told him that my ex-wife said that she refused to send the copy to him. The principal then said that he would be willing to take a risk and accept my word on the matter, and that I could send to him a copy of the Order. But he gave me specific instructions, of how to address the envelope, which would ensure that he, and only he, and not his office staff, could open the envelope.

On 8 March, I posted photocopies of the Family Court Orders of September 1988 to the principal.

On 15 March, I rang the principal. He told me he had received the copy, and told me that he had instructed all the members of his office staff to treat me as a 'normal' parent, and that they were to call Dary's class teacher, and Andrew's class teacher, to the phone, so that I could speak to them, should I phone the school and ask to do so.

On 18 March, I rang the school and asked to speak to Dary's teacher. The receptionist told that me that he was unavailable, and that he would ring me later. When I heard that, I thought that all the effort to get to speak to the teacher was being thwarted again. But later that day, I received the promised call from Dary's teacher, and we had a long discussion about Dary's schoolwork and his attitude. I also did the same with Andrew's teacher.

After all that, I was able to have something to talk about when, later, Dary and I and Andrew had some phone conversations.

For the next few weeks, I continued to have many talks to Ben by phone, every few days. We made plans for me to travel down south and stay in temporary accommodation, so we could see each other daily during the coming 1991 April school holidays.

On 11 April, I rang my ex-wife. She agreed to let Ben stay with me in a caravan that I would hire for two weeks in a nearby caravan park. She said Dary did not want to come and see me, and Andrew might come and stay for one night only. She told me she had moved to another house; she gave me the address. She said I could pick Ben up there on 19 April, the first day of the holidays. I said I would rather pick him up at his footy match, than at her house, but she insisted, so I agreed.

On 13 April, I rang my ex-wife again to confirm the holiday time arrangements. Andrew answered the phone. He said that she had gone out and he was not sure when she would be back.

On 14 April, at 7 pm, I rang to wish Ben a happy twelfth birthday. Andrew answered. He said that Ben was over at my ex-wife's brother's wife's place. I rang her at 7.30 pm, thinking that everything was fine, and that she had taken Ben over to her sister-in law's house for a combined birthday celebration with his cousin. I knew Ben and his cousin got on very well. But the sister-in-law told me that she was looking after Ben because my ex-wife was in the psychiatric hospital again, and that she was detained in the section of the hospital that housed potentially violent patients, and had been there for two days already, and would probably be there for at least another two days, but they did not know for sure how long she would be detained there. I asked why I was not told about this, seeing I had been arranging for Ben and my holiday together. The reason I was given was that nobody knew how to contact me.

Then I got to talk to Ben for his birthday, and I told him that we would still be staying in the hired caravan for the holiday time. Then I rang Andrew and told him off for not telling me the reason why my ex-wife was not at home, because I thought that he, at age sixteen, would have been aware of everything leading up to her detainment.

On 15 April, I rang my ex-wife's sister-in-law. She was still looking after Ben. She said I could pick Ben up from her place when I came down south.

On 19 April, I drove from Coober Pedy and went to pick up Ben, but he had gone home, because my ex-wife had been released from the psychiatric hospital and had taken him back. I went to her house. She asked me to come inside the house to wait, because Ben was out riding his bicycle somewhere, because, she said, they didn't know if I was still coming. I went in, and I waited in the house for about an hour. On the floor of the room there was hardly any place to walk, because of books, clothes, papers etc. Nothing had changed in the way she managed her house, even after ten years of not having me, the originally alleged handicap of a husband, around. Then she told Dary and Andrew to come out of their bedrooms and ordered them to "talk to your father". They came out and we talked. It was a very strained conversation.

She showed me a letter that said Ben had been selected in the local football league Under 15's training squad, preparing for an inter-league match. That was very impressive, because Ben was only just turned twelve. The letter said that if a boy missed any of the training sessions, without a parent telling the coach the reason, the boy would be precluded from the team. Training was to start on Sunday April 21. When I read this, I did not say anything, because I had planned to take Ben with me to a local church meeting.

Then Ben came home. I took him to my rented caravan, arranging to return in the morning to pick up Andrew and take him and Ben to play their footy matches for their local team.

On 20 April, Ben and I picked up Andrew and I took them to the football oval. During the matches, I caught up with the team manager, with whom I had been talking by phone from Coober Pedy about my sons' involvement in the club. I explained about not seeing Ben for a long while, and that I wanted him to be with me at church, instead of going to the first training session. He said that was fine, because family comes before football.

After the matches, I took Ben and Andrew back home. I sent Ben to get some extra clothes for church, while I waited in the car. My ex-wife came out. She asked me to come into the house, to discuss Ben not going to football training. She said she didn't want other people in the street to listen to the conversation.

I went in. She started shouting abuse at me, in front of Ben, saying that I was making Ben very upset by preventing him doing something he is good at. Ben looked upset. I tried to talk back to her to explain about the coach excusing Ben from the first training session, but I couldn't get through to her, because she kept shouting at me in front of Ben, bringing up matters that had been dealt with years ago in the Family Court. I said nothing, hoping she would stop shouting and let me say something. Ben looked upset.

She continued to shout at me, saying, "Look at what you are doing to Ben." Ben looked upset. She shouted at me again, "See, you can't say anything in your own defence. The truth hurts, and you can't stand it."

I thought that Ben would be thinking that I was what his mother said I was, because I just sat there, putting up with all the accusations like a naughty boy who has been caught out and is being told off by the teacher.

For years, I had always tried not to criticize my ex-wife in front of the boys in the manner that she was now doing to me. But I realized that if I didn't fight back (even in her house) she would succeed in the bluff of trying to get me to leave the house without Ben, and thus put an end to our holiday.

In a loud voice, I said, "Listen to me. Yes, the truth hurts, but you don't tell the truth. You are the one who has deceived the Family Court. The Family Court has acknowledged that."

Ben looked upset. My ex-wife shouted back at me, saying that she had legal custody of Ben, and that if I didn't let Ben go to football training, she would call the police to take me out of the house.

I shouted back, "Go on, call the police, but you are wasting your time, because they know you, and they won't take any notice of you. You tried that trick years ago, and they refused to come."

She shouted back, "That was years ago. There's new police here now."

I said, "OK, ring them, but it won't do you any good, because the Family Court knows you, and you won't get away with it. You are the one who is upsetting Ben. You are blaming me for it, and you are saying all these things in front of him, trying to convince him that I am the cause of him being upset."

She said nothing, so I continued, speaking calmly this time, because she seemed to be ready to listen. I said, "Ben can be excused from one training session. I've already talked to the coach about it, and they are happy about it. I've seen him play, and he is a good player, and after I go back to Coober Pedy, he can go to the rest of the training sessions. I've seen Andrew play too, but Ben is a good footballer. Andrew is average, but Ben is good."

She called Andrew in from his bedroom and said to him, "Did you hear what your father said? He said you are not much good at footy." She turned to me and shouted, "You're trying to make Andrew feel bad."

I quickly said to Andrew, "Do you feel bad for what I said?"

He said, "No."

I said to him, "You're good at upholstering. I've seen the bench press you made. The welding is average, but the upholstering is good. Your footy is average."

Andrew looked happy. Ben looked happy too. He got his clothes and we went off to the church. After that, we went to the caravan, where Ben stayed with me for a week. We had a good time. I was disappointed that Andrew only stayed one night, and even more disappointed that Dary did not come to visit, but the Lord was my ever-present Comforter.

Back home in my dugout in Coober Pedy, I had a time of reflection on my trip down south to see the boys. Overall, I was thankful to God for the experience. Dary was not happy with me, most likely because of my ex-wife's influence, but there was nothing I could do about that except be patient, and hope that one day he would be mature enough to re-evaluate our relationship. With Andrew, my relationship was one of mutual tolerance. At least he did not refuse to communicate with me. With Ben, our relationship was about as good as I could expect, considering I was never living in the same house as him.

I considered making an appeal to the Family Court to get sole custody for him, and to have him come to Coober Pedy to live with me. I wrote to my solicitor about this. He said that it was a possibility, but it would be conditional on Ben being happy to move to Coober Pedy. I thought about how good a footballer Ben was, and how much he liked playing, and how he might have a professional career opportunity. I thought about how great a difference it would be for him in Coober Pedy-there was no junior football competition. There was not even a grassed oval to play on-we played locally on a dirt oval which was strewn with rocks and broken glass.

I asked Ben if he would like to come and live in Coober Pedy with me. He said he would rather not move. I wrote again to my solicitor and told him about Ben's choice, and that I would not want to force him to come to Coober Pedy, mainly because of his football opportunity down south, and so I would not bother to make an appeal to the Family Court for custody of Ben.

Later in 1991, Ben and Andrew visited me at my home in Coober Pedy. I drove down south to pick them up. I stayed in a hotel. While I was there, I spent a few hours with Dary. We got on better than before. Ben and Andrew and I enjoyed our time together in Coober Pedy, and then I drove down south and took them back to their home. I spoke again with Dary while there. He was happy to spend some time with me. Wendy was cooperative. I thanked the Lord that, after ten years of frustration and battles, my three sons and my ex-wife and I were at peace with each other.

49

Dary and Andrew and Ben came to adulthood and went their separate ways.

By 1992, Dary had left school, and had left home, and had been working for about two years at part time jobs. He phoned me one day and asked if he could come to live with me. He told me he wanted to try again at Year Twelve in high school, in Coober Pedy. I agreed. I set up a study bench for him in one of my underground bedrooms. He came, and each day he rode his bicycle three kilometres to school. It was a great joy to see him ride off.

He kept at his studies for most of the year, but gradually, week by week, he got out of bed later and later, and his night time studying dropped right off. He seemed to have lost interest in trying. Disappointingly, he left without finishing the school year, and went back to live in the same house as my ex-wife.

In 1994, Dary came to live with me in Coober Pedy again. This time he stayed for two years, working at part time jobs, but again, he gradually lost interest in working, and life in general. Without a job, he could not support himself, but he wanted to continue staying with me. I agreed, but it became a great strain for me to have to pay for everything. Then he went back to live in the same house as my ex-wife again.

About a year later, during which time I had not heard from Dary, I had a phone call from a psychiatrist at an Adelaide psychiatric hospital, who told me that Dary had been detained there, had been diagnosed as schizophrenic, was on medication, was due to be released, and had told the doctor that he wanted to come again to live with me. The doctor asked me if that was alright with me. At first, I refused, because I did not want to be responsible again to pay for everything, and I did not want to try again in my life to cope with living with a mentally sick relative. But the doctor persisted. He explained that if I agreed to look after Dary, I could convert my Unemployment Pension to a Carer Pension, and Dary could get a Disability Pension. He also explained the behavioural manifestations of schizophrenia, a major one being an apparent attitude of apathy, which was associated with chronic clinical depression.

He told me about the various Service Providers available to families of schizophrenic people-the psychiatric hospital telephone 'hotline', the South Australian Carer's Association, the Association for Relatives and Friends of the Mentally Ill. He said that if Dary was willing to cooperate, he and I would be a father and son team slotted into a network of agencies, including the local General Practitioner, and visiting psychiatrists and psychologists, and Community Health Workers. He said that it may be possible to set up a regular video conference in Coober Pedy between himself and Dary, and me. He told me that there was funding available for local hospital care for Dary while I went down south for regular "Retreats", to stay at various accommodation facilities, paid for by the government. All this was a far cry from the days when "red-back spider" explanations were all that was available. I agreed to try.

Dary came to me. I took him for a government assessment, which resulted in him being granted a Disability Pension, and me, as his Carer, granted a Carer Pension. This meant that I no longer had to try to find employment.

For about the next eighteen months, Dary and I battled it out. It was not an easy time, but we slotted into the system, including local video conferencing, which was the first time that such a thing had been done in Coober Pedy, and thank God, we survived.

In 1997 Dary got well enough to look after himself, and he left my care, and ever since then, he has cared for himself, surviving on his Disability Pension, not being able to, because of "voices", hold down a job.

Andrew, having left school and worked in local part time jobs while staying at home for about a year, signed up in 1993 with the Australian

Navy, for six years. After qualifying as a Marine Technician, he lived on ship, and travelled extensively in Australian waters, and in the northern hemisphere. He saved his wages and put a deposit on an investment rental property in Australia, and engaged a land agent to manage rentals. Eventually he was able to pay off the mortgage. After discharge from the navy, his international appetite being whetted, he travelled in many countries for a few years, working part time, travelling a lot by bicycle, camping in a tent, doing a lot of recreational bushwalking in remote areas of the world.

When he returned to Australia, he continued with his adventurous outdoor lifestyle in many areas. In a remote area of Tasmania, he saw an opportunity to set up a backpacker style accommodation facility on pastoral land next to a National Park, a day's walk from an extreme sport coastal surfing beach. He bought the land and built the facility, and he has operated it ever since.

Ben stayed at home until he finished high school, and he continued to stay at home, doing some part time work. In 1998, he started full time work as a production line welder in a car manufacturing company in Adelaide. He moved out of home and rented a flat in Adelaide. He held the job for four years, and then resigned and travelled in Europe for a year, doing casual jobs. Then in London he got a full time job for two years as a labourer for a landscape gardener. Then he returned to Australia and stayed with Andrew, helping him build his backpacker facility, and he worked for a time on a boat for a professional fisherman.

When a major copper/gold mine started near Coober Pedy, the company offered locally based training courses, for local people, in preparation to work at the mine. Ben moved from Tasmania to Coober Pedy to try for enrolment in the course. He was accepted, and successfully completed the course, and he started work at the mine. The job was long hours, with a high pay packet. Ben saved his money and bought his own semi-dugout property in Coober Pedy, and a small rural parcel of land near the coast, about 800 kilometres from Coober Pedy, and got a mortgage on a rental property in Adelaide and engaged a land agent to manage tenants. Ben worked in the mine for about two years, but he wasn't happy in the job.

He finished up with the company, and started working locally, doing renovations and gardening. Then he started travelling around Australia.

He started talking about how he thought people were following him. To me, and Andrew, and my ex-wife, it seemed he was exhibiting behavior indicating mental sickness, perhaps schizophrenia. Ben denied any such thing whenever any of us suggested to him that he submit for an assessment of his situation. Eventually, his behavior in a public place one day apparently caught the attention of someone who was qualified to recognize that kind of behaviour and detain such people. Ben was detained, put in an ambulance and transported to a psychiatric hospital, where he was diagnosed as being schizophrenic. He was put on medication and detained in the hospital.

After a couple of months, he was released from the hospital, to care for himself. He found it difficult to hold a job. An employment agency which specializes in finding employment for schizophrenic people took him on, and from time to time he gets part time work through the agency. He now lives in the same house as Dary and my ex-wife, three schizophrenic people together, probably finding a mutual comfort in their shared life experiences.

50

I continued to live in my dugout on my block in Coober Pedy, in 1992, digging more rooms. I paid the fee to the government to convert it from leasehold to freehold.

I continued to receive an adjusted Unemployment Pension, while earning casual money from a land agent for cleaning up tenanted properties after tenants left, from selling scrap metal, raising chooks and selling eggs, working over summers as a swimming pool attendant, and selling consignment opal and my own opal gemstones from my opal mine, in a booth at the annual Royal Adelaide Show.

When the Coober Pedy Town Area expanded westward, as I thought it would, when I registered my opal claim, I converted my opal claim to an annual residential lease, and in 1995, I paid the government fee to convert the land from leasehold to freehold. I built a shed there, and then operated a Saturday morning retail fodder business in it.

When Dary left my care in 1997, I cancelled my Carer Pension and went on to a Newstart Allowance. I volunteered to do office work at the local Coober Pedy Times Community Newspaper, in lieu of trying to find employment. Soon after I started doing the volunteer work, the incorporated body which ran the newspaper received a government grant to move from being a printed newsletter to a tabloid newspaper. When a major Australian printer and newspaper publisher came to Coober Pedy to mentor the volunteer-run newspaper in its transition to tabloid in 2000, as the Coober Pedy Regional Times, I went from volunteer to part time there, as an advertising salesman, which then went to a full-time job as salesman and journalist. It was the first time in seventeen years in Coober Pedy that I had a full time job. I still also had my annual opal selling booth at the Royal Adelaide Show, scrap metal sales, egg sales, cleanup jobs, and fodder store sales. With saved money, I paid $3000 for a block of land in a seaside town about 700 kilometres from Coober Pedy, and then built a tin shed there to stay in for holidays.

I quit the newspaper job in 2002 after disagreements with the volunteer committee about publishing policies. I had money saved, and enough income from my self employment activities to survive without going back to any government unemployment benefit.

Recognising a need for an independent news publisher for Coober Pedy, I started my own regular media outlet, on the internet, calling it the Coober Pedy News. The main things I reported on were the activities of the District Council of Coober Pedy, because the Coober Pedy Regional Times, which relied heavily on funding from the Council, never attended monthly council meetings, and thus was never able to report objectively on the monthly council meetings.

For four years, I ran the internet news service. During that time, the local Coober Pedy Regional Times, still being run as an incorporated body by volunteers, failed to engage the District Council of Coober Pedy with any journalistic objectivity. My internet-only Coober Pedy News did that, but many local people did not look at internet. Only the ones who did so, kept abreast of local politics. Often in those four years, I appealed in prayer to the Lord to help me to understand why I should bother to continue, because, although the cost to me was minimal, there was no income. I believed that the Lord wanted me to continue, and to trust that there was a good reason why I should continue, and so I came to regard it as a free service to the community. Income from my other business activities was enough to pay my way.

Then one day, the local mayor contacted me to ask if I would be interested in buying the assets of the Coober Pedy Regional Times, and then to run it as a private business. I told him I was interested, but I would first need to see the financial records of the volunteer-committee-run incorporated body. I contacted the person who kept the records. He said that, as I was a friend, he would give me access to the records. What

I discovered was that the body was in serious financial difficulty, so I told the mayor that I was no longer interested.

About a month after that, the committee of the paper announced that a public meeting would be held the following week, to discuss ways of keeping the paper afloat, because it was in serious financial difficulty. On the night of the meeting, the assembled interested townspeople were told that they might as well go home, because, between the day of the announcement of the meeting, and the night of the meeting, the committee had ceased to function, as it had been discovered that the incorporated body was insolvent, and therefore could not continue to trade legally, and if it did so, the personal assets of the volunteer committee would have to be confiscated to pay for the debts of the body.

The townspeople, and the newspaper paid staff, were shocked to receive the news, and went home greatly disappointed, realizing that the town no longer had a local newspaper. It had been functioning in some form or other, run by volunteers, for nearly twenty years.

Contrastingly, I went home excited with the prospect of starting my own tabloid newspaper, grateful to the Lord for the strength and perseverance to have kept up my regular internet-only news for four years.

The next day I phoned the office of the South Australian division of the national newspaper publisher that came to Coober Pedy to help when the Coober Pedy Regional Times was starting. I spoke to the man in charge and told him that, as of the previous day, the town of Coober Pedy no longer had a newspaper, and I was interested in forming one. He said he would ring me back after he verified what I told him. Later that morning he rang back and said that his inquiries had backed up what I had told him. He said he would come to Coober Pedy very soon and help me get started.

He came, and suddenly I was confronted with such a steep learning curve that I hardly had time to sleep or eat for months, but Coober Pedy once again had a newspaper. My income increased about four times what it had been, on top of the other little business ventures that I had been doing for years. I no longer had any time to personally work on developing my two dugouts, and a block of land for, amazingly in the desert, horticulture, but I had plenty of income to hire two men to do the work. My life was spent on my computer. I ate out often.

Not long after I started publishing my fortnightly newspaper, demand from China for iron ore became so strong that old iron ore discoveries were opened again, several of them near to Coober Pedy. It was the start of a mining investment boom in Australia. Several Australian Stock Exchange listed mining companies started mining near Coober Pedy. The managing directors sought my favour as the editor of the Coober Pedy News, and I met with them over meals in local restaurants, and some came into my office. I was confronted with another steep learning curve-to write intelligently about mining ventures. I had to do lots of internet searches, and absorb many new technical mining terms, and to follow stock exchange daily prices. I found it very interesting, and many times each day, I stopped working on newspaper articles to follow price changes. Then I saw that it could be a possibility for me to earn money via the internet by trading in mining company shares. I invested several thousand dollars in shares in mining companies whose ventures were close to Coober Pedy.

In the following months, all of them showed a modest profit. One company that had diamond exploration leases near Coober Pedy interested me more than the others, because, a few years previous, I had read an old mining report about the discovery of a single diamond nearby, and I went to the area and prospected for diamonds, not finding any, but I found diamond 'indicators'-garnets and quartz crystals. The company had other diamond exploration leases several thousand kilometres away, in north-west Western Australia, but my interest was in the diamond exploration lease less than two hundred kilometres from Coober Pedy. I bought seventy thousand shares in the company at one cent each.

Several times each day while working on my computer on internet searches relevant to my newspaper articles, I would flick over to the stock exchange website to look at how my portfolio was going. Sometimes it would rise in value by a few dollars, another time it would fall by a few dollars. Then one day when I looked, I saw that my portfolio had risen by almost eight thousand dollars. My first thought was that the website had made an error, and I ignored it and went back to my article writing. But later in the day when I checked my portfolio again, I saw that the same massive rise was still there. On checking each of my portfolio companies, I discovered that my diamond exploration company shares had risen from one cent each to twelve cents each! On searching the internet, I found out that the company's diamond exploration lease in far off Western Australia had drilled up massive drill cores of high percentage iron ore, and the Chinese demand for Australian iron ore was in full flight. I sold my twelve-cent shares that afternoon. In following days, the same shares dropped a lot, and I bought them again, and then they rose again, and I sold them again. This happened several times. Another of my companies also rose sharply in value following their positive company press release, and I sold those shares too, as well as exercising my Options shares in the company.

Suddenly I had more than twenty thousand dollars sitting in my bank account! I was thankful that I trusted the Lord for strength to keep doing my internet-only news without pay for four years, because if I had stopped doing it, I would never have had the opportunity to start the Coober Pedy News newspaper, or to get involved in share trading.

I made another amazing and unexpected profit at that time-I received an offer of twelve thousand dollars for the seaside town property that I had bought for three thousand dollars. I declined the offer. The spectacular rise was unexplainable to me, so I took a couple of days off and went there to see what the situation was. I found out that there was a massive rise in real estate values in the town, and my property would probably fetch fifty thousand dollars in the current market. I asked an old-time resident why this had happened. He said that nobody saw it coming, that it was sudden, and was caused by two factors: a brand-new aquaculture business had just got established, and the rise in iron ore prices had made it economic to mine local iron ore bodies that previously were left untouched-fly-in, fly-out workers had seen that it was better to invest in, and live in, local houses, than to commute by air and live in on-site mining accommodation huts. I put my property on the market that day, with a local agent, and after about six months, it sold for forty-nine thousand dollars!

51

By 2009, I had been living for twenty-seven years as 'single again', alone, apart from several lodgers, most of whom turned out to be either conmen or thieves. I had always kept in mind what I believed to be a promise of God to me in 1982, that he would give me a wife again, still young but once rejected, that he would bring her to me, and that she would be a leader of women. A couple of times I thought that a woman who came to Coober Pedy was the one, and a couple of times a woman thought I was the one for her, but nothing developed. Many a time in my weekly Sunday church attendance, I looked around to see if my promised wife had turned up, but she never did.

In Coober Pedy, there were many Philippino women married to Australians, to migrants, and to those of British descent. Several times, married friends said to me that I ought to get a Philippino wife. I always said to them that I was not interested in getting a wife from the Philippines, simply for the sake of getting a wife. I said I would let God do the talking to me on that subject. Then one day I got an invite to tea at the home of a business friend whose wife was Philippino. Her sister was visiting Australia, and my friend and his wife were trying to 'marry me off' to her. I apprehensively went for the meal with them, which was very tasty, but I had to tell my friend's wife that I felt that her sister was too old for me.

Another time they invited me again, to meet another sister. I was aware what it was all about, and wary, but I went again, with the same result. Then I asked my friend's wife if she had any relatives a bit younger. She gave me a photo of an unmarried niece of hers, whom she said was twenty-four, forty years younger than me, and I took it home, saying I thought she would be good for my son Ben, rather than for me. But then I started looking longer at the photo, and I got interested in her. I went back to my friend's wife and said maybe after all I was interested in the niece myself. My friend's wife rang her niece and told her, and they agreed that it would be OK for me to contact her, on an internet messenger service.

I made the contact, and even though her English was difficult to understand, we had a pleasant conversation. I rang another day, and another day, and then I started ringing her daily. She always seemed interested. I became so dependent on the daily relationship that I decided to travel to the Philippines to meet her, with a possible outcome of marriage. I got a new passport and boarded a plane for the Philippines, travelling with her aunty, the sister of my business friend's wife, who was returning to the Philippines without an Australian husband.

As the plane was descending to land at Manila, I got quite worried, thinking that this could be the end of my life as a single man, which, after nearly thirty years, I was comfortable in. But short of jumping out of the plane before it landed, an impossible act, or else just disappearing into the millions of Manila when the plane landed, there was no way to avoid what was ahead of me, so I calmed down.

At the airport, when we first met, it looked to me that the girl was less interested in me than I was in her. I stayed in her aunty's home, and the niece and I saw each other every day, mostly in shopping malls, and we went on a three-day trip by jeepney to a rural province where many of her relatives lived. There were about fifteen of her relatives travelling with us, and a girlfriend from the college where she was a student. I paid for everyone and everything. On that trip, I got on better with her girlfriend than I did with her. The girlfriend and I even talked about her coming to Australia to get work, and I said I would help her any way I could.

I eventually concluded that the niece was not attracted to me, and so I told her that I did not want to see her anymore. That settled, I only had to wait for my return flight to Australia.

I went to a Supermall for window shopping and met a Philippino woman, probably in her late fifties. We got talking-her English was competent. She said she was widowed, and she was looking for a husband. I told her I was not interested, and I told her about my failed attempt to find a wife in the Philippines, and I told her about the niece's girlfriend and how I liked her a lot. The woman said I ought to contact that girl. I decided to follow her advice. I thought that if God was not going to bring me a wife, then I would have to find one for myself. But the old story of Gideon came back to me, and I set a condition-if I met the girl again, I would ask her to come to church with me on the following Sunday. If she said yes, that would be a sign to me that she maybe was God's choice for me.

I did not have a phone contact for her, but I knew how to walk the few kilometres to the college where she and the niece were students. I told the aunty, and she made me agree to phone her every hour, in case I got lost, or attacked and robbed.

I walked to the college and waited outside. The college was on a busy main road, very noisy, with jeepneys roaring past constantly. Many of them had bible scriptures painted on them, as did fences on properties. Many of the scriptures referred to the power of prayer, and to, "Pray Hard, it Works."

For four hours I waited outside the college, not even knowing if the girlfriend was attending that Friday afternoon, and many times I 'Prayed Hard', before the bell rang and the students came through the gates and onto the footpath. The girlfriend came out, with the niece, who walked past me, but the girlfriend said, "Hi, what are you doing here?"

I said I had come to ask her to go to a church meeting with me. A young man butted in to the conversation and said, "No, she can't come. She has family commitments." Well, that was my first 'fleece' answered, and the end of another of my attempts to find a wife in the Philippines.

The next day, the girlfriend rang me and said that her mother wanted to meet me. I thought that the reason was that she had told her mother that this nice guy from Australia had promised to help her if she came to Australia to work, and so the mother, out of concern for her daughter, wanted to meet me. I agreed to meet the girlfriend outside a supermarket close to her college, and from there she would take me to her mother's house.

I went there. She was waiting, and another girl was with her. She introduced me, saying, "This is my cousin Cristel. She's looking for a husband." She said that Cristel stayed with her, working as a live-in housemaid for her mother. I said hello and she said hello and that was the end of that conversation. She was dressed in very plain house clothes.

The girlfriend and Cristel and I went to the supermarket to buy food (which, of course, I paid for) for the evening meal at her mother's house. In the supermarket, the girlfriend went off on her own to select the items, while Cristel and I waited uncomfortably together. It seemed the girlfriend was away a very long time. Eventually we left the supermarket with a great amount of food, and went to her mother's house, where the mother and I talked for a long while, after which, I went back to the house where I had been staying.

The next day, Sunday, I went to a church that I had been to the previous Sunday, when I had talked about my visit to the Philippines in search of a wife. The churchgoers were interested to hear how my search was going, and I told them that I had failed to find a wife, whereupon a woman from the church set about befriending me, with, as I understood, an attempt to catch me for a husband, but I thought that she, like the two visiting Phlippino women in Australia, was too old for me, and I managed to escape unharmed.

In the afternoon, I texted the girlfriend. She didn't reply, but I received a text message from Cristel. She called me "Darling", and said she loved me. I was dumbfounded-how could she meet me on one day, and then, the next day, call me Darling, and say that she loved me? The text message ended with "MWAH", which I had never seen before. I thought it was probably an acronym for some local Philippino thing. I asked the daughter of the aunty what it meant. She puckered her lips and spoke the word, 'mwah', indicating a kiss. At least I then understood what mwah was, but I did not understand the 'Darling, I love you' part.

But I kept on thinking about the message, and it made me wonder what I was going to do about it. It made me wonder what sort of a woman would act like that. It bothered me for such a long time that day, that in the end, I just had to talk to God and ask, "What am I going to do about this?"

I felt that the Lord answered me thus: "I have just slammed two doors in your face. Now this door is open. Do as you wish." So I decided to take the opportunity handed to me, an opportunity for which I had made no effort at all to bring into being: I decided to ask the girl to marry me!

I contacted her, and she agreed to meet me the next day, in a takeaway food shop near the supermarket where we had spent an uncomfortable few minutes waiting for her cousin to do the shopping.

The next day, waiting in the shop for maybe half an hour past the arranged time, I got to thinking that nobody would turn up, and it was all a joke. Then Cristel arrived, with her aunty, and a man, who was apparently Cristel's uncle. The aunty said that Cristel's parents could not come to the meeting because they were working in a rural province.

Practically all the English conversation that followed was between me and the uncle, who spoke quite good English. The aunty's English was passable, and Cristel's was virtually non-existent. We chatted about the weather, and the traffic causing the late meeting, and ordered some French fries and ate them, and then the conversation stopped. It was an awkward silence. I knew why I had arranged the meeting, and maybe the others did too, but they were saying nothing. It was up to me to say something. My mind was racing with the thoughts of how ridiculous the situation was-had I gone crazy to be going to ask someone to marry me, whom I had met briefly for only one day-what if I ask Cristel to marry me and she says no-what if she has no idea what the meeting is about, and if she said no, how would I cope with three doors slammed in my face in as many days-what if she says yes-what would I have started, on such a short notice, in two people's lives-what if it would be better if I said nothing and we went our separate ways and I stayed single as I had been for many years.

Then I summoned up the courage, and blurted out to the uncle, "Look, I know you might think I am crazy, and it doesn't make any sense to me either, but I want to ask your permission to ask Cristel to marry me!"

With no hesitation, he said, "No worries." Then I asked Cristel, and she said yes!

My three-week tourist visa was about to expire. There was no time to arrange a wedding ceremony. With help from the uncle, a plan was agreed upon whereby I would return to Australia, get another tourist visa, come again to the Philippines within a fortnight, go to Cristel's home province, have the wedding, and grab a passport and visa for Cristel. Then she and I would go to Australia as husband and wife. It all seemed very straightforward and simple.

I returned to Australia, and over a coffee in a café in Coober Pedy, I excitedly told a married couple, the wife being Philippino, about the plan. They told me that it could not work like that, and that I would have to arrange everything according to the policies of the Australian Department of Immigration.

In 2012, after two years of working through the intricacies of both the Australian and the Philippines Immigration Departments, Cristel and I married.

We now live in my underground home in Coober Pedy. With us is Cristel's daughter Grace. We also have a home in the Philippines and a nearby block of land there on a mountainside. We travel there each year, and we stay in our home for about a month.

I have retired, on a restricted aged pension.

I have come to appreciate, from personal experience, the truth of the scripture in 1 Peter, chapter 5, verse 10, "And the God of all Grace, who called you to Glory in Christ Jesus, shall Himself, after you have suffered a little while, restore you, and make you strong, firm and steadfast."

The End

www.ingramcontent.com/pod-product-compliance
Lightning Source LLC
LaVergne TN
LVHW091534060526
838200LV00036B/607